HOMOEROTIC SPACE
The Poetics of Loss
in Renaissance Literature

HOMOEROTIC SPACE

The Poetics of Loss in Renaissance Literature

STEPHEN GUY-BRAY

UNIVERSITY OF TORONTO PRESS
Toronto Buffalo London

© University of Toronto Press Incorporated 2002
Toronto Buffalo London
Printed in Canada

ISBN 0-8020-3677-5

Printed on acid-free paper

National Library of Canada Cataloguing in Publication Data

Guy-Bray, Stephen
Homoerotic space : the poetics of loss in Renaissance literature

Includes bibliographical references and index.
ISBN 0-8020-3677-5

1. European literature – Renaissance, 1450–1600 – History and
criticism.   2. English literature – Early modern, 1550–1700 –
History and criticism.   3. Homosexuality in literature.   I. Title.

PR428.H66G89 2002   809′.93353   C2001-903691-4

University of Toronto Press acknowledges the financial assistance to
its publishing program of the Canada Council for the Arts and
the Ontario Arts Council.

This book has been published with the help of a grant from
the Humanities and Social Sciences Federation of Canada,
using funds provided by the Social Sciences and Humanities
Research Council of Canada.

University of Toronto Press acknowledges the financial support for
its publishing activities of the Government of Canada through
the Book Publishing Industry Development Program (BPIDP).

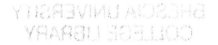

This book is for
my parents and my sister.

CONTENTS

ACKNOWLEDGMENTS

I have been working on this book for a long time and I have many people to thank. My most important obligations – first, last, and always – are to Tom Kemple, who has helped me since the beginning of this project. Both this book and its author are better because of him.

I would like to thank the Humanities and Social Sciences Federation of Canada, the University of Calgary, and Red Deer College for essential financial support during the writing of this book. I would also like to thank my colleagues in the English department at the University of Calgary and at Red Deer College, especially Nancy Batty, Susan Bennett, Jim Ellis, Jackie Jenkins, Paul Nonnekes, Mary Polito, Eric Savoy, and Jason Wiens. Many other people have helped in one way or another and I am very happy to have the opportunity to acknowledge them here: Peter Babiak, Julie Beebe, Stuart Blackley, Clint Burnham, Kegan Doyle, Mary Agnes Eagen, Mark Alexander Gabruch, David Galbraith, Donald Kemple, A.E. Leggatt, Robert K. Martin, Ian McAdam, Shane Rhodes, W.A. Sessions, Claude J. Summers, Peter Toohey, Terry Wood, and Paul Yachnin. Professor Kenneth Borris of McGill University very kindly sent me the galley proofs of his collection of essays on Richard Barnfield.

The secretaries of the English department at the University of Calgary were of great assistance in the final stages of this project. I owe a particular debt to the people who taught me the classical languages on which so much of this book depends: Anne McWhir, Janet Bews, Patti Schroeder, and Ian Begg. I would like to thank Suzanne Rancourt at the University of Toronto Press for her help, advice, and encouragement throughout the publishing process, John St James for his careful editing, the Aid to Scholarly Publications Programme, particularly Jessica Schagerl, for financial aid, and the two anonymous readers for their comments on my manuscript. Thanks to Karen Walker, my graduate assistant, for the index.

Portions of this book have been presented in different forms over a period of years at conferences and colloquia: the Association of Canadian College and University Teachers of English in 1997, the International Congress on Medieval Studies in 1999, the Pacific Northwest Renaissance Society in 1999 and 2000, the 16th Century Studies conference in 2000, the Group for Early Modern Cultural Studies conference in 2000, and colloquia at the University of British Columbia and the University of Calgary. I would like to thank the organizers of these sessions for the opportunity to try out some of my ideas and the participants and audience members for their comments and questions. Part of chapter 3 was originally published in somewhat different form in *English Studies in Canada*.

As my subtitle indicates, this book does not tell a particularly happy story, and loss – in particular, the deaths of young men – is one of its major topics. I want to conclude these acknowledgments by honouring the memory of some of those I knew who died too young: Maureen Kavanagh, John Booth, Bill Deacon, René Highway, Peter McGehee, David Richardson, David Saunders, Phil Eastmure, Doug Wilson, Teddy Nix, Rick Crocius, Alex Wilson, Kevin Chandler, Duncan Scherberger, Mark McChesney, Mark Shields, Robin Hardy, Michael Wade (whose knowledge of Latin poetry was of great assistance when I first started thinking about this project), and the incomparable Howard Pope.

HOMOEROTIC SPACE

The Poetics of Loss
in Renaissance Literature

Introduction

Illud peccatum horribile inter Christianos non nominandum

This horrible crime not to be named by Christians: this commonplace of medieval and Renaissance legal and theological discourse has often been used to end the discussion, but I want to use it to begin my discussion. In approaching this Latin tag I have been mindful of something Michel Foucault said in *The History of Sexuality*:

> [W]e must not imagine a world of discourse divided between accepted discourse and excluded discourse, or between the dominant and the dominated one; but as a multiplicity of discursive elements ... Discourses are not once and for all subservient to power or raised up against it ... We must make allowance for the complex and unstable process whereby discourse can be both an instrument and an effect of power, but also a hindrance, a stumbling-block, a point of resistance and a starting point for an opposing strategy.[1]

For my purposes, the two most significant aspects of the phrase 'Illud peccatum horribile inter Christianos non nominandum' are that sodomy is presented as something that Christians must not name and that the quotation itself is in Latin. If, as Foucault suggests, the distinction between accepted and excluded discourse is not absolute and one discourse can have more than one function, then perhaps this phrase can open up avenues of resistance as well as functioning as an instrument of control. Perhaps rather than reading this phrase as condemnatory we should see it as providing 'a starting point for an opposing strategy.' If we return to the phrase, then, we could see sodomy as something that can be discussed by people who are not Christians or even by Christians as long as they do so in Latin.

In this book, I want to look at some of the discussions classical literature gave rise to in the Renaissance, a time when, as has frequently been noted, Latin became increasingly important to curricula and Greek was introduced into western Europe as a subject of study.[2] Bruce R. Smith points out that in sixteenth and seventeenth century England 'Latin was the tribal language of educated men ... the language of law, diplomacy, and international trade. It was also the language of sexual knowledge.'[3] And, of course, Latin was the pre-eminent language of literature: both Latin and Greek literature provided the educated men of the Renaissance with knowledge about various kinds of homo-eroticism, knowledge that was, as a rule, accessible to them only in Greek or Latin. The legal condemnation I have cited is in Latin because Latin is a 'safe' language that is only understood by the educated; the irony is that the educated would have learned Latin largely by studying such texts as Virgil's second eclogue, with its famous depiction of a shepherd consumed by love for a beautiful youth.[4] In other words, we should imagine a situation in which educated men would come to make at least an implicit connection between sodomy and classical languages.

One of the best statements of this connection comes from an article on Marlowe by Claude J. Summers:

> From Greco-Roman history, literature, and myth came potent symbols and archetypes of homosexuality, including figures and pairs such as Ganymede and Jove, Patroclus and Achilles, Socrates and Alcibiades, Alexander and Hephaestion, Hercules and Hylas, Hadrian and Antinous, Orestes and Pylades, and Damon and Pythias, as well as Orpheus and Narcissus among others. The classical literature of homosexuality provided Renaissance writers and readers with a pantheon of homosexual heroes, a catalogue of images, and a set of references by which homosexual desire could be encoded into their own literature and by which they could interpret their own experience.[5]

To these heroes, images, and references I would add genres. In this book, I argue that certain classical genres – particularly the pastoral and the elegy – were frequently encoded as homoerotic. The use of classical literature was twofold: the features mentioned by Summers can be employed to express homoerotic themes, but they are also frequently found in Renaissance literature without any homoerotic implication. As a result, most Renaissance homoerotic texts cannot easily be separated from heteroerotic texts that also make use of classical themes, forms, or allusions. The centrality of classical literature to Renaissance education and culture provided a perfect cover for expressions of homoerotic desire.

The homoeroticism of many classical texts (including some of the most celebrated of them) was often given Christian interpretation or simply ignored. Nevertheless, these classical texts were read and taught and cited as examples of proper style and high art throughout the Renaissance and long after. An educated Englishman would thus have been exposed to a wide range of culturally approved texts in which homoeroticism plays an important part. My argument in the chapters that follow is that many Renaissance writers used classical models to construct their own homoerotic discourses. This theory is ultimately not susceptible to proof or disproof, of course. Still, I think that Renaissance writers were able to construct a homoerotic tradition out of the classical works that they had been enjoined to study, and that by following these classical models they were also able to continue this tradition. The homoerotic continuity between Renaissance and classical texts contrasted with the officially sanctioned continuity according to which, for instance, the English were the true inheritors of the Roman Empire.

In this study, I shall begin by looking at classical texts in which homoeroticism plays a part. This will not be an anthology of 'Greek love' dealing with every example of homoerotic poetry in classical literature. I concentrate on the most famous classical texts precisely because they are the most famous: they have most often been read, studied, and used as models for literary composition; indeed, they are the basis for later ideas of the classical tradition and, to some extent, of homoeroticism. I begin with the establishment of the pastoral genre in Theocritus's *Idylls*[6] and then turn to Virgil's development of this model in his eclogues and the connections he makes between loss and poetry. I then look at how a homoerotic and elegiac mode continues in the *Aeneid*. My first Renaissance chapter is on Castiglione's 'Alcon,' Surrey's 'So crewell prison,' and Milton's 'Epitaphium Damonis.' Surrey's poem is probably the most famous of the three, while both Castiglione and Milton are of course much better known for other works, but I think all these poems are interesting and influential versions of classical pastoral elegy. I then look at Renaissance pastorals (Spenser's *Shepheardes Calender* and, to a lesser extent, 'Colin Clouts Come Home Againe,' the pastoral poetry of Barnfield, and Browne's *Britannia's Pastorals*) and the problems faced by a lingering homoeroticism in a genre increasingly focused on heteroeroticism. My last chapter is on Beaumont and Fletcher's *The Maid's Tragedy* and Shakespeare's *The Winter's Tale*. I chose these works rather than the Renaissance poetic epic because these playwrights engage with the problem of the containment of the intense bonds among men that are the rule rather than the exception in the pastoral and military milieus depicted in the classical poetry I discuss. In a sense, both *The Maid's Tragedy* and *The Winter's Tale* take up where the *Aeneid* left off: with the transition to a milieu in which the norm is a relationship between a man and a woman. In the postscript to the book, one motivated partly by my desire for a happy ending, I return to Theocritus, to look at how the twelfth idyll suggests the possibility of a very different homoerotic tradition in literature – one that is only now beginning to be written.

I

In the past twenty years or so, attempts to trace a canon of homosexual works have tended to be dismissed as naive. Such attempts are naive if the assumption behind them is that there have always been men and women who were homosexuals in the sense in which we understand that word. I do not assume this, however. My assumptions, which are modest enough, are that there have always been men who were attracted to other men or who were interested in passionate bonds between men, that some of these men were both readers of poetry and poets, and that classical texts, written in a period in which it was relatively easy to discuss homoeroticism, have been of particular use to such men. This has certainly been true for me as a reader, since one of the ways in which I read classical texts is to find out something about the history of homoeroticism. For me, this is a vital part of the significance of these texts as cultural and as social documents. I want to assert my own right to do this along with the right of Renaissance poets to do the same. I am assuming that these poets saw the classical texts not merely as lessons to be learned, but also as storehouses of images and themes that could signify homoeroticism for the reader then and now. Further, I am assuming that readers who were also writers felt free to transform the material they read, to use it for their own purposes.[7]

My use of the term 'space' has been influenced by Michel de Certeau's work. His sociological analysis of everyday life and his analogy between using public places and using language provide a good analogy to my comments about reading and about making use of what one has read. De Certeau makes an important distinction between a place and a space:

> [S]pace is a practiced place. Thus the street geometrically defined by urban planning is transformed into a space by walkers. In the same way, an act of reading is the space produced by the practice of a particular place: a written text, i.e., a place constituted by a system of signs.[8]

De Certeau says that people who use public places 'trace "indeterminate trajectories" that are apparently meaningless, since they do not cohere with the constructed, written, and prefabricated space through which they move'; he goes on to say that although these movements form sentences that 'use as their *material* the *vocabularies* of established languages' and 'remain within the framework of prescribed *syntaxes*, these "traverses" remain heterogeneous to the systems they infiltrate and in which they sketch out the guileful ruses of *different* interests and desires.'[9] De Certeau's formulations are particularly helpful both because of the connection they make between spatial and linguistic considerations and because they present the use of large-scale systems as an act of interpretation. Consumers of texts, even of the famous classical texts central to Renaissance notions of culture, history, and identity, similarly interpret texts as they move through them according to their own 'interests and desires.' If a famous classical text is a public place open to all in the Renaissance who could read Latin, a reading that highlighted its homoeroticism – a reading that might inform a new poem – would turn that place into a space. I want to look at Renaissance texts as examples of 'the practice of a particular place.'

II

The Renaissance texts I shall discuss can all be classified as imitations, at least in the classical sense of the term. As Summers suggests, Renaissance writers tended to treat the great Greek and Latin texts in part as repositories of images, metaphors, themes, and plots. Their educations encouraged them to do so, as did the reading habits of their educated audience. As a result, in reading Renaissance texts, one is often aware of the classical original showing through. Given the increasing scarcity of instruction in Greek and Latin, many readers today originally learn classical texts through Renaissance ones, as I did myself. We may first have read Catullus because of *Volpone* or Theocritus because of 'Lycidas.' As Thomas Greene has pointed out, learning about the classics in this way can be problematic for conscientious readers:

> Reading imitations makes even larger claims on the historical imagination than most reading, and underscores even more cruelly our cultural solitude. It asks us not only to intuit an alien sensibility from a remote *mundus significans*, but also that sensibility's intuitions of a third.[10]

The latter is my interest: not so much to understand the *mundus significans* of the classical world as to try to figure out how that *mundus significans* appeared to the Renaissance. In this study, I am less concerned with what Theocritus, for instance, thought of homoeroticism than with how his depiction of it might be used by a reader from a society in which homoeroticism was more or less strictly regulated. Perhaps an example is in order. To readers brought up in Christian societies, characterizations of sexuality as either natural or unnatural will be only too familiar and will evoke the ideas of heterosexuality and homosexuality respectively. When these people read poems in which a sexuality whose object is undefined is depicted as opposed to nature (I am speaking of the first idyll) they will be likely to think that the eroticism in question is homoeroticism. I am looking for the presence in classical texts of what readers in societies influenced by Christian ideas of sexuality might read as the signs of homoeroticism.

As scholars, we may well want to point out that readings of this sort are wrong because they anachronistically assume that other cultures conform to the rules and customs of our own culture. This point is well taken and it is often crucial to stress cultural differences, but we should perhaps consider that a misreading of this kind may on occasion be more productive than a more correct meaning. For one thing, a misreading of this kind may lead to what Greene has called a mistranslation.[11] He is referring to the process by which Renaissance writers misunderstood the classical and medieval texts that they were imitating. These misunderstandings may be the result of imperfect knowledge of the language in which the original to be imitated was written or they may come from the poet's sense of what is useful for his own text. To use one of Greene's examples, misunderstandings of this kind are everywhere in Wyatt's translations of Petrarch. Because their divergences from the Italian originals are numerous and often startling (rather than despite this fact), Wyatt's poems stand on their own as literature in the way that more accurate translations, such as Robert M. Durling's excellent prose versions in his dual-language edition of Petrarch, do not. Furthermore, I am not solely concerned with texts here and one reason to approve of misreadings is that they are not only productive of new texts but also of a sense of new possibilities in life. Greek and Latin texts may be used to construct, or at least to adumbrate, an emancipatory sexual discourse. To put it another way, the textual motion of the strong reader can be translated into the literal motion of cruising, in which people sexualize the urban spaces they inhabit.

III

The homoerotic tradition I have suggested does not extend from ancient Greece to the sixteenth century in a continuous manner. This is partly because the Renaissance had a very different idea of homoeroticism. In Renaissance England, the term sodomy covered a multitude of actions; furthermore, there was, as Foucault has pointed out, no real equivalent for our contemporary habit of classifying people by sexual activity – except, at times, in a legal context, in which, again, a category of persons was identified with an activity.[12] The best account of the history of sodomy in this era is Alan Bray's *Homosexuality in Renaissance England*, which he followed with 'Homosexuality and the Signs of Male Friendship in Elizabethan England.' Both works are immensely valuable to anyone writing about homoeroticism in the English Renaissance, and they have informed much of my own work; but as my approach differs from Bray's, I would like to point out some of my divergences. Bray says, for instance, that 'the homosexual reformers of the late nineteenth century' assumed that Renaissance use of classical models implied 'a tolerant attitude to homosexuality.'[13] This view was, he goes on to say, 'a persuasive myth, but it was not sound history.'[14] Bray's use of the word 'homosexuality' here is obviously tendentious. Despite the title of his book, one of his main points is that homosexuality is a term that cannot legitimately be applied to a period like the Renaissance. Therefore, if we do not speak of homosexuality as having existed in the Renaissance, we will be expected to disagree with any statement that posits its existence. Still, although I do not feel that it is accurate to speak of homosexuality or of homosexuals in the Renaissance, I do feel that writers who had access to classical texts were able to use them to gesture towards other sexual possibilities than the ones officially promoted by their own churches or governments. As Summers points out, '[t]he context in which homosexuality is encoded in Renaissance literature always includes homophobia, yet the signs of early modern culture are more varied, subtle, and multivalent than any monistic culture can accommodate.'[15]

Bray goes on to dismiss the historical value of much of the homoerotic literature produced in the Renaissance by saying that it 'consisted of the conventions of Platonic friendship and of exercises which on analysis turn out to be based on classical models.'[16] Yet the special place of classical models in Renaissance England meant that these models were never just guides to correct style or use of imagery. Virgil and Homer, for instance, were not only considered to be great poets: they were also seen as people who had much to teach about how societies should be run and about what values and actions were to be prized by a society that, like sixteenth-century England, had imperial aspirations and compared itself to ancient Rome. In *Sodometries*, Jonathan Goldberg points out that the 'classical literariness' of a text cannot be said to guarantee 'that it would go unremarked.'[17] It may even be that the reverse is true. The English ruling class had been trained since early childhood to read classical texts very closely, and there has never been a successful way to foreclose readings that are not officially sanctioned.[18] We have no basis for saying that the classical models to which Bray refers were not also, at least at certain times and by certain people, seen as models in life as well as in art.

Despite Bray's ambivalence about literary texts, he makes frequent use of them in both his works. In *Homosexuality in Renaissance England*, after a discussion of various poetic and theatrical writings on sodomy, Bray says that '[w]hen all the purely literary and political elements in these writings have been discounted, we might be left wondering whether they are of any use at all as pieces of social observation.'[19] It is naive to think that any social observation is entirely without 'literary and political elements' – or, for that matter, that those elements can be neatly removed from a text. In fact, because their biases are easier to spot, avowedly literary and political texts may well be of greater use than seemingly impartial texts. Bray's implicit distinction between fanciful literary texts and a historical reality that can be recovered in some way has been ably criticized by Elizabeth Pittinger, who points out the 'double standard Bray applies to literary texts.'[20] While Bray sometimes makes very perceptive comments about the social uses of literature in the Renaissance, he tries at other times to separate literature and society altogether. In particular, his article 'Homosexuality and the Signs of Male Friendship in Elizabethan England' rests on an untenable polarization of sodomy and friendship. For instance, Bray devotes about one-quarter of his article to an explanation of how the fact that a man would speak of another man as his bedfellow and that he would speak of kissing him cannot be taken as proof of any sexual activity between the two.[21] This is obviously true as far as it goes, but what Bray does not appear ready to consider is that the use of such language is not proof that sexual activity did not take place. This is simple logic: two men who speak very affectionately of each other and who kiss each other are surely more likely to be having sex than two men who do not. Nor is the assumption that two people who were friends did not have sex any more plausible or historically rigorous than the assumption that they did.

The purpose of my book is not to settle the question of which Renaissance men were having sex with other men, although I would be happy to know. In one of the first books ever published on homosexuality and literary history, Rictor Norton pointed out that 'the critic of "homosexual literature" is under no special obligation to be an expert sleuth in detecting erotic innuendo.'[22] Rather than making a firm distinction between a sexual relationship and a friendship, I prefer 'to hypothesize the potential unbrokenness of a continuum between homosocial and homosexual,' to use Eve Kosofsky Sedgwick's famous formulation.[23] Despite the official condemnations of both the church and the state, men in the Renaissance do not in practice appear to have felt that sex between men was necessarily incompatible with what we would now think of as a conventional (heteroerotic) life. Furthermore, since it is almost always impossible to prove that sexual contact did or did not take place, my interest here is not so much in sex as in love between men, a love that can be subsumed under the heading of friendship but that often seems – not just for us but also for the Renaissance writers I shall discuss – to exceed this category. In the Renaissance, as I see it, the continuum that Sedgwick has hypothesized between men who are friends and men who are lovers was less broken than in our own time.[24]

A particularly good example of this conflation of categories that are to us so distinct can be found in Erasmus's *De copia*, a collection of phrases from classical authors, organized by topic. In section 119, which deals with ways of expressing love, Erasmus quotes from the first line of Virgil's second eclogue: 'Corydon ardebat Alexim' (Corydon burned for

Alexis). Romantic passion can also be found in some of the other citations (e.g., 'flagrat amore tui' [he burns with passionate love for you]), but is less certain in 'amat effusissime' (he loves immoderately) and is absent, as far as I can see, from citations such as 'tui tuorumque est observantissime' (he is extremely respectful to you and to your family).[25] It is obvious that Erasmus, at least in this context, was more concerned with the similarities among the various expressions of love than in differences of kind or degree (or, it would appear, in differences of gender). Furthermore, *De copia* is an educational text whose purpose is to help people to write in Latin. A sixteenth-century student who used it could have drawn the inference that the book sanctions the passionate love of a man for another man. One inference that any reader of any period can legitimately draw from the examples cited in this section is that the love of one man for another is not utterly removed from other kinds of love or even what we would now call esteem. For some people, section 119 may well appear to be a homoerotic space, or at least a place that can be transformed by a certain practice of reading; it certainly demonstrates that our contemporary ideas about the difference between romantic love and friendly love do not fit very well with Renaissance texts and lives. Furthermore, we should remember that romantic love and friendly love are not unchanging natural objects, but rather are frequently modified and always socially contextualized, as the variety of the phrases offered by Erasmus would indicate.

IV

Most previous analyses of the Renaissance use of classical homoerotic sources have concentrated on the myth of Ganymede, which is seen by both Leonard Barkan in *Transuming Passion: Ganymede and the Erotics of Humanism* and James M. Saslow in *Ganymede in the Renaissance: Homosexuality in Art and Society* as triumphant. Although my main concern is not with Ganymede – or, indeed, with triumph – the formulations of these critics, and of Barkan in particular, are useful to me. Barkan says that

> [w]e are dealing with a cultural series in three terms: the revival of ancient literary forms expressive of homosexual desire; the myth of Ganymede along with a tradition of interpretation that denies or sublimates the latent sexual content; a lived society in which pederastic or other homosexual relations may be undertaken.[26]

Barkan appears to see the tradition of interpretation as essentially repressive. I think that the homosexual desire here does not inhere in the ancient forms or texts themselves; rather, it inheres or can inhere in interpretation. Although the scholarly tradition has usually sought to rule out homoerotic content, often in doing so it has nonetheless admitted that such an interpretation is held by some people. Yet interpretation is not only a question of the official scholarly tradition: there is often a parallel tradition, unofficial and more open to discussions of sexuality. This parallel tradition can be found (or glimpsed) in poetry.

Barkan illustrates his third term, the relationship between literary forms and lived society, with an analysis of an anecdote from Cellini's autobiography about a dispute with the artist Bandinelli over both art and sexuality. The dispute ended triumphantly for Cellini in his creation of three new statues that proved his point and demonstrated his superiority as an artist:

> By making these three statues – Ganymede, Apollo and Hyacinthus, Narcissus – Cellini defines the tradition of antiquity. Foremost, of course, is the fact that it is definitionally homoerotic. True lovers of antiquity (unlike Bandinelli) are above all lovers and, more specifically lovers of the beauty of boys.[27]

Barkan goes on to point out that 'Cellini sets these works in a context of loss,'[28] and he develops this point in a crucial footnote:

> I do not mean to establish a Hollywood-in-the-fifties-style connection between homosexuality and despair. Still, in a volume that concentrates upon a triumphant story of male love, it is important to recollect how powerful is the mythic and mythological tradition that associates it with barrenness and death.[29]

In *Epistemology of the Closet*, Sedgwick makes a similar connection that she also develops in a footnote: 'One might look, for instance, to Achilles and Patroclos, to Virgilian shepherds, to David and Jonathan, to the iconography of St. Sebastian, to elegiac poetry by Milton, Tennyson, Whitman, and Housman, as well as to the Necrology of Vito Russo's *Celluloid Closet*.'[30]

I have no intention of discussing all these topics, but clearly the number of examples Sedgwick is able to come up with (and the list is far from complete) points to a long-lasting association of homoeroticism with early death. In his recent survey of Western thinking about death, Jonathan Dollimore says that 'the sexually dissident have known that the strange dynamic which, in Western culture, binds death into desire is not the product of a marginal pathological imagination, but crucial in the formation of that culture.'[31] According to this point of view, the elegy is not only the most obvious literary manifestation of this dynamic[32] but also a form central to our culture as a whole. Furthermore, what is lost in the elegy is not just the particular man whose death is mourned: as the elegy is, in its origins and in most of the examples we have, a poem that takes place in a pastoral setting, the poem also mourns the loss of the pastoral landscape. After all, the pastoral is a genre that begins in the classical period with such losses as the death of Daphnis in Theocritus's first idyll and the eviction of goatherds in Virgil's first eclogue; by the sixteenth century, with greater population density and greater governmental control of land and land use, the setting of the pastoral (a setting that is classical in both senses of the word) was clearly something that only existed in poetry.

V

Before I consider the association of the pastoral with loss I want to return briefly to the Ganymede myth. What interests me about this myth is how we have to think about it in order to consider it a triumphant story. Ganymede goes to Heaven and remains young and beautiful forever, but his lover on earth presumably wrote an elegy for him. The myth is triumphant only because Ganymede ends up in heaven. This may sound obvious, but the point is that happiness is elsewhere: in heaven, in the Ganymede myth; in the rural landscape, in the pastoral elegy and in pastoral poetry as a whole. In order to appreciate Ganymede's triumph, we have to acknowledge the imperfection of the world in which we live. Here, I am following Friedrich Schiller's famous views on the nature of pastoral art:

> If the poet contrasts the nature of art and the ideal of reality in such a way that the representation of the former preponderates and pleasure in it becomes the dominant emotion, then I call it elegiac ... Nature and the ideal are an object of sadness if the former is represented as lost and the latter as unattained.[33]

Schiller's point is that much of pastoral literature is inherently elegiac: the loss of the original rural paradise is irreparable, like the loss
of the beloved man in the traditional elegy. As Adam Parry put it in a
discussion of landcape in Greek poetry, 'Nature no longer tells us what
we are: it tells us what we are not but yearn to be.'[34] It is only in art that
our mythical former perfection and our mythical future perfection can
be apprehended.

In his influential recent book on pastoral, Paul Alpers make a distinction between Schiller, whose 'model of nature is the child and its
maturing,' and critics like Parry, for whom 'landscape [is] representative of nature and the issue it raises.'[35] Both views of nature are necessary conditions for the homoerotic tradition I want to examine. The
ability of pastoral poetry to recreate both a bygone place and a bygone
time allows for the creation of what I call homoerotic space: a safe,
because carefully demarcated, zone in which homoeroticism can appear. This kind of spatialization of sexuality is a traditional way of
talking about sexual practices. In his discussion of the discourse of
sodomy in colonial New England, Michael Warner points out that this
geographical separation is built into the word sodomy itself: '[l]ike
the much later coinage lesbianism, sodomy still implies, at however
fantasmatic a level, a map of sexual knowledges and exotic origins.'[36]
While in using the terms 'sodomy' or 'Philistinism' we support our
disapproval by conjuring up the other associations of Sodom or Philistia,
if we connect sexual activity between men to ancient Greece, it is
impossible to foreclose interpretations that connect that activity with
the many things we are supposed to admire about Greek civilization.
Authors have used the association of homosexuality with ancient Greece
as a way to present homoeroticism in a relatively positive light.[37]

Homoeroticism does have a space, then, but that space is always
elsewhere and usually textual. In his study of homoeroticism in English
literature, Paul Hammond notes that in some Renaissance texts, 'homosexual desire is either expressed within the continuum of public masculine relationships, or located in a privileged space.'[38] I would like now
to consider why the most common choice of setting for homoerotic
literature has been the pastoral landscape, which is, as Alpers's discussion of Schiller can be taken to suggest, both a different time – the early
years of a particular culture or the early years of the individual or both
– and a different place – the unspoiled landscape that is so different
from the civilized areas in which we live. The pastoral landscape is

doubly suitable for homoerotic space because, as Eleanor Winsor Leach points out in her study of Virgil, the relation of the landscape from which we are presumed to have come to the landscape in which we now find ourselves tends to be somewhat antagonistic:

> The garden of Eden and the golden age – the legendary ideals of the pastoral – are primitivistic, fertile, indeed maternal, intrinsically threatening to the security and identity of civilized man ... [B]y accepting and dramatizing the elusiveness of the garden, [the poet] renders it subject to control; it need not endanger his established selfhood or his allegiance to the imperfect world that he knows.[39]

All the features of the pastoral landscape and of the people who inhabit it may temporarily be recreated and celebrated – indeed, this is a necessary process, as civilization depends on the fertility (often metaphorically described as maternal) of the earth. Nevertheless, this landscape must be presented in such a way that human control of it is evident: civilization is largely defined by its effects on and differences from the pastoral landscape.

The fact that the pastoral setting is so clearly marked as remote has been seized upon as an opportunity by many writers, as David M. Halperin remarks: 'its usefulness was perceived to lie chiefly in satire or allegory. Pastoral afforded a vehicle for veiled comments on ecclesiastical or political matters.'[40] Shepherds are presumed to be free from social rules and restrictions and this freedom can be presented as something that we should envy. The operations of the state (the imposition of its will) are not absent from pastoral poetry, but they tend to appear as the intrusion of alien forces. Thus, state and ecclesiastical power are made to appear unnatural in the context of poetry that celebrates nature. This is not to say that pastoral poetry is inherently subversive: nothing is inherently subversive. My point is that, as Halperin suggests, pastoral poetry seems to offer an opportunity for stressing the extent to which the laws governing our lives may themselves be artificial. In Renaissance literature, the greater freedom afforded by the pastoral genre was usually employed by people who wished to make religious or political points, but the potential for homoerotic space was always present.

The use of the pastoral has been studied most recently by Curtis Perry. His excellent study concentrates on the Jacobean period and he makes a sharp distinction between the reign of Elizabeth and that of James. While much of what he says is valuable and his demonstration of the uses to which literature can be put is perceptive, the distinction between Elizabethan and Jacobean pastoral is problematic. In his discussion of the tension between the individual and society, Perry says that 'where they are addressed in Elizabethan pastoral, questions about the relationship between subject and society tend to be approached by exploring only the emotions and experiences of a particular individual.'[41] He develops this point a little later on:

> [T]he characterological focus of Elizabethan pastoral contributed to the domestication of social criticism, eliding its most telling and potentially subversive questions. Attention to the prodigality, love-sickness, or simply private depths of an individual character deflects attention away from the production of social problems.[42]

Perry's argument rests on a distinction between public and private that I feel is untenable. Although my emphasis in this book is not in historicizing the pastoral, I feel that it is important to note that an individual's 'private depths' are never only private. The love affairs of fictional shepherds may not seem to be of national concern, but surely the question of how much power national bodies such as the church or the state should have over private lives is a public issue. To me, what Perry refers to as 'the domestication of social criticism' is a very promising development indeed, as it implies the serious consideration of serious issues.

Near the beginning of his discussion, Perry remarks that '[p]astoral ... is a literary kind which tends to be explicitly concerned with "the allusive presences" of its predecessors; the sheer artifice and conventionality of pastoral attitudes and settings underscores the allusive as well as the innovative elements in each individual text.'[43] While I agree with Perry's comments on allusion, I want to make the point that the artificiality of pastoral poetry is itself a fiction. In its themes, characters, and settings, the pastoral is no more artificial than most other genres. It is hard to account for the fact that the pastoral is described as artificial while *Hamlet* and *The Tempest* are not, except by suggesting that a genre that presents agricultural labourers – some of the poorest people in the societies in which pastoral poets lived – as interesting, intelligent, articulate, and worth our attention is bound to be seen as artificial. To take shepherds seriously would involve rethinking the social structure of classical and Renaissance Europe. Still, this is the conception of pastoral poetry we have inherited, and as a result the pastoral can lead us to notice how unnatural art in general is. In particular, the pastoral's juxtaposition of natural and unnatural might prompt us to consider how it is that we decide which things go in which of those two catego- ries. For this reason, forms of sexual expression deemed to be unnatural have often found a place in pastoral poetry, as Gregory M. Bredbeck notes: 'In the sixteenth and seventeenth centuries one of [pastoral's] primary interests is its participation in fields of sexual deviation.'[44] In fact, 'fields of sexual deviations' could easily be the subtitle of many of the most famous pastoral poems. As I shall show later on, pastoral poetry (in particular, those pastorals that are elegies) often functions as a resistance to the supposed laws of nature rather than as a celebration of them, as has often been imagined. By highlighting the artificiality of poetry in general, a poet can suggest that when we speak about nature we are really speaking about different forms of 'social representation.'

Most of the pastoral poems I shall discuss are in fact pastoral elegies. Perhaps more than any other kind of poetry, this one has lent itself to expressions of the love of one man for another, or at least to celebrations of the youth and beauty of a dead or dying man. Micaela Janan has suggested that we can read Ovid's version of the story of Apollo and Hyacinth, one of the most famous tales of male love in the classical tradition, as a story about the pastoral elegy's origin: 'the beloved of the lover is, paradoxically, killed by him – and, in dying, yields him his new genre.'[45] Of course, the pastoral elegy was, although not under that name, a well-established form by the time of the *Metamorphoses*, but Janan's interpretation is highly suggestive. Almost all the famous pastoral elegies (and many of the obscure ones) are to some extent homoerotic. The double separation of the form from the society in which the poet lives – the separation inherent in the setting and the separation caused by the fact that the man who was beloved is now dead – gives the poet the space and the freedom to expatiate on the love of one man for another: homoerotic expressions may be excused as the hyperbole of mourning, especially since the classical precedent – in what is almost the legal sense of the word – for the genre as a whole is the well-known story of Apollo and Hyacinth, which was also the subject of one of Cellini's triumphantly homoerotic statues.

VI

Up to this point, I have concentrated on pastoral poetry. There is, however, another kind of poetry that has often provided poets with homoerotic space: war poetry. The connection between these two forms of poetry has been apparent since the beginning, as Judith Haber points out in her comments on Theocritus, who is considered to be the first pastoral poet:

> Throughout the *Idylls*, both the poet and his characters repeatedly recreate, in diminished forms, the heroism they leave behind. Attempts to evade this dilemma, moreover, merely succeed in reinforcing it: at its most extreme, the bucolic perspective becomes identified with and indistinguishable from the heroic.[46]

If we see pastoral poetry as in some sense growing out of epic poetry, then pastoral's tendency to become elegiac will seem even less strange. The lament for Daphnis, in what is considered to be the first pastoral poem ever, is thus connected to the laments for young warriors that form such a large part of both the *Iliad* and the *Odyssey* and that provide those poems with what we now call romantic interest. In both kinds of poetry, we could also give the name homoerotic space to the gap between the living and the dead, a gap filled with laments. It may even be that the nostalgia for country life that pervades so much pastoral is an extension of the regret for the loss of so many young men.

Both pastoral and epic are governed by strong, if not always easily defined, generic conventions; part of my aim in this study is to show how poems violate these conventions. In this I am following W. David Shaw's work on elegy, in which he points out that '[a]s elegists keep testing the conventions, little cracks or fissures begin to break apart what A.J. Greimas called the marks of "truth-saying" or veridiction in their language. It might be argued that, as students of elegy, we should be studying the history of these fractures.'[47] Indeed, that is part of my project here: I shall be concerned with the ways in which certain poems significantly disobey generic conventions. An attachment that seems to exceed the bounds of the homosocial and become homoerotic may be figured in a text as a poetic excess or even as a deficiency. For instance, we can see the generic difficulties of *The Winter's Tale* as exemplifying the disruptive potential of the homoerotic attachment that precedes the events dramatized in the play. Another example is the convention of the *consolatio*, in which the speaker of an elegy turns to a new object, typically the hope of literary success. An elegy that omits the *consolatio* makes the point that this new object (what Freud would call a substitute) is unacceptable. A literary transgression may be read as a metaphoric substitution for a social transgression or, at least, as a sign of that transgression.

The poems I shall discuss, however, do not merely violate conventions: they often conform to them; if they did not, we would not be able to recognize these poems as pastoral or epic. The conformity and the violation should be understood as parts of the same process. Tzvetan Todorov has said of genre that '[t]he fact that a work "disobeys" its genre does not make the latter nonexistent; it is tempting to say that quite the contrary is true ... The norm becomes visible – lives – only by transgression.'[48] This is the double bind: in order to object to a particular genre a poet still has to work within it, and for this reason it is difficult to determine whether the use of a particular convention is merely formal or if it signifies an acquiescence to the ideas behind the convention. Here again, I suggest that textual and social transgression are linked. Just as the poet must still write within specific genres, so he must still live within a specific society, and in order to do either or both he must conform to certain rules. We can now return to the passage from Foucault: 'Discourses are not once and for all subservient to power or raised up against it.' This time, we are approaching the quotation from the other side. The qualities in the nature and use of discourse that prevent it from being purely repressive also prevent it from being purely emancipatory. Since the Renaissance texts I shall discuss opened only a very small and temporary homoerotic space, I want to show not only the opportunities for expression they found and created but also the defeats they suffered and the dissatisfactions they felt.

For me, one of the most important connections between pastoral and war poetry is that both depict societies in which intense emotional relationships are more common between men than between men and women. Readers from societies ruled by Judaeo-Christian ideas of morality have found that pastoral poetry often depicts the homoerotic activity permissible to some extent between adolescents and war poetry often depicts the homoerotic activity permissible to some extent between men who find themselves temporarily without women. The homosociality of pastoral may also be a result of its origins in epic verse; the history of pastoral verse would presumably have been very different if it had evolved from a genre (like the lyric or the drama) in which women played a more important role. Unlike the farmer or the courtier, the soldier and the shepherd live on the margins of society in places where women are not usually found. In their different ways, both the soldier, in carrying out the orders of his country's government, and the shepherd, in tending his flocks (*pecunia*, property or money, derives from *pecus*, herd or flock), safeguard the interests of the society to which they often rather tenuously belong.

Both kinds of poetry take place in settings that are, as a rule, outside the society in which the poet and his audience live, but in both cases the setting is closely connected to that society and its sense of itself. Both war poetry and pastoral poetry could be said to be genres of origin because their settings tend to evoke the beginnings of the society in which the poets write. The pastoral setting may be presented as a simpler and more virtuous version of the court and city, a version that recalls the early days of the nation in question. There is often at least a tacit acknowledgment of the fact that the wealth of the nation is largely agricultural in origin. Furthermore, the peace of the rural world may be threatened by events in the civilized world, as it famously is in Virgil's *Eclogues*. In this case, the entire poem or series of poems may be read as critical of the civilized world. The implied contrast between the virtu-ous toil, simple diet, and unadorned clothing of rural labourers and the decadent lives of urban aristocrats is perhaps the most familiar political use of pastoral poetry, and for this reason much pastoral poetry has been read as forming part of a larger debate about the relative merits of the country and the city. The unproblematic homoeroticism of pastoral labourers in Theocritus and Virgil, which appears to be as much a part of the pastoral landscape as the people and animals who inhabit this landscape, would strike a Renaissance reader as perhaps the most obvious contrast between the classical pastoral world and the civiliza-tion of Renaissance Europe.

Although both forms of poetry lend themselves to serving as vehicles for the examination of the poet's world, the pastoral stage is usually presented as something that an imperial society has to some extent outgrown, for better or for worse, while war is tacitly acknowledged as a condition that cannot be outgrown. Indeed, war is one of the ways in which societies tend to define and assert themselves as societies. Never-theless, war poetry is, like pastoral poetry, a poetry of origins, as it often chronicles the process by which one tribe raises itself above its neigh-bours. Yet although war is always with us, the soldiers whose affection for each other is celebrated tend to be young men. As with pastoral poetry, war poetry takes place in a setting that is tied to youth and immaturity; but while the former depicts the youth of a society, the latter depicts the youth of individuals. Both pastoral and war poetry can provide homoerotic space because of their threefold distance: the geographical distance between the field – whether it is the meadow or the field of battle – and the city; the temporal distance between youth and maturity; and the metaphysical distance between the dead and the living. In my discussions of the *Aeneid* and, in my final chapter, of plays about courts, I concentrate on the texts' elegiac aspects because I see war poetry and the pastoral as both centrally concerned with loss.

I have referred to the poetics of loss in my subtitle because I see loss as characteristic of the poetry I discuss. The poetry is simultaneously the record of that loss and something that compensates for that loss. By testifying to the fact that what he documents has come to an end, the poet can declare his distance from the potentially dangerous story he tells while in substituting a poem for a homoerotic attachment he grants that attachment a textual survival.[49] This strategy would appear to be foolproof, but in practice it has not always been so easy for poets to separate themselves from the stories they tell. Sometimes the recompense offered by art may seem insufficient. As Dollimore remarks in his discussion of the poet C.P. Cavafy, 'aesthetic recompense only goes so far; the risk of desire is always there, and never more so than in the experience of loss.'[50] It is also a problem that, as Dollimore goes on to say, '[t]he risk of desire is also inside memory.'[51] The elegist, who sees in the death of the man he loves both a particular loss (that man is no more) and a general one (it is not possible to love another man in that way), resembles the protagonists of revenge tragedy whom Michael Neill has recently and memorably described: 'Alternately disabled by their inability to forget, and driven by their violent compulsion to remember, revenge heroes must wrestle to redeem their dead from the shame of being forgotten, even as they struggle to lay these perturbed spirits to rest, and thereby free themselves from the insistent presence of the past.'[52]

To commemorate the dead and, in a more general sense, to pay tribute to anything of value that has been lost, is a duty, but to remain stuck in the act of commemoration is dangerous. When Dido asks Aeneas to tell her the story of the fall of Troy, he says, 'Infandum, regina, iubes renouare dolorem.'[53] If the sorrow is unspeakable for any reason, to renew it may be fatal, especially if renewing sorrow means renewing desire. I take Dollimore's comment that the risk of desire is in memory to refer not only to the memory of a particular person but also to the cultural memory of a genre or form that is associated with homoeroticism. This, then, is the problem of the Renaissance writers I discuss: how to situate works within a homoerotic space without be-coming trapped in that space. In this book, I want to explore both the use these writers made of homoerotic space and how they negotiated their way through it.

CHAPTER ONE

Classical Pastoral and Elegy

Theocritus: Against Nature

Theocritus's idylls stand at the very beginning of the pastoral (or bucolic) tradition.[1] The Theocritean corpus as it has come down to us includes soliloquies, dialogues, and versions of famous mythical stories. Not all poems are set in the countryside, nor are all the characters in the poems in the same social class. Homoeroticism is important in many of the poems, but by no means in all. Finally, not all the poems in the corpus are by Theocritus. I have given this summary because Theocritus is an author who has been endlessly constructed and reconstructed and he has usually been read – at least by specialists in Latin or in modern languages – for what he can tell us about Virgil. I also read Theocritus for what he can tell us about Virgil and other later authors and I have also constructed my own Theocritus. In this part of this chapter, I want to look only at the first idyll, which has probably been the most influential of all, and the thirteenth, which tells the story of Heracles and Hylas. In being so selective, I have followed a common pattern in reading Theocritus. In keeping with the theme of my study, I have chosen the two that are arguably most concerned with loss.

Idyll I

The very first idyll of all is a sophisticated and self-reflexive poem. It is also, in part, a pastoral elegy. Two rustics, Thyrsis and an unnamed Goatherd, are lying in the shade during the midday heat, making music and complimenting each other:

Thyrsis.   Sweet is the murmur of the pine's music by the brook, and your piping is also sweet, Goatherd ...

Goatherd.   Sweeter, shepherd, is your song than the noise of the water falling from the rocks above.[2]

This opening tableau sets the scene for the *Idylls* and, indeed, for pastoral poetry as a whole. Theocritus sets up an implicit comparison between natural and artificial music and between instrumental and lyric forms of human music.[3] It is as if at the very beginning of pastoral poetry, nature had already lost to art and instrumental music to poetry. Theocritus praises poetry at the expense of nature; this binary opposition will become one of the most important topics of much, if not all, pastoral poetry.

Whatever our ideas may be about rustic solitude or the lonely lives of pastoral labourers, Theocritus presents pastoral poetry as something men do when together: these bucolic songs are performed in a homosocial setting. In what may be a survival from the genre's roots in epic poetry, poetry is also presented as something at which men compete. In a sense, then, the song contests that are so common in Theocritus and Virgil may be seen as pastoral equivalents to the great duels that structure the *Iliad*. As Peter M. Sacks remarks, '[M]any eclogues are obsessed with establishing who sits where,' that is, with questions of hierarchy.[4] Although this jockeying for both literal and metaphorical position may be friendly, Charles Segal is surely right when he points out that '[t]his most easeful of literary forms paradoxically has tension and antithesis as an inherent part of its mental world.'[5] Furthermore, tension and antithesis turn out to be the defining characteristics of the pastoral environment as a whole: the question of poetic superiority is often connected to questions of financial and social superiority, and the crucial antithesis – the one between the living and the dead – is, as even this first idyll demonstrates, never very far away. The loss that is the subject of my study is a basic component of the genre, as Paul Alpers has pointed out: 'Pastoral convenings are characteristically occasions for songs and colloquies that express and thereby seek to redress separation, absence, or loss.'[6]

The inset poem in the first idyll is entirely concerned with a particular loss: the death of Daphnis. His death has given rise to a large and varied body of criticism (partly because Theocritus tells us so little about his life), much of which attempts to reconstruct his life. This is probably due to the fact that (as Thomas G. Rosenmeyer shrewdly points out) the idyll 'shows the victim not dead but dying, with the result that the lament for Daphnis is at the same time, and perhaps more importantly, a protest of the victim *against* nature.'[7] This is one of the aspects of the first idyll that was not, as a rule, followed: in later pastoral poetry, it is more usual to protest against those who intrude upon the natural setting, like the soldiers in Virgil's eclogues. Here, however, much could lead us to consider the poem as a protest against nature. For example, the impossibilities or *adunata* in Daphnis's last speech are important precisely because the things he predicts are impossible and do not come to pass. Whatever Daphnis may hope, nature apparently does not care about human pain. Moreover, while these *adunata* are concerned with external nature, Theocritus also protests against what we consider human nature. Figures like Priapus, the Nymphs, Venus, and the Fates all represent aspects of external nature or human nature and all are indifferent or hostile to him. What is especially significant to me is that Daphnis's inability to live in the natural world is caused by his love. As Priapus's remarks suggest, the disjunction between the cowherd and his surroundings is most obvious in the realm of sexuality. To those raised in societies in which sexuality is categorized as either natural or unnatural, Daphnis's unnatural love will seem like that other kind of unnatural love, the kind that also cannot be discussed – or at least not by Christians.

Among so many shadowy things in the idyll, one thing that is clear is that Daphnis is unable to express himself sexually. His poetic expression can be seen as a substitute for sexual expression. In the introduction to his excellent translation of the idylls, Daryl Hine writes of the connection between sexuality and poetry in Theocritus:

> [N]aked sexual longing ... pervades the poetry of Theocritus ... Yet [this longing] is usually a frustrated longing, indeed is defined as such, an unrequited or intrinsically impossible passion ... The only remedy, our poet tells us more than once, is poetry; and poetry is its own reward ... If the shepherd is often an unhappy lover in Theocritus, he is always a triumphant poet.[8]

I would even say that the poet's triumph is largely the result of the lover's failure. In Theocritus, and I think this is true of many of the poets I shall discuss, poetry tends to come from losses of various kinds. Here, a double loss – Daphnis's failure at love and his death – gives rise to the first idyll, to all the other idylls, and ultimately, as we now know, to pastoral poetry itself.

The most obvious question to ask of an elegy is whose death is being remembered and what sort of man he was. In the case of the first idyll, almost all we know about Daphnis is his name. A character called Daphnis appears in other poems by Theocritus: in the second epigram he offers gifts to Pan; in the third epigram, he is about to be visited by Pan and Priapus; and in the fourth epigram he is the object of the poet's love. There are also other Greek poems that have a character called Daphnis. Still, these mentions do not add up to a cohesive literary character. In order to construct a character of this sort, Kathryn J. Gutzwiller has recourse to Parthenius's account of a man called Daphnis and, after discussing various theories about him, says that '[i]t is easier to assume (and it fits better with the words of Daphnis' visitors) that he is dying simply because he refuses to satisfy his love for the mortal girl [Xenea].'⁹ Gutzwiller's interpretation is typical of discussions of the poem, but some have seen the indeterminacy of the presentation of Daphnis in the first idyll as significant. For instance, Ellen Zetzel Lambert says that if Theocritus 'did inherit such a conception of the "woes of Daphnis," ... then we must be struck by the degree to which he departs from that traditional presentation when he tells the story himself in the first *Idyll*.'¹⁰ Segal also notices the difference between this Daphnis and the others, and says that 'a distortion of the myth in a poet as learned and sophisticated as Theocritus cannot but be intentional.'¹¹ The Daphnis of the first idyll is a character about whom almost nothing can be said with certainty; rather than trying to flesh out Theocritus's conception of him, we should consider the importance of his obscurity.

For me, one of the most striking aspects of Daphnis in the first idyll (and of his obscurity) is that his life, as opposed to his death, is literally unspeakable. In his book on elegy, W. David Shaw speaks of what he calls the ineffability topos: 'Since death is not an experience inside life, but an event that takes place on its boundary, every elegy sooner or later reaches the limits of language.'¹² We can relate the ineffability topos to the specific ineffability that is so puzzling in the first idyll, a poem that keeps returning to the limits of language. At the beginning, language is compared to the noises of nature and is praised for its sweetness rather than its sense. This may be true of the elegy itself, with its utterances that are formulaic (the refrain), non-verbal (the sounds of animals), not altogether clear (the speeches of Daphnis), beside the point (the speech of Priapus), or deceptive (the speeches of Aphrodite).

In order to supply the sense, we, like Daphnis's visitors, must make our own interpretations that we can never check against the truth. The central ineffability that causes all the others is the reason for Daphnis's sorrows. This reason, which clearly has something to do with sexuality and which cannot be expressed, will be reminiscent of homosexuality to readers for whom this is the thing that dare not speak its name.

In the course of the poem, Daphnis has several visitors both human and divine. It might be expected that they could tell us the nature of the sorrows of Daphnis, but they are also at a loss and have to resort to guessing. Even if the gods appear to be guessing, we might expect that Daphnis's fellow men would know something. Nevertheless, just after Hermes's appearance, Theocritus says, 'The cowherds, shepherds, and goatherds came, all inquiring what was wrong with him' (80–1). It is possible that Daphnis's sorrows, which are clearly caused by love, are caused by a kind of love that is so strange that neither the gods themselves nor the men who, like Daphnis, live and work in the bucolic landscape, are able to understand it. At any rate, this is one way to take Theocritus's statement that Daphnis 'was working on a bitter love, and he worked on it until the end of his life' (92–3). Theocritus never tells us what this bitter love is, but perhaps some indication may be found in the scornful epithet '*dyseros*' (85) that Priapus uses of Daphnis. As F.J. Williams has pointed out, the 'word ... has given rise to difficulties.'[13] Liddell and Scott define it as 'sick in love with,' except in the case of this line, where they say it means 'hardly loving, stony-hearted.' This must be a mistake, as the first meaning they give fits much better with the context. Daphnis is undeniably in love but there is something wrong with his love. One of Williams's comments is especially relevant to my analysis. He notes that in Greek poetry 'the word tends to mean "homosexual," but it is not always used in a very precise way.'[14] Thus, there may be some indication that Daphnis's sorrows are caused by love for another man. Whether or not this is the case, what Priapus's speech shows is that Daphnis is removed from the natural sexuality of animals and that his sorrows cannot be understood by the god who is supposed to represent the bestial sexuality within humans.

In his book on Theocritus, Frederick T. Griffiths suggests that Daphnis's problems are not the main focus of the poem anyway: 'The real movement of the poem is in the comparison of artifact to artifact, of one artistic medium to another ... with due attention to the sense of touch, smell, and taste as well.'[15] For this reason, the first idyll could be said to illustrate Hine's point about unhappy love and triumphant poetry, and I would relate this view to Rosenmeyer's comment that the idyll 'shows us that the pastoral elegy is not calculated to provoke grief, but to assuage it, with the reminder that the self (both the victim's and the mourner's) is only one of many, and that the tangible beauty counts for more than spiritual pain.'[16] The tangible beauty here is the poem itself, something which everyone can share and which we are introduced to as part of a social occasion. The spiritual pain is Daphnis's alone, however, and there does not appear to be anyone to mourn him. Thus, the unhappy lover and the triumphant poet are not the same person in this idyll: Daphnis's pain is Thyrsis's (and our) gain. By placing the elegy in the inset poem, Theocritus enables us to read the idyll as an ecphrasis that describes how a work of art is made and what it is made from.

The ecphrastic aspects of the idyll are clearest in the Goatherd's offer of a decorated cup as a reward for Thyrsis's song. This cup has been imitated in numerous poems and given rise to numerous studies.[17] At this point, I want to discuss only one feature of the cup's decoration: 'On it there is a woman wrought, as if by the gods, robed and with a circlet. Beside her two men with long hair argue, but their words do not touch her heart although she looks laughingly first at one and then at the other' (32–7). This is an enigmatic scene, but it does seem to bear various relations to the idyll. The two men arguing could be intended to suggest the Goatherd and Thyrsis (or any of the other pairs of rustics who engage in song competitions), especially since the expression I have translated as argue – *neikeious' epeessi* – means literally to strive with words or, even, to strive with poems. It may be that what the men say to the woman does not touch her heart because their words are not addressed to her. She may represent the object around which a poem is constructed, something that Theocritus carefully separates from the poem, like the cup itself. As well, the woman is dressed and has bound hair while the men's clothes are not mentioned and their hair is long. I take this to suggest that the woman is associated with culture while the men, at least visually, are associated with nature. This is surely significant in a poem that interrogates the relationship between humans and nature. We may also take the tableau to suggest that women – or, at any rate, a specific woman – may split up a male pair. Finally, the two men may seem to mirror Thyrsis and the Goatherd but, unlike them, they are at cross purposes: the placid homosociality with which the idyll begins is not depicted on the cup.

Whatever the significance of the picture, the cup itself is significant because it appears as a prize. Poetry, then, is something that can be evaluated and that can produce a material reward. The theme of poetic evaluation begins in the first lines of the idyll with the comparison of natural and human sounds and with the focus on the quality of sweetness, which is what Theocritus (or at least the Goatherd) most prizes in music. As Theocritus's use of forms of the adjective sweet gives us some insight into his theory of the relationship between what Hine called the unhappy lover and the triumphant poet, I want to look at his use of this adjective in greater detail. Sweet is the first word in the poem and it occurs seven more times. Thyrsis says that the sound of the pine is sweet (1) and that the Goatherd's piping is also sweet (2); the Goatherd responds that Thyrsis's singing is sweeter than the sound of falling water (7). Next, the Goatherd says that he will give Thyrsis goat's milk 'and a deep cup, coated with sweet wax' (27). These occurrences mark a progression, crucial to Theocritus's poetics, from natural sounds to human music and then to objects. The cup is both a work of art (and in some ways a tangible equivalent for singing) and, as I have said, a reward for good singing, but even the cup is not enough: the sweet wax is needed to make it a suitable prize. It is the wax that lifts the cup from a necessary domestic article to an *objet d'art* in a double sense, both an artwork in its own right and the objective of the competitors in pastoral song.

The adjective is next used in the description of Aphrodite as 'sweetly laughing' (95) just after Thyrsis says that Daphnis 'was working on a bitter love' (93).[18] Thus, the contrast between Aphrodite and Daphnis, which is the contrast between happiness and sorrow, is reflected in the juxtaposition of sweet and bitter.[19] The same juxtaposition appears in the description of her as outwardly laughing and inwardly stern. The extent to which Aphrodite is both literally and figuratively out of place in this scene is heightened by the fact that this is the only occurrence of the word sweet in the elegy itself. To me, the adverb shows that Aphrodite is out of place since her sweetness is, I think, insincere and since all the other mentions of sweetness have been in reference to natural things – the rustling of the pines, the falling water, the wax used to clean the cup – or to music, which is seen as having its origin in nature. Thyrsis seems to be recalling the juxtaposition of sweet and bitter when he uses the word after he has finished reciting the elegy. After saying farewell to the Muses, Thyrsis promises to sing a sweeter song later (145). This is his explicit acknowledgment of the incongruity between the sweetness of his poetry and the bitterness of its subject, an acknowledgment that I believe is made implicitly by the initial description of Aphrodite. Thyrsis is content to let the incongruity remain unresolved and his part in the first idyll ends on this entirely character-istic note of ambiguity.

The Goatherd has the last speech in the poem, however. He feels that Thyrsis's singing is already sweet and that in order to sing any more sweetly he will have to eat honey and 'sweet figs' (148). The idea of singing as arising spontaneously from the body recalls the comparison between nature and art in the opening lines. Human music arises from nature and is automatically compared to it. At the end of the idyll, moreover, sweetness is still the standard by which art is judged. The Goatherd is right: despite its sadness, the elegy is famous as one of the most beautiful poems ever written. The bitterness of Daphnis's love does become sweetness – but not for Daphnis. The first idyll is the defining example of the poetics of loss, and this is one of the reasons why it was so frequently employed in homoerotic verse. The death of a young man leads to a poem acknowledged to be a masterpiece. In a society opposed to homoeroticism, the death of the young man came to be seen as a necessary condition not just for the creation of the poem but for the self-creation of the poet as someone whose sexuality was above suspicion. Still – and I think this is characteristic of the poetics of loss – the losses are neither explained nor resolved. Within the frame of the poem, the cup may well strike readers as inadequate compensation for the painful death of Daphnis. As if to prevent the metamorphosis of loss into poetry from seeming too neat, Theocritus ends the poem by returning us to the world of work that has been halted by the midday heat. The Goatherd is forced to address his goats: 'You she-goats, cease leaping or the buck will be on you' (151–2). The verb here is *anastei*, which suggests rising up over someone (with a reference to erection that reminds us of Priapus's comparison of humans and goats in lines 88–9) and which can also mean to rise from the dead. I think the implication here is not that Daphnis will rise from the dead but rather that his sorrows have not disappeared. Although sexuality may be and often is the subject of poetry, it cannot, Theocritus suggests, be con-tained by it, no matter how sweet the singer or the song.

Idyll XIII

While the first idyll gives us an elegy without any of the usual informa-tion about the man who has died or the events leading up to his death, the thirteenth idyll gives us this kind of information without giving us the elegy itself. While the first idyll gives us an elegy for a cowherd recited by another cowherd in a moment of leisure, the thirteenth is the story of the abduction of Hylas, the lover of Heracles, during the voyage of the Argo. I read Idyll XIII in part as a meditation on the various forms of homosociality and on the ways in which these forms can and cannot be combined. For me, the parallel between Idyll I and Idyll XIII is stronger than that between Idyll I and Idyll VII, which is sometimes invoked as a way to explain the sorrows of Daphnis, as both the first and the thirteenth idylls are concerned with homoeroticism in a context of loss.

The poem begins, as does the first idyll (and as does epic poetry), *in medias res*: 'Love was not created for us alone, as we thought, Nicias' (1–2). The speaker supports his unexceptionable contention with an example from heroic literature: 'Even the brazen-hearted man, the son of Amphitryon, who stood his ground against the savage lion, loved a boy: graceful Hylas with flowing hair. Like a father with his beloved son, Heracles taught him everything that had made him virtuous and famous' (5–9). In the first nine lines of the poem, Theocritus gives us three kinds of relations between men: the friendship between the speaker and Nicias, who are presented as if they are in the middle of a conversation; the romantic love between Heracles and Hylas; and the familial bond between a father and his son (of course, the speaker and Nicias could be lovers or father and son as well). The most striking aspect of this passage is the heroic language, with patronymic and formal epithet, used to describe Heracles. In particular, the comparison between the savage lion and the beautiful boy underscores the uneasy coexistence of heroism and love. The comparison of Heracles' love for Hylas to that of a father for his son may strike some readers as incongruous, but the patronymic is actually odder, since just as Heracles is not Hylas's father, so Amphitryon was not Heracles' (his real father was Zeus). These incongruities and the many others like them have the effect of forcing us to consider the place of romantic love in the world and the merit of that love relative to other kinds of relationships.[20]

Theocritus tells us that Heracles spent all his time with Hylas 'so that the boy might be trained after Heracles' intentions, so that by proceeding well from the beginning he would turn out to be a trustworthy man' (14–15). As part of this training, Heracles takes Hylas with him to the Argo on the expedition for which 'were chosen the best men of all the cities' (18). At first, the relationship of Heracles and Hylas is compared to that of a father and his son; now, the two are going to be part of a larger company of heroes – that is, of men working together. Theocritus presents the love between Heracles and Hylas as closely connected to the two forms of homosociality most instrumental in tying a society like his together. The trouble begins when the Argonauts go on shore in Propontis, 'where the oxen of the Cians wear down the ploughs and broaden the furrows' (30–1). Once they have disembarked, the heroes turn their attention to preparing dinner and beds (32–6). I believe that in this passage Theocritus is signalling a shift from the heroic world of, for instance, Apollonius in his depiction of the voyage of the Argo to an agricultural setting similar to that of the first idyll. The presence of heroes in a pastoral setting adds a further incongruity to the idyll and a further aspect to the presentation of homosociality.

The description of the Argonauts and of their journey takes twenty lines (just over one-quarter of the poem). Once the Argo moors in Propontis, Theocritus returns to Hylas. Like the others, Hylas prepares for dinner: 'Golden Hylas went to fetch water for washing for his own Heracles and for unflinching Telamon, for the two companions always ate at one table' (36–8). Up to this point, Theocritus has stressed the closeness of Heracles and Hylas. Now he introduces Telamon, who is also, although in a different way, the companion of Heracles. In the syntax of the Greek original, Hylas's name is separated from Heracles, who is, by contrast, paired with Telamon (although admittedly Heracles is Hylas's 'own'). Furthermore, as Theocritus tells us that Heracles and Telamon 'always' ate together, the implication is that their relationship is of long standing. Mastronarde sees a contrast between Hylas and Telamon as essential to Theocritus's aims: 'Telamon ... is Heracles' companion in the epic world, whereas Hylas has been identified with tender beauty and an idyllic world.'[21] Heracles will eventually have to make a choice between 'golden Hylas' and 'unflinching Telamon.' One kind of homosocial relationship will drive out the other.

The crucial event in the poem occurs at the beginning of the second half and is heralded by what Segal has aptly described as 'uterine symbolism':[22] 'He soon found a spring in a hollow, around which grew many rushes' (38–9). It is at this point that the feminine irrupts into the poem: 'In the middle of the water the nymphs were preparing a dance, nymphs who take no rest, goddesses feared by the rustics' (43–4). As Hylas bends down to get water, the nymphs pull him in because 'love for the Argive boy had seized their tender hearts' (48–9). The epithet 'Argive' (this is the only time Theocritus refers to Hylas's origins) stresses the difference between the human Hylas and the nymphs; it also punningly reminds us of his status as an Argonaut at the moment that this association with the ship is severed. Hylas is unhappy but 'the nymphs took the weeping youth on their knees and soothed him with kind words' (53–4). At first, the nymphs are frightening figures who seem to represent a suitable challenge for a hero, then they fall in love, and in the final reference to them they have assumed a maternal role. The combination of lust and parental love parallels Heracles' feelings for Hylas: we may be intended to think that nymphs make better parents than a hero on a quest. On the other hand, the fact that they are 'preparing a dance' when we first hear of them may indicate that we are intended to see Hylas as a sacrificial victim. We may also be intended to connect them with the indifferent nymphs of the first idyll; perhaps just as the nymphs in the thirteenth idyll are indifferent to the love of Heracles and Hylas, the nymphs in the first idyll are indifferent to Daphnis's sufferings because they are caused by his love for a mortal or, more specifically, for a man.

Once the nymphs seize Hylas, Heracles becomes the focus of the poem (the presence of Hylas in the poem has been enough to remove Heracles from the central position that he occupies in most texts). Heracles wanders through the forest searching for Hylas and calling out to him: 'Those who love are tireless. He worked so hard, roaming over the hills and forests, that Jason's voyage was forgotten' (67–8). The verb meaning to work or to toil, which seems somewhat incongruous in context, actually points out how incongruous Heracles' love has made him. He neglects his real work (the work of heroism) to spend all his time with Hylas or, now, searching for him. The Argonauts wait for Heracles for a time, but 'he wandered, delirious; thus does the cruel god rend the heart' (71–2) and the Argonauts are forced to sail without him: 'so beautiful Hylas was counted among the blessed, while the heroes mocked Heracles as a deserter of the ship, because he left the Argo with its thirty benches. But he came barefoot to Colchis and inhospitable Phasis' (73–6). Halperin has suggested that the idyll is comic, at least as far as Heracles is concerned.[23] The idyll can be read as a rather elaborate joke on Heracles, who has failed to train up Hylas to a life of virtue (has failed even to safeguard him) and who has brought shame upon himself. When he does arrive at Colchis he is barefoot, which means he cuts a less than heroic figure. Yet as Griffiths points out, the word Theocritus puts in the mouths of the sailors – *liponautes* – may be 'proverbial as one of the worst epithets to acquire, given Agamemnon's dread of it,'[24] and the condemnation may be entirely serious.

Theocritus says specifically that Heracles 'left the Argo with its thirty benches.' The benches – more accurately, the thwarts – were first mentioned when the Argonauts disembarked at Propontis and 'prepared their dinners bench by bench' (32). The benches are both where the men work together rowing the ship and where they eat together. The word for bench is *zugon*, the cognate of the English word yoke. It has several common metaphoric extensions that share the basic meaning of a connection between two things. In Greek, as in many other languages, the word can be used metaphorically to mean love, as it does, for instance, in Theocritus's twelfth idyll: 'They loved each other with the same yoke [i.e., equally]' (XII.15). In the case of the thirteenth idyll, Theocritus's use of the word can be interpreted as a way of stressing the homosociality of the Argonauts. Love links them both as co-workers, as men engaged on a heroic enterprise, and as companions, at least for the term of the voyage. Just after Theocritus tells us that the men prepared dinner bench by bench he says that 'many prepared one bed' (33). (This means, as he goes on to tell us, that they all slept in one meadow.) Thus, the Argonauts are bound together both in the small groupings of men who sit at the same bench and as a whole. For them, the homosocial bond connects them not just to one other man but to a large group of men with a common purpose.

The connection among the Argonauts is the same connection that Heracles has had with Telamon, something that has been contrasted with his love for Hylas. But by searching for Hylas, Heracles isolates himself and loses both romantic love and heroic comradeship. In the beautiful passage in which he describes the disappearance of Hylas, Theocritus suggests that the effect it has on the Argonauts is opposite to its effect on Heracles: 'He fell all at once into the black water, just as a flaming star falls all at once from the sky into the sea and a sailor says to his companions: "Let out the tackle, boys. The wind is good for sailing"' (49–52). The simile of the falling star stands out by contrast with the general tone of the poem that is as a rule matter-of-fact, even to terseness (especially by comparison to its near contemporary, Apollonius's *Argonautica*). The famous episode of the clashing rocks is dealt with in only three lines, for instance (22–4). The star metaphor is like an excerpt from an elegy – the elegy we might expect for Hylas; but there is only room for an excerpt. The homoerotic elegy is superseded by the nonsexual homosociality of the sailors who must, always, sail on.

As Hylas falls he enters the dark world of women all alone, while the sailors move together as an all-male group on the surface of the water.

There is a symmetry between the men above the water who leave both Hylas and Heracles behind and the women below the water who take Hylas in. There is also a symmetry between the falling star to which Hylas is compared and the Pleiades, thought of as women, whose rising signals the safe season for navigation (see 25–8). These symmetries are reinforced by Theocritus's diction in this passage. In line 51, the sailor is imagined as speaking to his 'companions,' the same word used of Heracles and Telamon in line 38. In the next line, the sailor addresses his companions as 'boys,' the word used to describe Hylas four times, including line 6, before he is named. The word is also used three lines before this line and three lines after. The sailors work together in such a way that they combine the heroic – they are companions like Heracles and Telamon – and the homoerotic – they are boys like Hylas. In contrast, Heracles fails to maintain either kind of relationship and is an isolated figure at the end of the poem. He is isolated from romantic love by the nymphs who abduct Hylas and from his fellow heroes by the passage of time: the Argo simply cannot wait for him. Heracles, we could say, has been denied homoerotic space.

What is not always considered in discussions of this poem is that Theocritus presents the love between Heracles and Hylas as only one possible relationship between men. Although their love is ultimately unhappy, Theocritus suggests that this love occurs in different forms in male society as a whole and that the bonds that unite heroes are not so very different from romantic love. What connects the thirteenth idyll with the first is that both stress poetry and sexuality as male activities: the first idyll arises from the fact that Thyrsis and the Goatherd are companions and the thirteenth from the debate about love between the speaker and Nicias. Another important connection is that both poems are about loss. Both Daphnis and Hylas die – or more precisely they die to the human world, although in both cases there is at least the suggestion of apotheosis. The main lessons that later poets and readers in general could draw from this were that in the broadest sense love between men was an important part of Greek society, that narratives of male sexuality, when that sexuality is not directed at women, end in death, and, perhaps most important, that poetry has the power to turn death and loss into art and celebration. For people to whom death and loss were very likely consequences of homoerotic behaviour and even of homoerotic discourse, poetry's metamorphic power, as Theocritus demonstrates it, would perhaps have seemed a real compensation.

Virgil: Chronicles of Loss

Virgil's ten pastoral poems were not originally called eclogues, although that is now their official name, and the word has been used to describe thousands of more or less similar poems written in the two millennia since then. The term means simply extract, from the verb *eligo*; the use of the word to mean a pastoral poem is a mistake or, as I think, a productive misreading. The Oxford Latin Dictionary gives the primary meaning of *eligo* as 'To pull out, extract (weeds, etc.)' and the secondary as 'To select, choose, pick out (persons or things).' The commentators who first referred to the poems as eclogues clearly had the second meaning in mind, but the similarities and differences between the two meanings are instructive. The poems were not originally extracts, as they represented all of Virgil's first literary production and when they appeared they were complete in themselves; but they do appear short when set beside the *Aeneid* and like extracts in that ever since Virgil's death readers have thought of his work as a whole and poets and critics have used the trajectory of his writings as a model for a poetic career. The eclogues are now seen as extracts from a larger work, even if this larger work does not complete the eclogues or fill in the gaps between them.

The first meaning of *eligo* – to pull out or extract weeds and other things – is most obviously applicable to the eclogues because it is horticultural. In so far as the concern here is with tending plants rather than merely watching them grow, this sense of the word looks forward to the discussions of agriculture and arboriculture in the *Georgics*, and looking forward to the next work is typical both of Virgil and of his critics. In its metaphoric sense, this meaning of *eligo* has connections to some of the important themes of the collections. The background of much of the eclogues – most famously of the first and the ninth – is a rural landscape out of which the farmers are being pushed:

> uiui peruenimus, aduena nostri
> (quod numquam ueriti sumus) ut possessor agelli
> diceret: 'haec mea sunt; ueteres migrate coloni.'

(I have lived to see it happen to me [which I never feared] that the possessor of my dear field would say: these are mine, go away, old farmer; 9.2–4.)

Ultimately, it is pastoral poetry itself that is weeded out, as the last eclogue shows: 'Extremum hunc, Arethusa, mihi concede laborem' (Arethusa, grant me this last labour; X.1).

What the two meanings of *eligo* have in common is the idea of extraction as selection, of choosing one thing over another. This too relates to the subjects of the eclogues. Sometimes what is to be selected in these poems is a lover. In the second and tenth eclogues for instance, Virgil's emphasis is on the one who is not chosen, the one who loses. More often, what is to be selected is a song. To a greater or lesser extent, all the eclogues focus attention on the selection of a poetic repertoire, that is, on the question of what to sing and why to sing it. Furthermore, romantic and poetic selection are linked in these poems, and both are associated with the uprooting of pastoral labourers that gives the poems their chief historical background. The narrative situation that connects all these is one in which something has been lost. In a gloomier version of Theocritus's gloomy point that art comes out of loss, the songs the characters sing (and, by extension, the songs Virgil sings about them) come into being as chronicles of loss. I want to look at Virgil's preoccupation with various kinds of loss in the *Eclogues* to show how he associates both loss and the poetry that arises from it with homoeroticism in a way that has had long-lasting poetic effects. I have already referred to the fact that the pastoral labourers themselves are threatened with the loss of their land and livelihood. In the context of the poems this may be the most obvious loss, but there is another important loss here, one that becomes apparent through a consideration of Virgil's handling of the homosocial context of Theocritus's idylls. The idylls present a largely unbroken spectrum of relationships between men ranging from friendship to romantic and sexual love and including friendly rivalry. This world is present in the eclogues only in a fragmented form. Amicable and equal relationships between men give way to ones marked by differences in social and economic status. As a rule, the men of the eclogues meet to mourn when they meet at all.

Eclogue I

The opening of the first eclogue recalls the opening of Theocritus's first idyll:

Tityre, tu patulae recubans sub tegmine fagi
siluestrem tenui Musam meditaris auena;

nos patriae finis et dulcia linquimus arua.
nos patriam fugimus; tu, Tityre, lentus in umbra
formosam resonare doces Amaryllida siluas.

(Tityrus, reclining under the cover of a spreading beech you meditate the woodland Muse on a plain oatpipe: I am leaving the borders of my fatherland and my sweet ploughed fields. I am fleeing my fatherland: you, Tityrus, relaxed in the shade, teach the forests to echo lovely Amaryllis; 1–5.)

While in Theocritus the music is inspired by the natural sounds that surround Thyrsis and the Goatherd, here Tityrus teaches the woods to echo human song. The natural music of the first idyll has become a mere echo: nature is represented as the passive instrument of human desires and activities. The link between human and natural music – and, to some extent, between humans and nature as a whole – has been broken and music itself has become something that is imposed on the landscape, a form of arboriculture. At the very beginning of the collection Virgil signals his intention to move to the georgic mode.

The hierarchical relationship between humans and nature that is a necessary aspect of the georgic is reflected in the hierarchical relationship between the two men. The almost undetectable difference between cowherd and goatherd in the first idyll has become the crucial difference between Tityrus, a shepherd who still has land and animals, and Meliboeus, a goatherd who has nothing. While Tityrus can lie in the shade and sing, Meliboeus is landless and destitute and is forced to leave the land altogether in order to seek a living. Virgil makes a connection between pastoral work and pastoral song in the last lines Meliboeus speaks in this eclogue: 'carmina nulla canam; non me pascente, capellae,/ florentem cytisum et salices carpetis amaras' (I shall sing no songs; I shall not be leading you, she-goats, when you graze on flowering clover and bitter willows; 77–8). For Thyrsis and the goatherd music is performed in the intervals of labour. In contrast, even relaxing in the shade Tityrus teaches the woods with his song, while singing is part of Meliboeus's work – an accompaniment in both senses of the word. Virgil makes clear the precariousness of pastoral poetry in a society where the ability to live on the land is itself precarious and brings pastoral poetry under the control of political and military forces.

As Meliboeus's situation reveals, Virgil's pastoral world is from the beginning depicted as subject to the political disturbances that grip the entire Roman state. I think that it is in this sense that we are to take the word 'tegmine' (l. 1), which struck some of Virgil's contemporary readers as a solecism. In this line, the word refers literally to the spreading branches of the beech tree, but a 'tegmen' is more usually a covering and often both literally and metaphorically a shield (it is related to the word 'toga'). The beech tree is most importantly a shield from the noontime heat, but the image resonates (to employ a word that is crucial to the eclogues) with Meliboeus's reference later in the eclogue to soldiers: 'impius haec tam culta noualia miles habebit' (a merciless soldier will have these fields, so well tended; 70). Virgil's use of a word with military connotations to describe the basic setting of pastoral poetry, the very symbol of rural otium, should be taken as a sign that the pastoral world, is not a place of ease removed from the troubles of the political world, but rather a place subject to the needs and imperatives of that world. Rather than being the protectors of rural peace, soldiers are moving in and driving out the natives. Perhaps a shield is a better symbol of rural life in Virgil's time than the shepherd's crook or the decorated cup that Thyrsus wins in the first idyll.

One way to describe the differences between the first idyll and the first eclogue is to note that the friendly association of the two labourers in the idyll has given way to unequal relationships like the one between the peasant who still has land and the peasant who has no land or the one between the ruler and the peasant who presents a petition to him. The obvious inequality of the latter relationship is stressed by the manner in which Virgil presents it. Tityrus reports the words of the 'iuuenem' (young man; 42) who has granted him land as 'pascite ut ante boues, pueri; summittite tauros' (lead cattle to pasture as before, boys; yoke bulls; 45). In response, Meliboeus addresses Tityrus as 'Fortunate senex' (fortunate old man; 46). Virgil's stress in this passage on terms denoting age underlines the power of the political hierarchy, which can turn an old man into a boy and force an old man to submit himself to a young one. Large-scale and formally codified hierarchical relationships such as those that govern the Roman empire as a whole are the important forces in the world of the poem, and while Daphnis is visited by gods who speak to him more or less as an equal, Tityrus plans to worship a fellow human as a god: 'erit ille mihi semper deus, illius aram/ saepe tener nostris ab ouilibus imbuet agnus' (he will always be a god to me; a tender lamb from our folds will often stain his altar; 7–8). The homosociality based on friendship and on working together that characterizes Theocritus has been replaced by a

homosociality based on power (and, as lines 7–8 show, a power disguised as divine power) in which rustic characters like Tityrus and
Meliboeus have no share.

It seems that Tityrus can ill afford the lambs he plans to sacrifice.
Although Meliboeus appears to be sincere when he calls Tityrus fortunate, the adjective could be taken as ironic:

> ergo tua rura manebunt,
> et tibi magnia satis, quamuis lapis omnia nudus
> limosoque palus obducat pascua iunco.

(Therefore your lands will remain and be large enough for you, although
bare rock and marsh with muddy reeds cover all the pastures; 46–8.)

Also, when Tityrus offers Meliboeus a place to stay for the night, the
meal he offers is very modest: 'sunt nobis mitia poma,/ castaneae
molles et pressi copia lactis' (We have ripe apples, soft chestnuts, and
an abundance of pressed milk; 80–1). Tityrus is only marginally more
fortunate than Meliboeus, and his future only marginally less grim. His
kindness is all the more commendable for this reason and briefly returns us to the affectionate tone of the relationship in the first idyll. For
one night, the two men will be united in friendship rather than separated by the dictates of a far-off government. Thus, the depiction of
their relationship ends with an echo of the homosociality that is such an
integral part of the background of Theocritus's idylls.

Virgil ends the eclogue with a description of the world that surrounds Tityrus and Meliboeus: 'et iam summa procul uillarum culmina
fumant,/ maioresque cadunt altis de montibus umbrae' (and now the
very tops of far-off farmhouses smoke and larger shadows fall from
the high mountains; 83–4). These beautiful lines underscore the difference between the first eclogue and the first idyll. Not only does Virgil
reduce the two men resting in the shade at the beginning of the idyll to
one, he also chooses to end his poem at nightfall, while in the idyll very
little time seems to have elapsed and the poem ends with the two men
returning to work. Virgil emphasizes the impermanence and fragility of
the pastoral world; there is a sense in which the coming of night can be
seen as a parallel to the intrusion of political control into the landscape.
In Virgil's presentation of the scene, the two men are surrounded by
both natural and human barriers (the mountains and farmhouses respectively).[25] In contrast, the landscape of the idylls is altogether un-

specific and there appear to be no close landmarks or dwellings of any kind. What is most significant is that the shade that was a refuge from the heat at the beginning of the eclogue (and that provided the opportunity for the singing competition in the first idyll) is now something from which refuge must be sought. The ending of the eclogue suggests that poetry must give way to considerations of survival. The ease that Tityrus celebrates in line 6 is shown to be illusory and without it pastoral poetry starts to seem like a luxury that pastoral labourers cannot afford. The first eclogue is a poem that makes clear its indebtedness to the idylls of Theocritus, but Virgil concentrates on the loss that was only one part of the first idyll.

Eclogue II

The second eclogue is perhaps the most famous of all classical poems that deal with love between men. There is a tradition that the poem is autobiographical; probably the most energetic promoter of this tradition was the commentator Servius, who proposes several interpretations. The first is that 'Corydonis in persona Vergilius intellegitur, Caesar Alexis in persona inducitur' (Vergil is comprehended in the person of Corydon, Caesar is introduced in the person of Alexis).[26] Servius also suggests that Alexis may represent Alexander, 'servus Asinii Pollionis, quem Vergilius, rogatus ad prandium, cum vidisset in ministerio omnium pulcherrimum, dilexit eumque dono accepit' (the slave of Asinius Pollio, whom Virgil, invited to lunch, saw serving in all his great beauty, was delighted with, and accepted as a gift). After saying this, Servius returns to the theory that Alexis represents Caesar, who is 'formosum in operibus et gloria' (lovely in deeds and glory), or even Caesar's son, and suggests that Virgil is attempting to inspire Caesar's gratitude. Servius appears to be torn between his desire to read the second eclogue as autobiography and his wish to foreclose interpretations that stress Virgil's sexual interest in 'Alexis.' For instance, he follows his reference to gratitude with this comment: 'nam Vergilius dicitur in pueros habuisse amorem: nec enim turpiter eum diligebat' (for it is said that Virgil loved boys: he did not, indeed, delight in them in a shameful way).

Servius was an amazingly conscientious commentator, eager to shed light on any word that might be difficult and to provide as thorough as possible a background to the poems. He was concerned not just with explicating the poems but with furthering Virgil's reputation. To the

Romans of the late fourth century, Virgil was a poet who could be used as an example of the superiority of Latin culture, but the explicit homoeroticism of the second eclogue had apparently become something that had to be dealt with in order for Virgil to appear suitable to readers in an increasingly Christian empire. This concern, of course, only intensified with the years as Virgil became one of the authors boys read in order to learn Latin. The difficulties posed by the relative frankness of classical authors are most amusingly presented in Byron's account of Don Juan's education. Juan's mother and tutors try to gloss over the pagan aspects of the great classical works. They feel trepidation about Ovid, Anacreon, Catullus, Sappho, Lucretius, and Martial, '[b]ut Virgil's songs are pure, except that horrid one/ Beginning with "Formosum Pastor Corydon."'[27] The homoeroticism of the second eclogue, then, is an ineluctable fact that must be accounted for by all those who regard Virgil as one of the cornerstones of the classical tradition.

In the rest of the note, Servius attempts to relegate the homoeroticism to a secondary position. While he said earlier that the original of Alexis was the slave of Asinius Pollio, he now describes him as his boy and adds that 'Corydona a Vergilio ficto nomine nuncupari ex eo genere avis, quae corydalis dicitur' (Virgil gave Corydon a name invented from that kind of bird that is called corydalis). Now the stress is on art and not on the beauty of the original of Alexis. Servius goes on to say that 'Vergilium gratum se futurum existimasse, si eum laudaret, cuius forma Pollio delectabatur, qui eo tempore transpadanam Italiae partem tenebat et agris praeerat dividendis' (Virgil thought that he would be rewarded if he praised the boy in whose beauty Pollio, who in that time held land in the part of Italy north of the Po and presided over the division of fields, delighted). By praising Pollio's boy Virgil could presumably hope to do well in this division. The reference to the division of agricultural lands also serves to link the second eclogue with the first. The homoeroticism of the story of Corydon is ultimately reduced to the level of a poetic fiction no more important than the choice of the name itself. To obtain material rewards by flattering a powerful man may seem to compromise Virgil's dignity, which Servius is at such pains to establish, but centuries of critics have felt that homoeroticism is the only thing that really tarnishes a poet's reputation.

I have discussed Servius's footnote in detail because it affords an excellent example of the various strategies with which commentators of all periods have attempted to control the homoeroticism of a poem that must nevertheless be studied. Also, I think Servius is at least

partially right. There is a connection between the agricultural dis-
placements of Virgil's time, which he commemorates in the first eclogue, and the romantic narrative in the second eclogue, which is
introduced at the very beginning: 'Formosum pastor Corydon ardebat
Alexin,/ delicias domini, nec quid speraret habebat' (The shepherd
Corydon burnt with love for lovely Alexis, his lord's beloved; and he
had no hope; 1–2). Corydon's love is presented as hopeless and Virgil
gives us two reasons for this: first, the contrast between the rustic
Corydon and the lovely Alexis;[28] and second, the fact that Alexis is the
lord's beloved. Corydon is presumably a shepherd who works for a
large landowner, the 'dominus' of line 2 and, in one way or another,
Alexis works for him too. Virgil takes the intrusion of the world outside
the pastoral world that was such a prominent feature of the first eclogue and makes it an intrusion into the personal life of the pastoral
labourer.

It is thus not merely the case that romantic and material loss or
dispossession are paralleled, but also that they are connected to each
other and to the making of poetry. Eleanor Winsor Leach points out that
'the unsuccessful singers and the reasons for their failure are a major
issue in the interpretation of the *Eclogues.*'[29] We can see many kinds of
failure in the poems. It could be said that singing comes from failure
rather than from leisure or, at least, from such partial success as Tityrus
has achieved (although as we have seen, Meliboeus appears to have
stopped singing altogether). After telling us that Corydon knew he had
no hope, Virgil adds

> tantum inter densas, umbrosa cacumina, fagos
> adsidue ueniebat. ibi haec incondita solus
> montibus et siluis studio iactabat inani

> (Nevertheless, he came continually to the dense and shady-topped beeches.
> Alone there, with vain desire he hurled this disordered speech at the
> mountains and woods; 3–5.)

Corydon's singing takes place under beech trees, as does Tityrus's, but
the relationship between the singers and the setting is very different,
however. Tityrus is stretched out in the shade singing what is apparently a love song echoed by the trees, and the scene as a whole is an
echo of Theocritus. The disturbance in the first eclogue comes from
another rustic who approaches Tityrus with his complaint. In the sec-

ond eclogue, the singer himself is the disturbance. Corydon's song is disordered and is characterized by vain desire. Corydon does not partake of the otium that Tityrus enjoys and, as Judith Haber remarks, he 'seems, initially, to be completely cut off from the normal pastoral routine.'[30]

One sign of Corydon's isolation is that he sings his song at noon, when both animals and humans seek shelter:

Thestylis et rapido fessis messoribus aestu
alia serpyllumque herbas contundit olentis.
at mecum raucis, tua dum uestigia lustro,
sole sub ardenti resonant arbusta cicadis.

(Thestylis pounds garlic, wild thyme, and fragrant herbs for reapers tired by the fierce heat. But while I trace your steps under the burning sun, the vineyards echo the hoarse cicadas to me; 10–13.)

Corydon stresses his isolation from pastoral society; perhaps more importantly, the musical relationship between humans and nature set up in the first eclogue is inverted. While the woods echoed Tityrus's song, here they echo the shrill noise of the cicadas. The human is the audience to this music, rather than its creator. At the same time that he stresses Corydon's powerlessness, however, Virgil presents a landscape that is more under human control than was the case in the first eclogue, where houses were 'procul.' In the second line of the second eclogue, we were told of a lord (a local figure rather than the Roman emperor whom Tityrus reveres). Now Virgil tells us of reapers and the echoes come not from woods but from vineyards. In other words, the *Eclogues* are already moving towards the *Georgics*, and as the landscape becomes tamer, the home of pastoral poetry is threatened and the pastoral poet himself – in this case, a pastoral poet singing of his love for another man – is increasingly out of place.

I want now to concentrate on one aspect of the contrast between naivete and sophistication that is embodied in the contrast between Corydon and Alexis. This contrast is to a great extent an inheritance from Theocritus's eleventh idyll, which is Virgil's chief source here and which tells the story of the cyclops Polyphemus and his unsuitable love for the lovely Galatea. In the idylls as they have been transmitted, this tale of unsuccessful and ludicrous heteroerotic courtship is followed by the triumphantly homoerotic '*Aites*' and then by the story of Heracles and Hylas, in which women end a loving relationship between two men. Profiting from this juxtaposition, Virgil transfers the theme of a male unsuccessfully attempting to win the love of someone higher in status from a male-female couple to a male-male one. For Theocritus, homoeroticism may be associated with loss because of the vicissitudes of life or the hostility of others, as in the story of Hylas; Virgil builds loss into homoeroticism and pastoral poetry.

The contrast between Corydon and Alexis can be seen most clearly in the gifts Corydon offers Alexis. These begin with 'duo nec tuta mihi ualle reperti/ capreoli' (two kids I found in a dangerous valley; 40–1). Corydon may want to stress his courage in going into a dangerous valley, but it is obvious that this chance finding of livestock is in direct opposition to the developed agriculture of the world of the poem. It is tempting to identify these kids with the twin kids Meliboeus was forced to leave behind in the first eclogue. His description of where he left them ('inter densas corylos ... silice in nuda' [among dense hazel thickets ... on bare rock; I.14–15]) could certainly apply to a dangerous valley. In any case, my point is that what appears to Corydon as good fortune can be read as a sign of the end of his and Meliboeus's way of life. Other gifts also suggest a connection between the first two ec-logues. After the kids, Corydon offers flowers and food – 'cana ... tenera lanugine mala/ castaneasque nuces' (tender peaches with whitish down and chestnuts; 51–2) – and then gives up altogether: 'rusticus es, Corydon; nec munera curat Alexis,/ nec, si muneribus certes, concedat Iollas' (you are a rustic, Corydon: Alexis does not care for gifts, and, if you contended with gifts, Iollas would not yield; 56–7). The food that Corydon offers is similar to the food that Tityrus offers Meliboeus at the end of the first eclogue, but in the first eclogue, the modest meal allows the poem to end with a reaffirmation, however temporary, of the bond between the two men whose luck has been so different. Here, by con-trast, the food and the other gifts Corydon has to offer are shown to be unable to bridge an economic gap between men.

Defeated by the power of the material inducements of the society that controls the pastoral world, Corydon next tries to win over Alexis by praising the woods:

> quem fugis, a! demens? habitarunt di quoque siluas
> Dardaniusque Paris. Pallas quas condidit arces
> ipsa colat; nobis placeant ante omnia siluae.
> torua leaena lupum sequitur, lupus ipse capellam,

florentem cytisum sequitur lasciua capella,
te Corydon, o Alexi: trahit sua quemque uoluptas.

(Ah madman, whom do you flee? Even gods and Dardanian Paris have
lived in woods. Let Pallas, who established citadels, care for them herself;
let woods please us above all. The savage lioness pursues the wolf; the
wolf itself, the she-goat; the playful she-goat pursues flowering clover;
and I you, o Alexis: each is led by his own pleasure; 60–5.)

Corydon uses the pun Paris/Pallas to present cities as places of violence. Although the judgment of Paris took place in the woods where
Paris was a shepherd, the Trojan War took place in and around the
citadel of Troy, which was, of course, eventually destroyed with the
help of Pallas Athena herself. To the destruction of Troy and the
violence of cities Corydon opposes a chain of violence that involves
animals rather than humans, that gradually decreases in ferocity (note
the difference between 'torva' and 'lasciva'), and that is ultimately
contained in the pastoral image, already used by Meliboeus in I.77–8, of
the goat nibbling plants to which Corydon's love can be compared.[31]
    Corydon depicts the pastoral world as a place in which even violence
is linked to order rather than disorder and in which homoerotic desire
is presented as part of that order. The conclusion he draws from his
contemplation of the natural world ('trahit sua quemque voluptas')
could be used as the slogan of sexual libertarianism. Yet the otium
Corydon invokes is only temporary, and just as the tired reapers must
return to the fields, so Corydon must return to work:

a, Corydon, Corydon, quae te dementia cepit!
semiputata tibi frondosa uitis in ulmo est:
quin tu aliquid saltem potius, quorum indiget usus,
uiminibus mollique paras detexere iunco?
inuenies alium, si te hic fastidit, Alexin.

(Ah, Corydon, Corydon, what madness seized you! You have a half-
pruned vine on a leafy elm: why not at least prepare to plait something
useful from osiers and flexible rushes? You'll meet with another Alexis, if
this one scorns you; 69–73.)

Leach remarks that '[b]oth Cato ... and Varro ... mention basket-making
as an important part of farm-work, since harvesting and storage require

numberless baskets.'[32] Corydon's work is thus eminently plausible, but it is important to remember that both training vines and weaving baskets are farm work: that is, they are associated with agriculture rather than with tending sheep, with the georgic rather than with the pastoral. I think it is significant that in the first eclogue reeds were cited as one of the disadvantages of Tityrus's land (I.48), whereas in this new economy they can be turned to use.

Putnam suggests that Virgil intends to establish a parallel between weaving and poetry: 'The word *semiputata* also has the secondary implication of "half considered" and seems in this sense to balance *incondita* in line 4.'[33] Both Corydon's song (the second eclogue itself) and his work are unfinished, poorly thoughtout. Although Corydon ends the poem by expressing his hope for better luck in romance, it is the work that predominates: the vine will become 'putata,' but there is no sense that Corydon's speech will become 'condita.' Both the work and the eclogue come from the loss of Alexis in a way that recalls, for instance, the creation of Theocritus's thirteenth idyll from the loss of Hylas, but Virgil's handling of this topos is very different. Although Hylas is taken from Heracles, the two men were lovers, while the dramatic context for the second eclogue is that Corydon never had a chance with Alexis. Furthermore, instead of a polished mini-epic like the idyll, Virgil gives us a poem that he is careful to present as 'incondita.' Ultimately, pastoral poetry as a genre will seem 'incondita' to Virgil; although he continues to depict loss, the losses in question give rise to increasingly weighty compensations for which a basket is no longer a suitable image.

The Last Eclogues

As the sequence progresses, Virgil becomes increasingly restive (most famously in the rather plaintive beginnings of the fourth and sixth eclogues), until in the last two eclogues he shows quite clearly that the time for pastoral is over. As the ninth eclogue opens, Lycidas hails Moeris, 'Quo te, Moeri, pedes? an, quo uia ducit, in urbem?' (Moeris, where are your feet taking you? To town, where the road goes?; 1). Instead of the repose of the first eclogue, however temporary it may be, we have motion towards town; furthermore, as the road apparently only goes in one direction, the motion, which is also the motion of Virgil's poetic career, is inevitable. In response, Moeris reveals that his land has been given away and he has been evicted (he is thus in the

same situation as Meliboeus in the first eclogue). Lycidas's reaction
shows that he still believes in the power of pastoral song:

> Certe equidem audieram, qua se subducere colles
> incipiunt mollique iugum demittere cliuo,
> usque ad aquam et ueteres, iam fracta cacumina, fagos,
> omnia carminibus uestrum seruasse Menalcan.

> (I had surely heard that by singing Menalcas saved all your land from
> where the hills begin to slope down in a gentle incline from the ridge to the
> water and the old beeches, whose tops are now broken; 7–10.)

In the first line of the first eclogue, the beech provided a 'tegmen' for
Tityrus as he sang; in the third line of the second eclogue, the 'umbrosa
cacumina' of the thick beeches shade Corydon as he sings of his love for
Alexis. Now – and Virgil's use of 'iam' can be taken to mean that the
occurrence is very recent – the tops of the beeches are broken and, by
implication, the singer is unsheltered in both senses of that word.

In his correction of Lycidas, Moeris points out the futility of pastoral
song:

> Audieras, et fama fuit; sed carmina tantum
> nostra ualent, Lycida, tela inter Martia quantum
> Chaonias dicunt aquila ueniente columbas.

> (You had heard that, and such was the report; but Lycidas, our songs do as
> much good among the weapons of Mars as Chaonian doves when the
> eagle comes; 11–13.)

Although Virgil never gave us any reason to think that pastoral poetry
did have any sort of political power, he did present it as a consolation.
Now even this aspect of pastoral poetry seems to have been lost.
Throughout the eclogue, Moeris resists Lycidas's requests for a song
and even claims that he is now unable to sing:

> Omnia fert aetas, animum quoque. saepe ego longos
> cantando puerum memini me condere soles.
> nunc oblita mihi tot carmina, uox quoque Moerim
> iam fugit ipsa

(Age takes everything, even the mind. I remember as a boy often passing the long day in singing. Now I have forgotten all those songs: even Moeris's voice itself is going; 51–4.)

Moeris's words may be taken as mere modesty, but in the context of the eclogues as a whole the stress on loss cannot be ignored. More immediately relevant, however, is Moeris's final refusal to sing: 'Desine plura, puer, et quod nunc instat agamus' (No more boy, and now let us do what is urgent; 66). This recalls the ending of the second eclogue, in which Corydon returns to work, but the difference is that Moeris and Lycidas recall the traditional male couple of pastoral. Although Moeris's words can be seen as an appeal to homosocial solidarity, that homosociality is now focused on work rather than on poetry.

The sombre nature of this eclogue is particularly apparent when one compares it to its source, Theocritus's seventh idyll, which tells the story of three friends, the most prominent of whom is called Simichidas, who are on their way to a harvest feast. As they go along, they meet a goatherd called Lycidas, who proposes a singing match. After both he and Simichidas sing, Lycidas awards the latter the prize and the three friends go on to the feast through a beautiful fertile landscape and the poem ends with praise of the wine the friends are drinking. All the characters seem blissfully contented with their lot and there is no hint of insecurity: the humans are presented as being in complete accord with their setting. As well, the idyll gives us more than one kind of homosociality: the love between Lycidas and Ageanax that is the subject of the former's song, the friendship between Simichidas and his companions, and the brotherhood of Phrasidamus and Antigenes, whose farm is the setting for the festival. There is no suggestion here that any sort of dispossession of pastoral labourers is even possible. As I understand it, the comparison suggests that the world of the eclogue, in which men are bound together (if at all) only by work, in which there is no time for singing, in which singing has in any case no power, and in which dispossession is a fact of life, should be seen as the ruins of the world of the idyll. Perhaps most telling is the difference between Virgil's Lycidas and his namesake:

    et me fecere poetam
Pierides, sunt et mihi carmina, me quoque dicunt
uatem pastores; sed non ego credulus illis

(the muses made me a poet too; I have my songs too; the shepherds also call me a bard: but I am not willing to believe them; 32–4.)

Despite fulfilling all the conditions necessary to be a poet, Lycidas has no confidence in his status as a poet – perhaps because he has no confidence in the status of pastoral poetry. It may well be that it is no longer worth having the opinion of 'pastores.'

The tenth eclogue develops the ninth's suggestions that the time for pastoral poetry has ended. Virgil begins by stressing that this is his last pastoral poem:

Extremum hunc, Arethusa, mihi concede laborem:
pauca meo Gallo, sed quae legat ipsa Lycoris,
carmina sunt dicenda; neget quis carmina Gallo?

(Arethusa, grant me this last labour: little songs, but which Lycoris herself may read, must be sung for my Gallus; who would deny songs to Gallus?; 1–3.)

What is important here is not merely that pastoral poetry is described as labour,[34] but also that this labour is for Gallus. In the earlier eclogues, the beneficiaries of pastoral labour and of pastoral poetry were not specified. Now, Virgil directs his poem to a real person who would have been known to his readers. This is an indication both of the power the urban world has over the countryside and of the power of one literary genre over another since Gallus wrote erotic elegies.[35] The Latin erotic elegy (which has nothing to do with elegy in our sense) deals with love between a man and a woman. In conjunction with Virgil's avowed intention to write for a female audience, this aspect of Gallus's poetry suggests that homoeroticism itself is in the process of being lost.

The contrast between the pastoral and the erotic elegy runs through the whole eclogue. Gian Biagio Conte describes this eclogue as having an 'essentially metaliterary character,'[36] and this is most clearly demonstrated in Virgil's highlighting of the pastoral poem as poetic construct in the tenth eclogue. This is his strategy throughout this eclogue, but it is clearest in a passage from the speech by Gallus that occupies almost half of the poem. We learn that just as Virgil is preparing to give up writing pastoral poetry Gallus is considering adopting the genre: 'ibo et Chalcidico quae sunt mihi condita uersu/ carmina pastoris Siculi modulabor auena' (I shall go and play what I wrote in Chalcidic metre on the oatpipe of a Sicilian shepherd; 50–1). To emphasize the difference between genres, Virgil gives each its geographical origin: pastoral poetry is traced to Sicily and erotic elegy to Chalcis in Euboea, the home of the poet Euphorion. Virgil's stress in this passage is on the technical side of poetic composition. His use of 'auena' recalls the beginning of the first eclogue, in which the reference is to Tityrus as poet, but the verb there is 'meditor,' which presents composition as meditation or reflection. Here, however, Virgil uses 'modulor,' which implies technical adjustment. As Leach suggests, the point is that 'bucolic poetry no longer passes for a spontaneous emotional utterance but is acknowledged as a definite literary mode.'[37] Gallus's comment implies that one can choose to be a pastoral poet and, therefore, one can choose not to be one.

Gallus's adoption of the pastoral mode is of short duration: 'rursus concedite siluae' (once again, give way o woods; 63).[38] Gallus anticipates Virgil's own decision to leave the pastoral scene, but the tenth eclogue is not merely a contrasting of pastoral and erotic elegy. Part of the metaliterary nature of the poem comes from two pastoral intertexts: the first idyll and the second eclogue. The allusions to Theocritus begin after the preamble:

Quae nemora aut qui uos saltus habuere, puellae
Naides, indigno cum Gallus amore peribat?
nam neque Parnasi uobis iuga, nam neque Pindi
ulla moram fecere, neque Aonie Aganippe

(What groves or dale held you back, Naiads, when Gallus perished from unworthy love? For neither the summit of Parnassus nor Pindus nor Aonian Aganippe caused you any delay; 9–12.)

Putnam points out that the difference between this passage and Theocritus I.66–9, on which it is clearly based, is that the allusions in the tenth eclogue are to places associated with poetic inspiration.[39] I read this difference as indicating Virgil's desire to acknowledge his indebtedness to the pastoral tradition in the context of a more general exploration of poetry, one that ends with a decision to write no more pastoral poems. I would even say that Virgil presents himself as being held back by groves and dales (that is, pastoral landscapes) from attaining the heights of Parnassus (that is, epic poetry).

In her comparison of the many resemblances between the tenth eclogue and the first idyll, Christine G. Perkell points out that the fates of Daphnis and Gallus are not parallel, but rather precisely opposed. Although speaking paradoxically in the language of defeat, Gallus, in fact, compelled by love of Lycoris, abandons his pursuit of death and chooses life. The *Eclogue* poet, by contriving this difference from his Theocritean model text, throws emphasis on Gallus's decision to live, to love, to engage vitally even in difficult experience.[40]

By dying, Daphnis becomes part of the world of pastoral poetry, one of its stock characters, and he is used in this way by Virgil in the fifth eclogue. In contrast, Gallus is able to gesture beyond the pastoral genre in a way that is helpful to Virgil. One way to sum up the difference between Daphnis and Gallus is to say that Daphnis gives rise to a poetics of loss while Gallus gives rise to a poetics of survival. In the next chapter, I shall discuss Virgil's use of the poetics of loss in the *Aeneid*, a work that has to be concerned with survival; for now, I want to show how Virgil uses his own second eclogue in much the same way as he uses the first idyll: as a text that must be invoked and then rewritten for poetic development to occur.

Some of the resemblances between the second and tenth eclogues are verbal or thematic. The most obvious of these is the one between II.14–16 and X.37–41. In both passages, the speaker regrets his inability to choose more willing partners even if those partners are perhaps less beautiful; in both cases, the speaker imagines one potential female lover and one potential male lover. Perhaps more significantly, Putnam suggests that we can read Gallus's dismissal of the pastoral setting ('rursus concedite siluae') as a version of – or response to – Corydon's rather defiant endorsement of it ('nobis placeant ante omnia siluae'),[41] an endorsement that is not even convincing in the context of the poem, as Alexis is not likely to be persuaded and Corydon himself must leave the woods to return to the farm. The most important resemblance between the eclogues is that both end with passages in which the speaker turns from singing to pastoral labour. Corydon's return to this work is presented as a recognition that his love for Alexis has led him into a dereliction of duty. The second eclogue thus ends with a presentation of unrequited love and the expression of that love in poetic form as distractions from the life of agricultural labourers. The parallel passage at the conclusion of the tenth eclogue (which is, of course, the conclusion of the eclogues as a whole) presents poetry very differently:

Haec sat erit, diuae, uestrum cecinisse poetam,
dum sedet et gracili fiscellam texit hibisco,
Pierides

(It will be enough, Pierian goddesses, for your poet to have sung this while
he sat and wove a basket from slender mallow; 70–2.)

Here, poetic composition accompanies rather than disrupts pastoral
labour. The finished poem is depicted as equivalent to the basket that is,
as the ending of the second eclogue tells us, an object of use. In this
presentation of poetry as an activity that has its role to play in other
more obviously useful activities we see not only a shift to the georgic
mode but also the humble beginnings of the role poetry will play in the
establishment of the Roman empire in the *Aeneid*.

One of the ways in which we can read this passage as indicating
Virgil's preparations for a shift in genres is in his return to direct
address. While the beginning of the tenth eclogue was addressed to
Arethusa, a specifically pastoral figure who is a nymph rather than a
goddess, in the closing section of the eclogue Virgil addresses the
'Pierian goddesses' or muses, figures of much greater importance in
the pantheon than Arethusa and, of course, patronesses of various
forms of art and scholarship. The dedication to the muses adds to
what Conte calls '[t]he eclogue's metaliterary depth ... [which] allows
it to achieve an *exploration of the boundaries* of a poetic genre.'[42] In the
case of the tenth eclogue, these boundaries are shown to be partly
geographic. Instead of the fields and mountains of particular rural
districts, we have references to various parts of the empire and to
other seasons than the endless spring of the pastoral world. A further
boundary is between the homosociality of the eclogue and the
heteroeroticism of Gallus's world. Virgil and Gallus are linked by
their affection and because they are both poets; their bond recalls the
homosocial bonds that unite many of the paired characters in the
earlier eclogues. On the other hand, the bond between Gallus and
Lycoris is the bond between poet and female poetic subject typical of
erotic elegy. Conte suggests that 'Virgil's considerate interest in Gallus
is directed less to his friend as such than to his friend as elegiac poet,
whose sufferings *are* his poems, so that saving him would mean saving him from his elegies.'[43] The situation is even more complex, however, as Virgil simultaneously saves Gallus from erotic elegies and

himself from pastoral poetry. In the context of the eclogues, this incursion into the world of the erotic elegy is another sign of impatience with the pastoral mode.

Conte's formulation of Virgil's feelings for Gallus as 'considerate interest' understates what Virgil actually says at the end of the eclogue when he entrusts his poem to the Muses:

> uos haec facietis maxima Gallo,
> Gallo, cuius amor tantum mihi crescit in horas
> quantum uere nouo uiridis se subicit alnus

> (You will make these words great for Gallus, for Gallus, love of whom grows in me hour by hour just as the green alder pushes up at the beginning of spring; 72–4.)

Virgil's declaration of love is stressed by the repetition of the spondaic 'Gallo' and by the fact that this love breaks the boundaries of the pastoral genre. By enlisting the aid of the Muses in making his words 'maxima,' Virgil seems to be aiming at a larger fame than a pastoral poem or a pastoral poet would normally achieve. The power of Virgil's love for Gallus is emphasized by the comparison to the growth of a tree in spring. A.J. Boyle notes that the alder is used in the sixth eclogue to depict the sorrow of Phaëthon's sisters and draws the inference that 'the poet's love for Gallus seems to be allied not to passion but to compassion.'[44] But Virgil's presentation of the alder as shooting up also suggests erection and there seems to be no reason to choose only one of the emotions Boyle mentions. The linking of passion and compassion here prepares us for the role of elegy throughout the *Aeneid* and recalls Erasmus's linking of phrases that to us suggest very different kinds of relationships in section 119 of *De copia*.

Putnam points out that '[t]he image of growth is not common in the pastoral.'[45] In invoking ideas of growth and the passage of the seasons, particularly as they relate to trees, Virgil prepares us for the focus on agriculture and arboriculture in the *Georgics*. We can even mark a movement towards arboriculture in the fact that while Tityrus merely teaches the woods to echo the name of the woman he loves, Gallus actually proposes to carve his love on the trees (53–4). After the reference to growth, however, Virgil returns to his goats:

surgamus: solet esse grauis cantantibus umbra,
iuniperi grauis umbra; nocent et frugibus umbrae.
ite domum saturae, uenit Hesperus, ite capellae.

(Let us rise: shade is hard on singers, the shade of junipers is hard,
and shade harms fruit. Go home full, Hesperus comes, go home she-goats;
75–7.)

Virgil states that the goats have been fed as a way of formally discharg-
ing obligations and strengthening our sense of pastoral poetry as 'labor.'[46]
As in the first eclogue, the shade signals the end of the pastoral day, but
the shade that prompted Tityrus and Meliboeus to go in at the end of
the first eclogue was accompanied by the smoke of hearth fires and
balanced by the shade in which Tityrus sang at the very beginning of
the eclogue. Here, shade is only depicted as harmful both to humans
and to their crops.

While previously the pastoral world had been largely outside time
and the threat to it had come from outside, Virgil now places the
pastoral world within political time and strengthens the connections
between pastoral society and the society that surrounds it. He is thus
able to present the turn toward the georgic mode (and, through the
georgic, to the epic) as a logical and inevitable development rather than
merely as a shift in genre, and to present a conscious poetic decision as
a natural process. In turning toward the epic, and in particular to the
Aeneid, a story of the triumph of Rome, Virgil might seem to leave the
poetics of loss behind, since the epic's steady forward momentum
leaves little time for the contemplation of losses. Nevertheless, Virgil is
unable ever to transcend the elegiac mode. In the next chapter, I want to
look at his continued examination of the complex relationships between poetry and loss and at his continued association of homosociality
and elegy, even in what is in some ways a very triumphant narrative.

CHAPTER TWO

The Aeneid and the Persistence of Elegy

Before I turn to the *Aeneid* I want to look once more at the eclogues. While I think that the tone of the eclogues as a whole is elegiac, the fifth eclogue is the only one to contain a real elegy in the modern sense – in fact, it contains two. Two shepherds, Menalcas and Mopsus, meet and decide to sing. They both sing elegies for Daphnis. The use of the name Daphnis and many features of the elegies can be taken as part of Virgil's extended homage to Theocritus, but there are a number of important differences. Most obviously, Theocritus's Daphnis is still alive (in fact, much of the first idyll is composed of his own words), whereas Virgil's Daphnis is dead even before the song begins and Mopsus uses the past tense even to describe the mourning: 'Exstinctum Nymphae crudeli funere Daphnin/ *flebant*' (The nymphs *wept* for dead Daphnis's cruel death; 20–1, my emphasis). These lines set up a further difference, because while the nymphs of the first idyll are absent and unsympathetic, the nymphs of the fifth eclogue share in the general mourning for Daphnis. This is in keeping with Virgil's stress in this eclogue on harmonious relations between humans and the natural and divine aspects of the countryside in which they live.

The harmony between humans and the natural world is most evident in Mopsus's address to Daphnis:

uitis ut arboribus decori est, ut uitibus uuae,
ut gregibus tauri, segetes ut pinguibus aruis,
tu decus omne tuis.

(As vines are the glory of trees, grapes of vines, bulls of herds, and crops of fertile ploughed fields, you are the sole glory of your people; 32–4.)

Daphnis is presented as part of a larger group (humans) that is itself presented as part of a natural world under cultivation, and the emphasis is on fertility. With Daphnis's death, however, the natural harmony described in these lines has been lost. The basis for this passage is the *adunata* in the first idyll, but whereas those *adunata* underscore the extent to which Theocritus's Daphnis is isolated from the world around him, the *adunata* in the fifth eclogue appear to indicate that Virgil's Daphnis is in some way a deity upon whom the success of agriculture depends. In my discussion of Theocritus, I suggested that his Daphnis could be understood as someone who rebels against the sexual system. Virgil's version makes Daphnis one of the guardians of that system, since we can consider agriculture and marriage parallel insofar as both represent the harnessing of natural forces in the name of civilization.

At the end of his lament, Mopsus explicitly presents Daphnis as the tutelary deity of the countryside:

> spargite humum foliis, inducite fontibus umbras,
> pastores (mandat fieri sibi talia Daphnis),
> et tumulum facite, et tumulo superaddite carmen:
> 'Daphnis ego in siluis, hinc usque ad sidera notus,
> formosi pecoris custos, formosior ipse'

(Strew leaves on the ground, cast shadows on the springs, shepherds [Daphnis orders such things to be done for him], and make a mound and to the mound add an inscription: 'I am Daphnis in the woods, known from here to the stars, guardian of a lovely flock, more lovely myself; 40–4.)

Menalcas takes Mopsus's elegy as his starting point and continues the story by depicting Daphnis in heaven (56–7), saying that because he is in heaven the world has once again become peaceful (58–61), declaring Daphnis a god (64), vowing to dedicate altars to him (65–75), and ultimately comparing him to Bacchus and Ceres (79–80). Once Menalcas has finished his song, the two shepherds exchange presents: Menalcas gets a shepherd's crook and Mopsus gets a pipe. The singing contest appears to have ended harmoniously in a draw.

The fifth eclogue marks the end of the first half of the collection. As numerous commentators have noted, Virgil appears to have intended it to bring together many of the themes of the four eclogues before it. I want to look at his presentation of the male couple in this half of the eclogues. First of all, the meeting of the two shepherds in the fifth eclogue recalls similar meetings in the first eclogue (Tityrus and Meliboeus) and the third (Damoetas and Menalcas). As in those eclogues, we are presented with a male couple connected by both occupation and singing. Yet whereas Tityrus and Meliboeus seem to be friends, they are divided by the former's relative prosperity and by the fact that the latter is dispossessed. We might expect a certain amount of hostility from Meliboeus, but it never becomes apparent and the eclogue ends with a gesture of solidarity. In the third eclogue, Damoetas and Menalcas are shepherds and appear to be socially and materially equal. They are clearly at odds and they begin by trading very crude insults, but this exchange eventually becomes a ritualized singing match formally adjudicated by a third party. This situation is repeated in the fifth eclogue, with the difference that there is no open hostility between the men.

The first, third, and fifth eclogues concern male couples in which both men are fairly humble pastoral labourers. Between the first and third eclogues, we have a story of a shepherd's love for a man who is the lover of someone much higher in rank; between the third and fifth, we have a poem that tells us that the whole world will change through the birth of a boy. As a whole, then, the first half of the eclogues narrates a shift towards greater social complexity, and while the characters remain in the pastoral world our sense of that world as merely part of a larger world is intensified: Daphnis, as Mopsus tells us, is known from the woods to the stars. At the centre of this progression is a succession of different kinds of male couples: the labourers of the first, third, and fifth eclogues; Corydon and Alexis; Alexis and Iollas in the second eclogue; the poet of the fourth eclogue and the male infant; Virgil and the (hypothetically) male reader. The effect is to present the male couple as the central unit of the society described in the eclogues. This male couple can occupy many points on the homosocial continuum, but most of the couples are connected by the pastoral labour the men perform, even though this labour is performed in solitude, while homosociality flourishes during breaks in labour. Bonds between men thus exist in some sense outside of the pastoral labour that sustains the world of the *Eclogues*.

From this point of view, the fifth eclogue is particularly significant. It presents, once again, two shepherds who take advantage of some moments of leisure to sing, but in this case the songs become hymns to someone who has been transformed into an agricultural deity. Since Virgil's Daphnis is not merely a shepherd, but rather someone who can help shepherds if entreated to do so (Menalcas says 'sis bonus o felixque tuis' [O be good and favourable to your people; 65]), male homosociality now functions in the service of agricultural labour. Although the dead man is acknowledged to be beautiful, his beauty is introduced as a sort of correlative to the beauty of his flock and ultimately appears as one of the attributes befitting a god. Thus, what could have been the story of a man's love for a beautiful man (like the love of Corydon for Alexis) becomes the admiration of humble shepherds for someone far above them in status (like Tityrus's reverence toward Octavian). Virgil turns Theocritus's enigmatic narrative of sexual rebellion, which stresses its subject's alienation from the natural world, into religious poetry with a practical purpose in the increasingly agricultural world of the *Eclogues*. The harnessing of homosociality is one of the distinctive features of the *Aeneid* and of the *Iliad* before it.

The Death of Patroclus and the End of the *Iliad*

The elegiac character of the *Aeneid* is partly due to Virgil's own fondness for that mode and partly a consequence of the epic's Homeric origins. From the Greek point of view the *Iliad* tells of a rare moment of unity in which a great enemy was utterly defeated and many Greeks distinguished themselves. For Virgil, however, the elegiac nature of the poem would predominate because he was telling his story from the Trojan point of view. The *Iliad* to him was at least partly a lament for Troy itself. Ideally, a lament should end with a moment of renewal which reassures us that whatever or whoever was lost was not lost in vain. Something must be given to us to make up for what is gone. What is given to the surviving Trojans is a new kingdom in Italy, but the *Aeneid* stops just short of showing us this. Since the poem tells of the founding of a second Troy, Virgil is faced with the problem of containing the elegiac mode on which he has relied for most of the poem. I shall return to the question of the place of elegy in Virgil's epic, but first I want to sketch out a way of reading the *Iliad* that emphasizes the many elegiac moments in what is already a grim poem even for those who sympathize with the victors.

These moments occur most frequently and most importantly in the story of Achilles and Patroclus. The elegiac tone dominates the last nine books of the *Iliad*, although Homer begins to prepare us for it in the first line of the poem: 'Sing, goddess, of the wrath of Achilles son of Peleus.'[1] Achilles is angry because Agamemnon has taken Briseis, a female captive whom Achilles had claimed. With this line, Homer sets up a parallel between Menelaus and Achilles, who are both men whose women have been taken. The strife between Achilles and Agamemnon is thus a purely Greek equivalent to the larger strife between Greeks and Trojans over the possession of Helen.[2] But Achilles and Agamemnon never get past the stage of talking; meanwhile, the war continues. And continues and continues: for two-thirds of the *Iliad*, Achilles sits in his tent fending off peace offerings while the war rages on indecisively. Since both Achilles' personal destiny and the destiny of the poem itself require action, Homer has to restore him to the battlefield on which he will – must – die. To this end he uses Patroclus, Achilles's beloved companion, and we eventually learn that Achilles' wrath at the death of Patroclus is ultimately more important than his wrath at Agamemnon.

There is an extensive body of criticism, some of it almost as old as the *Iliad* itself, on the exact nature of the relationship between Patroclus and Achilles. Much of this criticism centres on speculation over whether the two heroes were sexually involved and, if they were, which was the *eromenos*, or beloved, and which the *erastes*, or lover. Although there can never be a final answer to these questions one way or the other, it is reasonable to draw conclusions about the relationship based on what Homer actually says. The most level-headed conclusions have been drawn by David M. Halperin, who points out that 'Patroclus performs many of the functions for Achilles that a wife or female normally performs in the Homeric world'; he goes on to show that the reverse is also true: 'at Patroclus's funeral, Achilles, as chief mourner, cradles the head of his dead comrade (23.136–7), the same gesture that is performed by Andromache at Hector's funeral (24.724). So each, in a sense, is wife to each.'[3] The intensity of this relationship is crucial to the *Iliad*, since it is Achilles's grief for Patroclus that finally leads him back to the battlefield and allows the poem (and the larger story of the Trojan War) to end in triumph for the Greeks.

This process begins at the beginning of the sixteenth book, when 'Patroclus came to Achilles, the shepherd of the soldiers, weeping hot tears' (XVI.2–3). As Achilles will not fight, Patroclus wants to be allowed to lead the Myrmidons into battle. In the conversation that follows, Achilles reveals his lack of solidarity with the Greeks: 'Father Zeus and Athena and Apollo, oh that none of all the Trojans and none of the Argives might escape death, and that we two might escape the destruction and destroy the sacred towers of Troy' (XVI.97–100). This attitude is dangerous. For one thing, the Greeks were fighting both against the Trojans and against their own tendency to split into factions. Achilles's individuality, which is of course also what makes him such a hero, increases this tendency. The epic depends on great heroes, but they are expected to function as members of larger groups. Achilles' comments here suggest that the only group of which he is a member is the one consisting of himself and Patroclus. While some kinds of homosociality actually promote solidarity, ones that are too intense actually militate against it, as we saw in Theocritus's telling of the story of Heracles and Hylas. Homer's task here is to turn this particular homosocial bond into a source of social cohesion.

Homer achieves this cohesion by having Hector kill Patroclus at the end of the sixteenth book; the seventeenth is mainly concerned with the battles for his corpse. As in the works of Virgil, friendly and romantic forms of homosociality are replaced by hostile ones, a process Homer emphasizes by his use of parallels and echoes, which I shall summarize briefly. First, Patroclus goes into battle wearing Achilles' armour, directly substituting for Achilles, at least in the eyes of the Trojans who see him. In this conflict, Menelaus kills 'a man called Podes, son of Eëtion, a rich and brave man. Hector honoured him above all, since he was his dear companion at feasts' (XVII.575–7). Then, Apollo takes the form of Phaenops, 'dearest to [Hector] of all foreigners' (XVII.583–4), to tell Hector of Podes' death. Hector kills Patroclus and takes Achilles' armour, while the Greeks are able to recover Patroclus's body and Menelaus sends Antilochus to tell Achilles what has happened. Later, Achilles tells Thetis that he wants to kill Hector because of Patroclus's death; when she points out that his own death will follow soon after, he retorts, 'May I die at once, since I was not able to help my companion when he was killed' (XVIII.98–9). Finally, Achilles takes Patroclus's body back to his ships.

Patroclus's return to fighting inaugurates all these parallels and echoes, some of which are poetic formulas. The verbal repetitions are matched by the correspondences in the plot. In order to bring about the fight between Hector and Achilles on which the *Iliad* depends, Homer begins with the deaths of the men dearest to the two heroes. Significantly, although Hector himself kills Patroclus, it is Menelaus who kills Podes. On one level, this underlines Achilles' separation from the action of the war; on another, Menelaus is himself a proxy for his brother Agamemnon, whose feud with Achilles began the poem. This feud is the first example in the poem of hostile homosociality, just as the bond between male family members (such as the one between the Atreides) is the first example in life itself of friendly homosociality. The important difference between a familial homosocial bond and an elective one is that while the latter may cut two men off from their society, as we have seen with Achilles and Patroclus, the former serves (in theory, at any rate) to connect men to larger social and political groups. The best example of this is the Trojan War itself, to which the various Greek states contributed armies under the generalship of Agamemnon because of an affront to Agamemnon's brother.

The story behind the mustering of the Greek armies is significant to our understanding of the function of both homosociality and heterosociality in the *Iliad*. In order to prevent the civil strife that Agamemnon feared would follow Helen's choice of Menelaus as husband over almost all the other Greek kings, he made the suitors swear to help Menelaus if anyone seized Helen. When Paris abducted Helen, the Greeks were bound to protect Menelaus's rights as husband: the Trojan War is the inevitable consequence of the rape of Helen. This concatenation of events allows Homer to depict heteroeroticism as divisive – potentially so in the case of Helen's choice of a husband and actually so in the case of Paris's love for her – and homosociality as cohesive. Homosociality is not always enough, however. In his analysis of the *Iliad*, Neal H. Bruss says that the poem 'depicts a moment when a social order which commanded intense loyalty became inadequate for two of its best members [Achilles and Agamemnon] and was forsaken by them.'[4] In Bruss's view, Agamemnon forsakes the social order because of his desire to be high king; Achilles does so because he is, after all, better than everyone else. It is one of the outstanding ironies of the *Iliad* that the qualities that equip Achilles to be its hero prevent him from doing anything heroic for most of the poem, and that the qualities that equip Agamemnon to be a leader among men drive him to alienate the best of his men.

While Agamemnon eventually reconciles himself to the (homo)social order, Achilles' own homosociality (or at least its most intense form: his love for Patroclus) does not draw him back to the battle while Patroclus is alive. This is the best illustration of Bruss's point: the 'intense loyalty' required for social cohesion is expressed in strong homosocial bonds, but if these bonds are too strong, the result will be intense loyalty only to one other person. We see in the last books of the *Iliad*, for example, that it is only when his love can only be expressed elegiacally that Achilles can fight again. In fact, his grief makes him an even fiercer warrior, as the Trojan Lycaon discovers when he begs for his life: 'Fool, do not talk of ransom, do not harangue me. Before Patroclus met his fatal day, it was preferable to me to spare Trojans and I sold many over seas, but now none at all shall escape death' (XXI.99–103). This death is particularly significant since Lycaon, as one of the fifty sons of Priam, can be seen as a substitute for Hector. As the continual slaughter gradually depopulates the battlefield, the fact that Achilles and Hector are the central male couple of the *Iliad* becomes increasingly clear. The enmity between Hector and Achilles replaces the love between Patroclus and Achilles as the poem's primary homosocial bond.

Achilles' savagery continues unchecked until the beginning of the twenty-third book. Although he recovers Patroclus's corpse, he does not perform the necessary funeral rites. At the beginning of this book, Achilles addresses his dead companion: 'Hail Patroclus, even in the palace of Hades. All that I have promised I shall now fulfil. I shall drag Hector here and feed him raw to dogs and cut the throats of twelve beautiful sons of Troy before your pyre – such is my anger at your death' (19–23). The barbarous treatment of Hector's corpse is, like the refusal to show mercy to Lycaon, an example of Achilles' estrangement from his society. It is left to the ghost of Patroclus to remind Achilles of his obligations: 'Bury me quickly, so that I may cross the gates of Hades; for now the spirits, the phantoms of the dead, keep me away and will not let me cross the river' (71–3). Patroclus' status as an outcast in the lower world mirrors Achilles's status in the upper world, cut off from human society. In asking for a proper funeral, Patroclus is asking Achilles to return to his society, to participate once more in the homosocial order. Achilles' grief has led him to ignore the normal customs and requirements of his society.

The ghost of Patroclus tells Achilles that he regrets that 'no longer as living men, far from our beloved companions, will we sit together making plans' (77–8) – a description that heightens our sense that their bond worked against social cohesion, as what was once the privacy of a couple becomes the painful solitude of Patroclus in the lower world and of Achilles in the upper world – and makes a final request that recalls their life together: 'One more thing I ask of you, if you can be persuaded: do not lay my bones far from yours, but together, as we were reared' (82–4). Patroclus is writing his own elegy here, or at least assembling the materials for it, at the same time that he reminds Achilles of his own mortality. When Patroclus says, 'The hateful hour of death allotted to me at my birth overwhelmed me,' he adds that 'your own fate, godlike Achilles, is to die under the walls of the noble Trojans'

(78–81). Patroclus also reminds Achilles that he is member of a family, first by speaking of his own adoption by Achilles' father (89–90) and then by returning to his wish that his ashes be placed in the same urn as Achilles'. He even specifies the urn: 'the golden amphora that the queen your mother gave' (92). The stress on Achilles' mortality and on his parents reminds him that he is human and shares the requirements and limitations of all humans. The requirement to give Patroclus a proper burial is the most immediately pressing; it symbolizes the larger requirement, which is to act, once again, in a way that conforms to the rules of Greek civilization.

One aspect of Patroclus's explanation of how it was that he came to be brought up with Achilles is particularly interesting. Patroclus tells us that when he was still a child, he killed another boy: 'Like a fool, not wishing to do so, I killed the son of Amphidamas when I got angry as we both played dice' (87–8).[5] This brief and somewhat puzzling anecdote is significant in various ways. For one thing, it is another example of friendly homosociality becoming hostile, as a game between boys turns into murder. As well, Patroclus characterizes himself as foolish and this picture of him as dangerously headstrong may be intended to influence our opinion of his fatal decision to fight in Achilles' armour. In a larger sense, the fact that a game of dice could cause a boy's death is a comment on the other causes of violence in the poem: the abduction of Helen, the quarrels over Briseis – perhaps even the death of Patroclus. We are perhaps being invited to consider these things as similarly trivial and to see the violence on which epic depends as incommensurate with its causes. Such an analysis would make the deaths of the poem even more tragic and would heighten the elegiac tone that characterizes the endings of both the *Iliad* and, as we shall see, the *Aeneid*.

Patroclus's ghost is only partially successful in bringing Achilles back to the social order. Although he does bury Patroclus (the funeral games are the chief subject of the twenty-third book), Achilles is still alone and disconsolate:

> As soon as the funeral games were over, all the soldiers dispersed to their ships. Some thought of dinner and others enjoyed sweet sleep, but Achilles wept, remembering his beloved companion, and sleep the conqueror of all could not overpower him. He tossed to and fro, longing for Patroclus's great strength and good courage, all they had done together and the pains they had suffered, the wars and the dangerous seas they had come through. (XXIV.1–8)

Every day Achilles drags Hector's corpse around Patroclus's tomb and then returns to his tent, letting Hector 'lie outstretched, prone in the dust' (18). This description recalls the description a few lines earlier of Achilles as sometimes lying prone in his efforts to sleep (11); it is also very close to the description of Achilles just before the ghost of Patroclus appears: 'he stretched out prone in the dust beside the bier of the son of Menoetios' (XXIII.25–6). In both cases, Homer refers to Patroclus by his patronymic and he uses almost the same words.[6] The linking of Achilles and Hector simultaneously foreshadows Achilles' death and increases our sense of Achilles and Hector as the most important couple in the poem by this point in the story.

All the issues I have been discussing come together in Priam's visit to the Greek camp, which is in my opinion the most moving scene in the whole *Iliad*. When Priam enters Achilles' house, he finds him with two of his soldiers, 'who busied themselves near him. He had just finished his meal' (XXIV.475–6). The fact that Achilles is once again eating and that he is not alone (even if the men with him are not there as companions) indicates that he is beginning to return to normal. Priam's visit completes the process begun by Patroclus's ghost. Before speaking, Priam 'kisses [Achilles'] terrible, murdering hands, which had slain so many of [Priam's] sons' (478–9). In his speech, Priam asks Achilles to think of his father, speaks of all the sons who have been killed, and ends by saying, 'But respect the gods, Achilles, and have mercy on me. Think of your father: I am more pitiable by far, for I have dared to do what no other mortal man on earth has yet done: I have touched with my lips the hand that killed my child' (503–6). Achilles is clearly struck by Priam's courage in coming to the Greek camp and by the fact that he was willing to kiss his hand, but the most important aspect may be the references to Peleus. Like Patroclus, Priam wants Achilles to see himself as a member of a family. If Achilles can be brought to remember his own emotional ties and practical obligations as a son, he will be sympathetic both to other people's ties and obligations and to his own obligations as a member of the Greek force.[7]

Priam's speech works. Moved by the thought of his father, Achilles begins to relent: 'He took his hand and gently led the old man away. They both remembered: curled up at Achilles' feet, Priam wept copiously for the murderous Hector; but Achilles wept now for his father, now for Patroclus. Their wailing went quickly through the house' (508–12). Achilles' sorrow leads him to restore Hector's corpse to the Trojans, who give it a proper burial; it is with this burial that Homer ends the *Iliad*. The main subject of the last few books of the poem is thus not battles or victories or even primarily the deaths of heroes; instead, Homer tells the story of attempts to ensure that people are properly buried. We can see this as a change from the genre of the epic, which is concerned with deeds and therefore has a strong forward momentum, to the genre of the elegy, which is chiefly retrospective. At the end of the poem, Achilles has lost his most important homosocial bond (his love for Patroclus) and his first homosocial bond (his love for his father, whom he will never see again). All that remains to Achilles is the temporary bond with the man whose sons he has killed, and both Achilles and Priam will soon be dead themselves. Although the pastoral elegy is traditionally considered to be something a poet writes at the beginning of his career, what Virgil learned from Homer is that because of the very nature of epic plots, the epic never moves far from elegy.

Nisus, Euryalus, and the Uses of the Male Couple

As I have suggested, the *Aeneid*'s elegiac tone is partly due to the fact that Virgil is concerned with the losing side in the Trojan War. Nevertheless, under Aeneas's leadership the exiled Trojans are clearly bound for glory throughout the poem and Virgil might be expected to emphasize this. He does not: the narrative begins with the famously tragic love story of Dido and Aeneas. The prophecies that figure so prominently in the second and third books make the love story even sadder, since they show that the affair is destined to end soon. While in the *Iliad* women serve primarily as conduits for relationships between men, I think that Dido embodies the possibility of a heteroeroticism that is an end in itself. When she kills herself she is eventually replaced as the female love interest by Lavinia. The problem with Lavinia is not only that she is a very shadowy figure in contrast to the vividly characterized and sympathetic Dido, but also that Aeneas's desire to marry her leads directly to war. Lavinia's function (which is really all she has) is very like the function of Helen and Briseis in the *Iliad*. By contrast, Dido embodies a chance for peace, a way out of the epic cycle of endless violence. In the end, the love of Dido and Aeneas does lead to war, since as Dido prepares to die she calls for revenge: 'exoriare aliquis nostris ex ossibus ultor' (let some avenger rise up from my bones; IV.625). The Punic Wars testify to Aeneas's ability to turn peace into war and demonstrate the inability of heteroeroticism to serve as an alternative to the wars required by the epic genre.

Both the love scenes between Aeneas and Lavinia, which could act as a replacement for the love scenes between Aeneas and Dido, and the Punic Wars, which are Dido's elegy (in that they are the concrete result of a painful death), are deferred until after the poem's conclusion. With Dido's death, heteroeroticism ceases to be an important force in the *Aeneid* and it is replaced by homoeroticism. Yet the problem with heteroeroticism is not that it leads to death, although it does, but that it threatens to end the story before Aeneas achieves the status on which Virgil's claim to be an epic poet rests. Dido is an impediment to him as well as to Aeneas. For both, the solution is to turn to men, and when Virgil cites Ganymede as one of the reasons for Juno's anger, he may be intending to prepare us for the shift to male homoeroticism in the fifth book. Michael C.J. Putnam points out that one of the differences between the *Iliad* and the *Aeneid* is that in the latter poem Ganymede appears 'not as youthful cupbearer to the gods, ... but rather as the rival of Juno whose jealousy spurs her to action.'[8] Virgil begins to develop the implications of this depiction in the fifth book by giving us a series of intense relationships between men. Jasper Griffin says that Virgil tries to put an 'essentially homosexual sensibility at the service of the patriotic purposes of his poem.'[9] This seems to surprise him, but pressing homoeroticism into patriotic service is, as we have seen, essential to the *Iliad* and even to armies in general. In both poems, love between men makes it possible for the epics to end, but it can only do so when expressed elegiacally.

The 'homosexual sensibility' Griffin mentions is displayed most prominently in the deaths of beautiful young men that occur so frequently in the last third of the *Aeneid*. Gian Biagio Conte says that 'in the interests of truth, the *substance of the content* of the *Aeneid* must be made of what is [*lugron*] (sorrowful); on the other hand, for literary reasons, that same content must be organized in a form that is functional to epic communication.'[10] In the remainder of this chapter, I want to look at Virgil's organization of his sorrowful material and at how he uses this material to advance the plot. A good starting point is provided by K.W. Gransden, who points out that Virgil emphasizes these deaths by his use of vatic empathy, that is, by addressing the dead men directly (specifically, Euryalus, Nisus, Pallas, and Lausus).[11] My discussion will concentrate on these deaths, but I shall also look at the death of Turnus, who, for all his youth and beauty, is denied vatic empathy.

The story of Nisus and Euryalus begins in the fifth book. We are introduced to them at the funeral games that mark the first anniversary of Anchises's death. Virgil thus situates them in a context of mourning that is also an affirmation of familial bonds and the occasion for friendly competition. He gives them pre-eminence in his catalogue of men about to run a race and presents them as a couple:

Nisus et Euryalus primi,
Euryalus forma insignis uiridique iuuenta,
Nisus amore pio pueri

(first were Nisus and Euryalus, Euryalus remarkable for his beauty and flourishing youth, Nisus for his gentle love for the boy; V.294–6.)[12]

Nisus and Euryalus replace Aeneas and the ubiquitous (if never particularly individualized) Achates as the *Aeneid*'s most prominent male couple. More importantly, in the first four books Aeneas has been the only man allowed to be beautiful. Euryalus is the first in a series of beautiful men who figure prominently in the second half of the poem; what eventually becomes clear is that, with the exception of Aeneas, whose beauty apparently forms part of his epic stature, the price of male beauty is death.

Nisus and Euryalus are introduced to the reader as participants in one of the races in the funeral games for Anchises. Nisus leads until 'leui cum sanguine Nisus/ labitur infelix' (unlucky Nisus falls on slippery blood; V.328–9). After this, he cannot hope to win.

non tamen Euryali, non ille oblitus amorum:
nam sese opposuit Salio per lubrica surgens;
ille autem spissa iacuit reuolutus harena

(Yet he did not forget Euryalus or their love: for rising on the slippery place he placed himself in the path of Salius, who fell backwards on the packed sand; V.334–6.)

Euryalus, who had been third, is thus able to win. Salius understandably protests, but 'tutatur fauor Euryalum lacrimaeque decorae,/ gratior et pulchro ueniens in corpore uirtus' (Partiality protects Euryalus, and his becoming tears; his excellence is more pleasing because it comes from a beautiful body; V.343–4). In the end, Aeneas makes sure that everyone gets a prize. The episode demonstrates the power of male beauty and the strength of homoerotic bonds. Aeneas is able to keep hostility out of competition between men, but this will soon be impossible. The atmosphere of affectionate homosociality that characterizes the funeral games will soon be gone forever as the poem slides into war. Furthermore, as Virgil makes only too clear in the second half of the *Aeneid*, a young man's beauty will no longer be able to help him.

When Nisus and Euryalus next appear, after the war has begun, Virgil describes them differently: 'Nisus erat portae custos, acerrimus armis' (Nisus was the guardian of a gate, very fierce in fighting; IX.176); and 'comes Euryalus, quo pulchrior alter/ non fuit Aeneadum Troiana neque induit arma' (his companion Euryalus, than whom there was none more beautiful among Aeneas's men or among those who bore Trojan arms; IX.179–80). Nisus is now defined by his role in the war, and while Euryalus's beauty is still stressed, he is presented as the companion of Nisus rather than as his lover and his own status as a warrior is made clear. The war has begun the process of swallowing them up, and with them the possibility of peaceful homosociality that they exemplify. This process will soon be complete and will not be confined to Nisus and Euryalus. The ninth book is a turning point: after this, the elegiac tone predominates. R.D. Williams says in his book on Virgil that '[i]n the last three books of the *Aeneid* Virgil's plot is clearly intended to echo Homer's in the *Iliad*.'[13] Williams sees the important echo as being between Patroclus and Pallas, but I think one of the distinctive features of the *Aeneid* is that Virgil provides multiple echoes and thus amplifies Homer's elegiac tone. Mark Petrini has commented on the resemblance between Pallas and Euryalus, for instance: 'Vergil's account of Aeneas and Pallas ... frames the episode of Nisus and Euryalus in Book 9 and reproduces in larger scale and with broader significance the themes of the miniature at its center.'[14] Virgil's vatic empathy alludes simultaneously to the *Iliad* and to other parts of his own poem.

Nisus conceives a plan to launch a solo surprise attack on the Rutulians by night. When Euryalus begs to be allowed to go with him, Nisus reminds him of his family:

neu matri miserae tanti sim causa doloris,
quae te sola, puer, multis e matribus ausa
persequitur, magni nec moenia curat Acestae.

(Nor will I be the cause of such sorrow to your unhappy mother, my boy, who alone of all the mothers dared to follow and refused to stay behind great Acesta's walls; IX.216–18.)

Unlike the appeals to familial bonds in the last books of the *Iliad*, this appeal is unsuccessful and Euryalus accompanies Nisus on the ill-fated raid. In this case, love between men overrides familial bonds. Virgil does not appear to endorse this decision, however, nor are familial bonds the only ones at stake. Nisus's plan is obviously reckless for military reasons. That even he is aware of this is revealed by the question he asks just after informing Euryalus of the plan: 'dine hunc ardorem mentibus addunt,/ Euryale, an sua cuique deus fit dira cupido?' (Do the gods cause this ardour in our minds, Euryalus, or does each man's fierce desire become a god to him?; IX.184–5). The question is never really answered and here, as in the case of Achilles after Patroclus's death, a homosocial bond is so intense that it supersedes all other bonds. Nevertheless, the question has profound subversive potential in a poem that ceaselessly reaffirms the role of the gods, and particularly so if we answer it with Corydon's 'trahit sua quemque uoluptas.' We can interpret both Nisus's decision to leave his post and Euryalus's decision to leave his mother as subversions of military and familial obligations respectively.

Euryalus's death at the hands of the Rutulian Volcens is the occasion for one of Virgil's most beautiful passages:

> uoluitur Euryalus leto, pulchrosque per artus
> it cruor inque humeros ceruix conlapsa recumbit:
> purpureus ueluti cum flos succisus aratro
> languescit moriens, lassoue papauera collo
> demisere caput pluuia cum forte grauantur.

> (Euryalus falls into death: blood flows over his beautiful limbs; his neck, collapsing, lies on his shoulders just as a purple flower cut down by a plough sinks and dies, or as poppies weighed down by heavy rain bow their heads on their weary necks; IX.433–7.)

Virgil draws on the resonances of this image with its sources in Homer, Catullus, and Sappho. In Catullus XI, the poet is speaking of his love; in XLII, of a virgin about to be married.[15] By specifying a purple flower where Catullus simply has 'flos,' Virgil draws attention to his and Catullus's source, Sappho's description of a maidenhead after the wedding night: 'Like the hyacinth in the mountains which shepherds tread underfoot, and the purple flower on the ground.'[16] The hyacinth is especially appropriate in the description of Euryalus's death, as it has associations that are simultaneously homoerotic and elegiac.[17] The fusion of these images thus places the death of a young man in battle in an erotic context: a warrior's death is presented as a kind of erotic consummation.

Connected with this is the fact that Virgil's version of these images stresses the idea of fertility. The plough that cuts down the flower in both poems by Catullus is, after all, an agricultural tool, and rain is necessary for plants. Indeed, although Catullus presents the plough as dangerous (in its pure state the flower is 'nullo conuolsus aratro' [torn by no plough; LXII.40]), rain is presented as contributing to the flower's beauty: 'mulcent aurae, firmat sol, educat imber' [the breezes caress, the sun strengthens, the rain raises up; LXII.41]). As well, the fact that both Catullus LXII and Sappho 105 are epithalamia could be said to recuperate Euryalus's homoerotic allure for heteroeroticism and thus ultimately for reproduction. As Susanne Lindgren Wofford remarks, the image 'shifts the readers' attention from the absoluteness of heroic death to the circular temporality of the flower.'[18] Virgil links human life to the georgic cycle in a way that has important implications for the *Aeneid*. The loss of a single flower is hardly tragic, especially if the flower is destroyed by the plough that helps to harness natural fertility for human needs: both the flower and Euryalus are what military analysts call acceptable losses. Presenting Euryalus's death and the others like it as both inevitable and necessary is part of an attempt to present ideology (here, the belief in the establishment and maintenance of the Roman empire as an absolute good) as natural.

These reflections are no comfort to Nisus, who is now alone. His solution is to form a new bond based on hate rather than on love: 'in solo Volcente moratur' (for Volcens alone he stays; IX.439). Once again, affectionate homosociality is replaced by hostility. As with the link between Achilles and Hector created by the killing of Patroclus, this new bond is of brief duration. Nisus chooses to die in avenging Euryalus rather than live without him. He quickly gets his wish; in fact he even manages to die in an iconographically significant manner: 'tum super exanimum sese proiecit amicum/ confossus, placidaque ibi demum morte quieuit' (then, himself pierced, he threw himself on his lifeless friend, and there he finally rested in peaceful death; IX.444–5). This is Nisus and Euryalus's final sexual act and the tableau reaffirms the homoerotic bond that appeared to have been destroyed by Volcens. Gransden says that 'Nisus and Euryalus have remained lovers in a world of war and conflict: the fragile ... eroticism of pastoral has not merely survived transplantation into heroic epic, it has flowered and flourished.'[19] In a sense, Volcens completes the process Virgil began in his description of the two men in Book IX as a soldier and his companion, rather than as the amorous couple they clearly were in Book V. The paradox here and in the depiction of homoerotic bonds more generally, is that homoerotic affirmation can only be achieved by the death of at least one member of the couple.

It is to Nisus and Euryalus as a couple that Virgil pays tribute in the first display of vatic empathy in the second half of the *Aeneid*:

> Fortunati ambo! si quid mea carmina possunt,
> nulla dies umquam memori uos eximet aeuo,
> dum domus Aeneae Capitoli immobile saxum
> accolet imperiumque pater Romanus habebit.
>
> (Happy pair! if my poems have the power, no day will ever remove you from time's memory, while the descendants of Aeneas live by the steadfast Capitoline rock and a Roman father rules; IX.446–9.)

By dying and by dying together, Nisus and Euryalus have achieved poetic immortality. This power is only granted conditionally, however, and the condition is that their memory will last as long as the Roman state does. Nisus and Euryalus's love has been pressed into political service. The homoerotic space Nisus and Euryalus occupy is created by the need to establish a new Trojan realm. Furthermore, the state whose survival will ensure their survival is described as ruled by a father and peopled by the descendants of Aeneas. At the same time that Virgil celebrates Nisus and Euryalus he returns to the fertility dependent upon heteroeroticism, and thus carefully closes off this homoerotic space in the same way that one would seal a tomb.

Pallas and Lausus

In his next displays of vatic empathy, Virgil moves from Nisus and Euryalus, who die together, to Lausus and Pallas, who never meet. I shall begin with Pallas, as his role in the *Aeneid* is considerably larger than that of Lausus. Pallas is the son of Evander, who as king of the Arcadians in Italy has achieved the position to which Aeneas aspires. This is only one of the connections between the groups, as we see in the first description of Evander's kingdom:

sol medium caeli conscenderat igneus orbem
cum muros arcemque procul ac rara domorum
tecta uident, quae nunc Romana potentia caelo
aequauit, tum res inopes Euandrus habebat.

(The fiery sun had reached the middle of the circle of heaven when they
saw far away walls, a fortress, and a few roofs which Roman power has
now raised to heaven; then it was Evander's, a poor place; VIII.97–100.)

A great deal of fighting lies ahead, but Aeneas has finally entered his
promised kingdom. Petrini notes that 'Aeneas' journey to Evander's
kingdom ... is a movement into the cultural past ... This journey is also
defined metaphorically as a return to youth.'[20] Our sense of the cultural
past is heightened by the fact that Arcadians are of course associated
with pastoral poetry. Virgil might appear to be going backwards, but
the rest of the poem makes it clear that he evokes pastoral associations
in order to employ them in the service of the epic. Virgil's strategy can
be seen in the fact that the site of Rome is now under the rule of
Evander: Aeneas and his descendants will eventually have to displace
him as well as Turnus, who emerges in the second half of the poem as
Aeneas's main enemy.

We are thus introduced to the Arcadians in a way that makes clear
that they will be superseded. As in traditional elegy, this loss leads to
something far better: the splendour of imperial Rome. The elegiac tone
is deepened (at least in retrospect) by the fact that the first Arcadian
Aeneas and his men see is the young Prince Pallas, who conducts them
to his father. Before we learn much about Pallas, however, Evander
reveals a further connection between the Arcadians and the Trojans:

tum mihi prima genas uestibat flore iuuentas,
mirabarque duces Teucros, mirabar et ipsum
Laomedontiaden; sed cunctis altior ibat
Anchises. mihi mens iuuenali ardebat amore
compellare uirum et dextrae coniungere dextram;
accessi et cupidus Phenei sub moenia duxi.

(Early youth had then covered my cheeks with down, and I marvelled at
the Trojan leaders and at the son of Laomedon himself; but Anchises
walked taller than all. My mind burnt with youthful love to address the
man and join my hand to his; I approached him and with desire I led him
under the walls of Pheneus; VIII.160–5.)

In effect, this story provides a historical precedent for the relationship between Aeneas and Pallas. Evander's ardent and fondly remembered love for Anchises inaugurates a sort of hereditary homoerotic bond between the dynasties.

Partly for this reason, when Aeneas asks Evander for help in the war against the Rutulians, Evander, among other things, gives Pallas to him:

> hunc tibi praeterea, spes et solacia nostri,
> Pallanta adiungam; sub te tolerare magistro
> militiam et graue Martis opus, tua cernere facta
> asdsuescat, primis et te miretur ab annis.

> (As well as these, I shall add our hope and comfort, Pallas; with you as leader, let him become accustomed to bear warfare, the painful work of Mars, to witness your deeds: let him admire you from his early years; VIII.514–17.)

This represents yet another stage in the harnessing of homoeroticism. Evander's love for Anchises turns, after the passage of many years, into a relationship between the sons of the two men. This is the first of the substitutions in this passage, reminiscent of the substitutions I discussed with reference to the *Iliad*; the second is that ardent young love is replaced by the bond between a general and a man who serves under him. Finally, as Gransden points out, 'Evander's offer of his son Pallas parallels and doubles Latinus's offer of Lavinia.'[21] The substitutions in this passage are all in the direction of greater utility to the war effort. The homoeroticism of the context is contained by the demands of war.

Virgil's first reference to Lausus is brief but telling: 'Lausus, quo pulchrior alter / non fuit excepto Laurentis corpore Turni' (Lausus, than whom none save Laurentine Turnus had a more beautiful body; VII.649–50). The phrasing of the description anticipates the description of Euryalus's beauty in IX.179–80, while the reference to Turnus emphasizes that Lausus is on the wrong side at the same time that it reminds us of Turnus's beauty. Male beauty becomes more and more important in the *Aeneid* as death makes it less and less common. It is obvious that Pallas and Lausus are doomed, and it might seem logical to assume that they will kill each other and die together in a hostile recension of the Nisus and Euryalus story, especially as they fight near each other in Book X. Virgil has other plans, however:

> nec multum discrepat aetas,
> egregii forma, sed quis Fortuna negarat
> in patriam reditus. ipsos concurrere passus
> haud tamen inter se magni regnator Olympi;
> mox illos sua fata manent maiore sub hoste.

(They did not differ much in age or in their outstanding beauty, but Fortune denied them return to their fatherlands. Yet the king of great Olympus did not permit them to fight each other: their fates await them shortly under greater enemies; X.434–7.)

The two youths are themselves substitutes for Aeneas and Turnus, who are, after all, the leaders of the opposing armies as well as the most beautiful men in the poem.

Pallas is the first to die, but Virgil delays the pathos of his death until the funeral scene. What is most noteworthy about his death scene is Turnus's arrogant behaviour and his taking Pallas's baldric as the spoils of conquest. On the baldric is embossed the story of the fifty daughters of Danaus who (with the exception of Hypertemnestra) murdered their husbands on the wedding night. As Conte suggests, our understanding of the story of the Danaids affects our understanding of Pallas's death: 'Turnus's act of tearing the baldric from Pallas's body strikes a painful similarity between the death of the youth on his first day at war and the death of the fifty bridegrooms on their wedding night.'[22] In both cases, what we see is the deaths of young men at what should have been the beginning of their adult lives. The comparison also sets up a connection between death and sexuality. We can understand this connection as a general statement or we can look at its specific application. Virgil's emphasis on male beauty and on the emotional bonds between men should lead the reader to expect a love story, if not between Pallas and Turnus, then at least between Pallas and Aeneas. The fact that we get a killing instead indicates to us that death has replaced sexuality as the agent of plot development – a substitution that is implicit in the death of Dido at the end of Book IV.

In the case of Lausus, Virgil arouses pathos even before the death itself, since the moment of vatic empathy comes before Lausus is killed. Virgil tells him that he will not be silent about 'mortis durae casum tuaque optima facta' (the disaster of your cruel death, and your great deeds; X.791). There is also a great deal of pathos in the death itself. The tenderness of this scene, coming as it does so soon after the death of

Pallas, sets up a comparison between Aeneas and Turnus and consequently has the effect of showing how much nobler a figure Aeneas is
than Turnus. Aeneas has the capacity of showing tenderness to the
enemy:

> At uero ut uultum uidit morientis et ora,
> ora modis Anchisiades pallentia miris,
> ingemuit miserans grauiter dextramque tetendit,
> et mentem patriae subiit pietatis imago.

> (But when the son of Anchises saw the expression and face of the dying
> man – his face was strangely pale – he sighed deeply in compassion and
> extended his right hand. The memory of his paternal love came to his
> mind; X.821–4.)

As the use of the patronymic suggests, Aeneas naturally thinks of
himself as a family man as well as a warrior; in this respect he is
superior to Achilles, who has to be reminded of his family.

Aeneas also naturally thinks of his opponents as belonging to families, as his description of himself as 'pius' in his address to Lausus
indicates:

> quid tibi nunc, miserande puer, pro laudibus istis,
> quid pius Aeneas tanta dabit indole dignum?
> arma, quibus laetatus, habe tua; teque parentum
> manibus et cineri, si qua est ea cura, remitto.

> (Unhappy boy, for such great deeds what can dutiful Aeneas now give
> fitting such a nature? Keep the arms in which you rejoiced; I give you back
> to the ashes and spirits of your parents, if spirits care for these things;
> X.825–8.)

Aeneas's concern for Lausus is all the more apparent because of the
touching phrase that raises the possibility that the ghosts of Lausus's
family will have no interest in the spoils of war. The pathos of the
passage is increased by the description of Lausus as 'miserande puer';
just over thirty lines earlier, Virgil had called him 'iuuenis memorande'
(youth who must be remembered; X.793). The two alliterating vocatives
make the point once again that the subject of memory is often misery.
Yet perhaps the most important aspect of this scene, insofar as it pre-

pares us for the poem's conclusion, is Aeneas's decision to leave Lausus's armour intact as a tribute to the young man's bravery. Aeneas's magnanimity (in both its original and its later English sense) forms a very effective contrast with Turnus's arrogant despoiling of Pallas's corpse and with his cruel reference to Evander: 'mea dicta referte/ Euandro: qualem meruit, Pallanta remitto' (report my speech to Evander: as he deserved, I return Pallas; X.491–2).

Virgil's delaying of the full pathos of Pallas's death slightly obscures the parallel between Pallas and Lausus. A more obvious parallel from the funeral scene itself is with Patroclus. There are other parallels in the lines describing Pallas on the bier: 'qualem uirgineo demessum pollice florem/ seu mollis uiolae seu languentis hyacinthi' (like a flower, either a soft violet or a drooping hyacinth, plucked by a girl's hand; XI.68–9). These lines recall the metaphor used to describe Euryalus, but there are some crucial differences. In the first use of the metaphor, the flower was either an unspecified purple flower or a poppy; now the hyacinth, a flower associated with homoerotic elegy, is named. The earlier flowers were either weighed down by rain or cut down by a plough, but this one is plucked by a girl.[23] The image is gentler and the flower will presumably be used for personal adornment. Euryalus's death was presented in a manner that had georgic associations; Pallas's death is aestheticized. Charles Martindale asks whether 'the eloquent pathos of the *Aeneid* ... reconcile[s] us to human pain, as in the lovingly-evoked deaths of Euryalus or Lausus, and in a rather sinister, aestheticized way?'[24] I would suggest that the sinister aspect is not the aestheticization in itself, but the fact that it indicates increasing subordination of homoeroticism – and of the beautiful young men who inspire it – to the demands of war. Readers of the poem must work out their own answer to Martindale's question, which is one of the most important questions to ask of the poem, but reconciling us to human pain is part of the task of the elegy. The change from lovingly evoking deaths to lovingly evoking funerals represents a further stage in the process by which the elegy helps along the work of empire.

Aeneas approaches the body of Pallas with an offering:

tum geminas uestis auroque ostroque rigentis
extulit Aeneas, quas illi laeta laborum
ipsa suis quondam manibus Sidonia Dido
fecerat

(Then Aeneas brought out two robes stiff with gold and purple that Sidonian Dido had happily made for him with her own hands; XI.72–5.)

The robe that was made and presented as a sign of love here serves the purpose of a different love. The passage demonstrates both the turn from heteroeroticism to homoeroticism and the fact that the motion of the plot depends on endless substitution. In fact, the robes themselves recall one of the presents given to Dido by Aeneas when they first meet: 'pallam signis auroque rigentem' (a tunic stiff with golden symbols; I.648). The wording is similar, and the use of 'palla' can be taken as a play on words, although one that obviously cannot be appreciated in the first book. The presents Aeneas gives Dido were 'Iliacis erepta ruinis' (snatched from the ruins of Ilion; I.647) and include Helen's veil (I.649–52) and Ilione's sceptre (653). Aeneas is clearly a man who can use anything: the destruction of his native city, love tokens from a woman who killed herself because of him. Ultimately, the most important thing both Aeneas and Virgil use – the former for military reasons, the latter to advance the plot and to create the moments of pathos in which he excelled – is the recurring trope of the beautiful man who dies young.

I do not mean to suggest, however, that Aeneas is unfeeling. The robe that was given to Aeneas as a love token is given by him to Pallas for the same reason. Our sense of Aeneas's tenderness in this scene is heightened by the fact that one robe remains. This material evidence of Dido's joyful love for Aeneas becomes the material evidence of Aeneas's sorrowful love for Pallas. As I have pointed out, these changes – a man for a woman, sorrow for love – are typical of the *Aeneid* as a whole. What could have been a wedding robe becomes a shroud for Pallas and the corresponding robe becomes Aeneas's widower's weeds. Aeneas leaves after a brief speech to Pallas that calls our attention once again to the process of substitution:

nos alias hinc ad lacrimas eadem horrida belli
fata uocant: salue aeternum mihi, maxime Palla,
aeternumque uale.

(The same dire fates of war call me hence to other tears: hail forever, great Pallas, and farewell forever; XI.96–8.)

In this scene, Virgil has already returned to the flower simile used of

Euryalus and the unmistakable allusion to Catullus CI further heightens the emotion of the scene and strengthens the connections among Dido, Euryalus, and Pallas. All these characters have been beautiful and have been associated with love; all have been left behind by the poem's relentless movement, a movement that we now see primarily as a progress to 'alias ... lacrimas.'

Turnus and the End of Elegy

The deaths of Pallas and of characters such as Camilla and Lausus, who have functioned as substitutes for the leaders, remove all obstacles in the way of the final conflict except one:

> continuoque ineant pugnas et proelia temptent,
> ni roseus fessos iam gurgite Phoebus Hibero
> tingat equos noctemque die labente reducat.
> considunt castris ante urbem et moenia uallant.

> (They would have begun to fight immediately, to brave battle, but rosy Phoebus bathed his tired horses in the Iberian sea and brought back night as day passed. They take up their positions in front of the city in their camps and fortify their walls; XI.912–15.)

This is the only book of the *Aeneid* that ends with the end of day. Virgil's return to a scheme in which the passage of time delimits the action recalls the first eclogue, in which contact between men shifts from outdoors to indoors as night falls; as well, the armed camps and fortifications of Book XI replace the villas of the eclogue. The love that unites Nisus and Euryalus or Aeneas and Pallas has its origins in the pastoral genre and extends even to the enemy, as we see in the death of Lausus. As the day ends, so does this friendly homosociality: Turnus will have no share in it.

Virgil's handling of the duel between Aeneas and Turnus illustrates one of the most striking differences between the *Aeneid* and the *Iliad*. The duel between Achilles and Hector is obviously a precedent, but Homer does not end his poem with this event. The very last line of the *Iliad* is 'Thus they honoured the burial of Hector tamer of horses' (XXIV.804). In concluding his epic, Homer chooses to stress its elegiac aspect. One of the reasons for this is that Achilles himself, like Hector, is doomed to die. In contrast, Aeneas is doomed to live and to establish a kingdom. There can be no fellow feeling between him and Turnus, since they are in competition for the hand of Lavinia and the control of Latium. Gransden points out that 'Dido was the chief of the *impedimenti* which beset Aeneas's Odyssey: Turnus is to be the chief of the *impedimenti* which will beset his Iliad.'[25] They are also in competition because of their beauty. Wendell Clausen notes that Aeneas 'is described as "ante alios pulcherrimus omnis" (4.141) and Dido ... as "forma pulcherrima Dido" (1.496). Nowhere else is Aeneas so described. In fact, the phrase occurs only once again, in 7.55, of Turnus suing for the hand of Lavinia.'[26]

These citations emphasize Turnus's role in the *Aeneid*'s homosocial economy. First of all, his replacement of Dido as the main obstacle to Aeneas's success underlines the poem's turn from women to men. This movement from women to men is repeated in the death of Camilla, who has been Aeneas's most dangerous enemy in the eleventh book, and the resulting shift in focus that returns Turnus to the centre of the poem's events. His beauty also plays a role in the poem's economy, since Virgil's repetition of 'ante alios pulcherrimus omnis' occurs at the moment that Lavinia's status as the object of contention is made clear. Turnus is at once like Aeneas (his enemy) and Dido (the precedent for his enmity). His beauty also links him to Aeneas and to such figures as Euryalus, Pallas, and Lausus. I said earlier that male beauty appears to be fatal to its possessor except in Aeneas's case, where it contributes to his epic stature. In other men, beauty only contributes to the elegiac tone Virgil invokes at their deaths. Still, although the combat between Turnus and Aeneas is inevitable, the form it takes further develops the poem's homosociality. When the fatal combat that ends the *Aeneid* comes, it is not motivated by the competition for Latium or for Lavinia, but rather by the death of Pallas.

In his book on Roman epic, Philip Hardie argues that at the end of the *Aeneid* Virgil gives us 'two versions of Pallas opposing each other, Aeneas as the agent of Pallas's revenge and Turnus as the young warrior who, by foolishly dressing in the sword-belt of Pallas, has consigned himself to the same premature and pathetic death in battle as his victim.'[27] These two versions correspond to the two possibilities for the place of elegy at this point in the epic's development: the epic can either end elegiacally, as the *Iliad* does, or it can leave the elegiac mode behind. Until now, Virgil has found the elegiac tone very useful: it has provided many of his celebrated moments of pathos and the movement from elegy to elegy has provided most of the plot of the second half of the poem. Nevertheless, elegies celebrate homosocial attachments, and while Virgil has turned from heterosociality to homosociality in order to advance the story, I think he would still want to stress that the maintenance of a kingdom – as opposed to its establishment – requires heteroeroticism. In a sense, the ending of the *Aeneid* can be read as repeating the movement from bonds between men to fertility in the service of the state that takes place over the course of the *Eclogues* in order to prepare us for the *Georgics*. In order to demonstrate this parallel, I want to look at the poem's ending in greater detail.

The *Aeneid* can only end elegiacally if Hardie's second version of Pallas – Turnus as a man who dies prematurely and pathetically – is given expression by the poet. We might well think that this would be the case and that Aeneas's slaying of Turnus would produce a scene similar to his slaying of Lausus, but this is not what happens. In fact, Turnus very nearly lives. After Aeneas wounds him, he pleads for his life:

> uicisti et uictum tendere palmas
> Ausonii uidere; tua est Lauinia coniunx,
> ulterius ne tende odiis.

> (You have conquered and the Ausonians see me, the conquered, extending my hands; Lavinia is your wife, do not let your hatred extend further; XII.936–8.)

Turnus emphasizes that Aeneas has won both the woman and the king-dom for which he was fighting and that he has no reason to kill Turnus. The speech almost works, but then Aeneas notices that Turnus is wearing Pallas's baldric and he kills him. His refusal to be moved by pity has come in for a good deal of criticism and it has the effect of changing our sense of the love triangle that has motivated the events of the second half of the *Aeneid*: the struggle between Aeneas and Turnus over Lavinia turns into a struggle between Aeneas and Turnus over Pallas.

The best illustration of Hardie's comment comes when Aeneas no-tices Pallas's sword-belt on Turnus's shoulder:

> ille, oculis postquam saeui monimenta doloris
> exuuiasque hausit, furiis accensus et ira
> terribilis: 'tune hinc spoliis indute meorum
> eripiare mihi? Pallas te hoc uulnere, Pallas
> immolat et poenam scelerato ex sanguine sumit.'

(When Aeneas stared at the remembrance of savage sorrow, the booty, he was inflamed with fury and terrible rage: 'Are you who wear the spoils of my dead comrade to escape me here? Pallas kills you with this wound, Pallas exacts this punishment from your guilty blood'; XII.945–9.)

The two versions of Pallas are face to face, but the men can be seen as versions of other characters too. To describe Turnus's death Virgil uses the line with which he described Camilla's: 'uitaque cum gemitu fugit indignata sub umbras' (and with a groan the offended soul flees to the shades below; XI.831, XII.952). In using the line once again, Virgil forces us to consider Camilla and Turnus together as a defeated pair in opposition to the victorious pair of Aeneas and Lavinia. This also makes it harder for us to consider Turnus in connection with Euryalus or Pallas or Lausus, even though there are so many obvious similarities – and particularly between Turnus and Lausus, who were allies. By simultaneously excluding Turnus from vatic empathy and linking him with Camilla (who is also excluded from it), Virgil signals the end of his use of the elegiac mode. The fact that Turnus wears Pallas's sword-belt is not interpreted as suggesting other resemblances. Instead, Aeneas interprets it as a sign of their difference, as his own repeated identification with Pallas in this passage shows: only Aeneas can be like Pallas. This is an important point in Virgil's gradual abandonment of elegy, since Turnus really is like Pallas, Euryalus, and Lausus. The *Aeneid* has depended on a whole class of persons who seem to exist only to become elegiac subjects. The killing of Turnus demonstrates that elegy no longer has a place in Virgil's epic.

Clausen refers to the killing of Turnus as a 'final, terrible act of *pietas*.'[28] The act shows *pietas* because it avenges Pallas, who was entrusted to Aeneas by Evander, but I also take Clausen's comment to mean that by killing Turnus Aeneas finally ends the homosocial world of elegy that has dominated much of the poem and returns to the sphere of family life, of being dutiful (*pius*) to one's family. From this point of view, the *Aeneid* at its conclusion recalls not the *Iliad* but the *Odyssey*, whose hero has to lose all his male companions so that the poem can end with a tableau of family life. The sexual reunion between Ulysses and Penelope is the sexual gratification that has been deferred for twenty-four books. The marriage between Aeneas and Lavinia does not have this place, however. After the tragic love affair with Dido, Aeneas has been chiefly occupied – militarily and emotionally – with a series of young men. Although Nisus and Euryalus are granted a death that is also a consummation, other men have died alone and Aeneas himself has remained alone, mourning young men whose beauty is almost equal to his. As Rachel Falconer suggests, the ending of the poem changes all that: 'Aeneas finally does embrace a substantive body, that of Turnus, but only to stab him in a fit of rage.'[29] The *Aeneid* thus ends with a gesture that simultaneously affirms and ends homoeroticism: the paradoxical status of homoeroticism mirrors the paradoxical status of the genre of elegy within the epic. I believe that one of the lessons Renaissance writers learned from the ending of the poem is that death is the price paid for the embrace of two men.

CHAPTER THREE

The Space of the Tomb

Although many of the most famous English poems are elegies, the tradition of elegiac poetry in English is not ancient. There are some Old English poems that are often called elegies, but it was only in the sixteenth century that English poets began to produce a body of poetry that is elegiac in the sense that the Greek poems lamenting the deaths of Daphnis or Moschus are elegiac. This may in part be due to the fact that most English poets before the sixteenth century would only have been able to read these poems in translation. In this chapter I want to look at three Renaissance elegies: Baldassare Castiglione's 'Alcon,' the Earl of Surrey's 'So crewell prison,' and John Milton's 'Epitaphium Damonis.' Both Castiglione's and Milton's poems are in Latin: I think Castiglione wrote in Latin mainly because he was self-consciously imitating a kind of poetry that he associated primarily, and perhaps solely, with the classical era (obviously this is one of Milton's reasons as well). Although the *Book of the Courtier*, Castiglione's most famous work, was written in Italian, his poetry is in Latin. Perhaps for him, as for so many, the vernacular was the language of public affairs, while Latin provided entry into a private world.[1]

Castiglione may seem an odd choice for a book on English responses to and uses of the classical tradition, but my point is that even though 'Alcon' itself has never been a well-known work, its influence on the English elegiac tradition through Milton has been incalculable. And indirect: I am not claiming that poets like Gray and Tennyson read 'Alcon' (the paucity of available editions makes that unlikely), but they did read 'Lycidas.' While many of the features of 'Lycidas' come directly from Theocritus and Virgil, many, I believe, are filtered through

'Alcon.' I have chosen to discuss 'Epitaphium Damonis' rather than 'Lycidas' partly because I think it is an excellent poem that has been unjustly neglected, but chiefly because, although the question of how well Milton knew Edward King is still a matter for debate, no one denies that Milton and Diodati were very close friends and that the elegy he wrote for Diodati is much more personal than the elegy for King. In her excellent discussion of the poem, Stella P. Revard contrasts Milton's two elegies: 'The anonymity of "Lycidas" falls away, however, in "Epitaphium Damonis" when Milton takes on the person of the classical Thyrsis and pours his heart out – in Latin.'[2] Because 'Epitaphium Damonis' is more personal than 'Lycidas' and because it is in Latin (and those two aspects of the poem are connected) it shows more clearly its relation to the classical tradition and to other Renaissance uses of that tradition such as 'Alcon.' For Renaissance poets, the elegy was pastoral in its genre and Latin in its language; by examining two Latin pastoral elegies from the Renaissance, then, we can get a clearer sense of the transition from the classical to modern elegy.

It is really Surrey who stands out in the context of this chapter, not only because he wrote in his native language but also because he drew more on native poetic traditions than on Latin or Greek ones. Later English elegists, who have been influenced by 'Lycidas,' have tended to follow classical models; in my discussion of Surrey I want to give some sense of what a more purely English elegiac tradition might have looked like. Although my emphasis in this book is on Renaissance English uses of the classical tradition, I am also interested in the larger question of the use poets make of the poetic traditions open to them. In any case, I think that even though Surrey's model is more likely to be Chaucer than either Virgil or Theocritus, his elegy has many similarities both to Castiglione's and to Milton's. Surrey's poem is concerned with homoerotic space just as much as the others are, and all three poets are concerned with the question of how (and where) the dead man is to be mourned and what sort of position the poet has in relation to this dead person who was neither a spouse nor a blood relative. There is really no equivalent for this sort of question in Theocritus or Virgil, but it becomes one of the central concerns in the English elegiac tradition – a sign, as I see it, of the increasing scrutiny of relations between men that has been one of the distinguishing features of Western society since the classical period and which has reached fever pitch in the last century or so. In these poems written at the beginning of our elegiac tradition, we can see the first attempts to find a place for homoerotic relationships in a militantly heteroerotic society.

Before I turn to the poems themselves, I want to summarize once more what the advantages of the classical tradition were for Renaissance poets. In his article on lesbian elegy in the Renaissance, James Holstun says that the lesbianism expressed in these poems is not threatening 'for it becomes vocal only as elegy.'[3] The love between Iolas and Alcon, between Surrey and Richmond, and between Thyrsis and Damon can become vocal as elegy, not only because an elegy describes what is past but also because elegies are art. Artistic works can create a space for the expression of emotions that are unacceptable in the world in which the artist lives, and the presence of a work of art arising from the relationship between the male couple is a sign that the relationship, whatever its nature, was worthwhile. The specifically pastoral nature of many elegies increases the distance between the poet and the dead man he loved. In her book on pastoral, Susan Snyder neatly distinguishes between temporal and spatial orientation in pastoral poetry: 'In the first mode pastoral bliss is back then, but in the second it is over there.'[4] Both kinds of separation apply in the pastoral elegy and prevent the elegist from too close an identification with the often homoerotic world he describes and celebrates. 'Alcon,' 'So crewell prison,' and 'Epitaphium Damonis' all to a greater or lesser extent engage very seriously with the question of the various kinds of distance between the poet and his subject. Although 'So crewell prison' is not a pastoral poem, in its re-creation of the boyhood of Surrey and Richmond and in its emphasis on the castle in which that boyhood was passed it is clearly concerned both with 'back then' and with 'over there.'

'Alcon'

Castiglione wrote 'Alcon' when he was still in his twenties, and while *The Book of the Courtier*, which he wrote two decades later, has been famous ever since, 'Alcon' has always been obscure. In recent years, *The Book of the Courtier* has often been discussed as one of the books that mark the entry into the Renaissance (or Early Modern): the book's very existence is seen as a sign of the self-fashioning that we now consider typical of that period, whatever we may call it. In contrast, Castiglione's Latin poetry, which is difficult even to find, has seemed remote from our concerns. Yet many of the issues that have attracted scholars to Castiglione in the last twenty or thirty years can be found in 'Alcon.' Richard L. Regosin begins his excellent analysis of *The Book of the Courtier* by summarizing the critical discussion of Castiglione's juxta-position of life and art; he makes the point that despite our increasing interest in the disjunction of those two categories, 'we continue to evince a faith in the ultimate ability of art and the aesthetic to allow us to reconcile or to transcend life's contingency and to overcome difference.' Regosin goes on to state that '[w]hat is at stake in Castiglione's book is the complex nature of the work of art – both as literature and as life – and its problematical status as it seeks to make life over or to give itself life.'[5]

The issues Regosin raises are crucial to 'Alcon,' in which Castiglione addresses the question of whether art can be any compensation for the losses of death. This question is not, of course, unique to the Renaissance. As we have seen, it is in many ways the central concern of Theocritus's first idyll and of most elegies written in the tradition he was held to have founded in that poem.[6] Yet while Theocritus's narrative frame permits the first idyll to take place at a certain distance from the death of its subject and thus to concentrate as much on questions of poetry as on questions of personal grief (a strategy Virgil follows in the fifth eclogue), no such distance exists in 'Alcon.' In his article, Salemi dismisses 'Alcon' as one of 'the usual exercises of the Renaissance Latinist.'[7] I hope to demonstrate that 'Alcon' is more than merely an exercise or even a creative imitation. Although 'Alcon' clearly has many similarities both to the first idyll and to the fifth eclogue, Castiglione puts in doubt one of the central points of the classical poems: the belief that art is a compensation for the death of a beloved man. This doubt is an important feature, not just of 'Alcon,' but also of the poems by Surrey and by Milton that I shall discuss later, and of most of the best-known English elegies of the following centuries. As I pointed out in my introduction, the omission of one of the standard features of a genre (in this case, the *consolatio*) can have great significance. To refuse the consolation offered typically by the hope of poetic fame or the pleasures of women is to imply that the loss of a man one loves is a loss for which there is no compensation. I think that the omission of the *consolatio* can be taken as a refusal both of a poetic convention and of conventional ways of living.

In an essay on her early poetry, Adrienne Rich said that for her 'formalism was part of the strategy – like asbestos gloves, it allowed me to handle materials I couldn't pick up bare-handed.'[8] Castiglione's use of a classical form and of a classical language may well have had a similar use for him. In his 1935 comparison of 'Alcon' and 'Epitaphium Damonis' (still the only detailed discussion of this subject), Thomas Perrin Harrison, Jr stresses 'Alcon''s autobiographical nature. He says that the poem commemorates 'Falcone, companion of his youth,' that Castiglione was in Rome when Falcone died in July 1505, and that as Castiglione 'alludes to the death of his brother Jeronimo [called Leucippus in the poem], it is concluded that the author wrote the poem during his visit to England.'[9] This biographical background has an important relation to the poem itself. 'Alcon' is centrally concerned not just with the grief caused by death, but also with the compounding of that grief by the absence of the speaker: absence becomes an important theme in the poem. The data supplied by Harrison also raise the question of homoerotic space. One sort of homoerotic space is provided by the fact that the poem is about a dead man, a second by the pastoral setting, a third by the use of Latin rather than Italian, and a fourth by the fact that Castiglione (at the time of composition a man in his late twenties already embarked on his successful career as a diplomat) is mourning the 'companion of his youth.'

In his manipulation of and engagement with classical poetry Castiglione places the poem in a literary homoerotic space from the beginning:

> Ereptum fatis primo sub flore juventae,
> Alconem nemorum decus, et solatia amantum,
> Quem toties Fauni et Dryades sensere canentem,
> Quem toties Pan est, toties miratus Apollo,
> Flebant pastores.[10]

(The shepherds mourned for Alcon, the ornament of the groves and the comfort of lovers, seized by fate in the first flower of youth, whom the fauns and dryads so often heard singing, whom Pan and Apollo so often admired; 1–5.)

Castiglione presents Alcon as an inhabitant of the pastoral world who is also a singer. His singing has been admired by both Pan and Apollo, that is, by a deity associated with pastoral songs and by one associated with a higher type of poetry altogether. Nor is this the only difference between the two gods: in legends Pan is primarily heteroerotic while Apollo is primarily homoerotic. There is thus in these opening lines a conscious balancing of elements, which can also be seen in the mention of fauns (male) and dryads (female). Castiglione is careful to differentiate the world of his poem from the homosocial worlds of the first idyll and the fifth eclogue. The fact that the subject of the sentence, which is delayed for as long as possible in the Latin, turns out to be 'shepherds' may seem to refer to that homosocial world, but I would argue that here as well Castiglione, having set up the genre and gender balances I have mentioned, chooses this plural subject in order to emphasize a community rather than a couple.

Up to this point, the poem appears as a cautious recension of a homoerotically charged original, but the speaker of the poem is unable to maintain this level of caution and the group of mourners is immediately narrowed to an individual: 'Ante omnes carus Iolas/ ... / Crudeles Superos, crudeliaque astra vocabat' (More than all the others, beloved Iolas called to the cruel gods and stars or called the gods and stars cruel; 5, 7). These lines bring 'Alcon' closer to the world of the dying Daphnis, who also protests against both the divine and the natural order. Castiglione makes these protests explicitly a little later in the poem:

Quis Deus, aut quis te casus miser abstulit? ergo
Optima quaeque rapit duri inclementia fati?
Ergo bonis tantum est aliquod male numen amicum?
Non metit ante diem lactentes messor aristas,
Immatura rudis non carpit poma colonus:
At fera te ante diem mors nigro immersit Averno.

(What god or unhappy accident took you away? Does hard and cruel fate then seize everything that is best? Is some divine will sometimes friendly and sometimes bad to the good? The reaper does not reap the juicy corn before its time, the farmer does not pick the immature green fruit: yet cruel death has plunged you into black Avernus before your time; 27–32.)

In the first part of this passage, Iolas considers several possibilities: Alcon's death could have been caused by a god ('Deus' and 'aliquod ... numen') or by fate ('fati') or even by chance ('casus'). Iolas wants both to protest against the gods and to suggest that they are not the most powerful force in the pastoral world. Furthermore, when he turns to natural images, he does so in order to point out the folly – one could even say bad management – of whoever or whatever is responsible for Alcon's death. It is the death itself that violates the natural order, not Iolas's emotions.

In the lines that follow the first mention of Iolas, Castiglione compares himself first to a nightingale (8) and then to a turtle dove:

qualis socia viduatus compare turtur,
Quam procul incautam quercu speculatus ab alta,
Immitis calamo pastor dejecit acuto.

(Like the turtle dove deprived of its spouse when a stern shepherd sees the incautious bird and brings it down from a tall oak with a sharp arrow; 9–11.)

The shepherds who mourned Alcon have now become a single, hostile man (particularly hostile to lovers, apparently), a change that heightens our sense of Iolas's isolation. Furthermore, it is becoming clear that his is a double isolation: from the dead and from the living. The pastoral community that was so prominent in the idylls and eclogues is now no sooner mentioned than it is shown to be illusory. As the second half of the poem demonstrates, the speaker's only real community has been with Alcon and to a much lesser extent with Leucippus, who is also dead. Although the beginning of the poem may recall the world of the frames of the first idyll and the fifth eclogue, in which agricultural labourers are united in grief, Castiglione quickly places the reader in a setting that is more similar to the one in which Theocritus's Daphnis finds himself.

The images of this passage are connected to love and to art. For instance, the nightingale is traditionally associated with romantic love as well as functioning as a symbol of natural art. In this part of the comparison, Iolas simultaneously attempts to give his lament the status of art and to present it as natural and understandable. By comparing his grief to that of a mother whose child is lost, Castiglione anticipates and fends off the suspicion that Iolas's grief is in some sense excessive or improper. This discretion is immediately lost in the second comparison, however, in which the dead man is metaphorically presented as a spouse.[11] The turtle dove has long been one of the commonest symbols of wedded love. Unlike the sound of the nightingale, the sound of the turtle dove is not usually seen as art, but Castiglione returns to the theme of art by having the shepherd shoot down the dove 'calamo ... acuto.' In context, these words mean 'with a sharp arrow,' but they could just as well mean 'with a shrill reed.' The 'calamus' is one of the basic instruments of the pastoral singers in poetry. We can see this play on words as a suggestion, in keeping with the poem as a whole but sharply different from both Theocritus and Virgil, that art is linked to death rather than being a compensation for it.

The references to the nightingale, the turtle dove, and the calamus are all part of a background that is not particularly different from many other pastoral poems of the period or earlier; as I have said, the themes of 'Alcon' and the questions posed by the poem recall the first idyll. Castiglione does make more specific use of two classical poems, however, and I want to look at these before turning to a general discussion of the poem. One instance of intertextuality begins in one of Castiglione's few uses of a time scheme for the events of the poem:

> decedens jam Sol declivis Olympo
> Occidit, et moriens accendit sidera coelo;
> Sed tamen occiduo cum laverit aequore currus,
> Idem iterum terras orienti luce reviset.

(now the departing sun inclines to Olympus and falls, and in dying kindles the stars in heaven, yet when it sets and its chariot washes in the sea, it will return again as before with light for the eastern lands; 57–60.)

References to natural cycles are often reassuring and may symbolize the restoration of order (as they do at the end of Virgil's sixth eclogue). In the case of elegies, these cycles are often adduced as evidence that life does go on even though individuals must die.

As so often in 'Alcon,' however, this passage gestures towards some sort of acceptance of, or reconciliation to, divine and natural order only to break down:

> Ast ubi nigra semel durae nos flumina mortis
> Lavere, et clausa est immitis janua regni;
> Nulla unquam ad Superos ducit via, lumina somnus
> Urget perpetuus, tenebrisque involvit amaris.

(But once the black streams of hard death wash us and the gates to the cruel kingdom are closed, no path ever leads to the gods above, perpetual sleep drives out the light and it [the path] is covered in bitter darkness; 61–4).[12]

The breakdown of this attempt to find consolation is emphasized by the intertext from what is possibly Catullus's most famous poem:

> soles occidere et redire possunt:

nobis cum semel occidit brevis lux,
nox est perpetua una dormienda.

(Suns can set and return, but if ever our brief light sets, we have a perpetual
sleep; V.4–6.)

Castiglione's lines are so close to the original in both theme and diction
that they could be called a paraphrase. Castiglione's version is longer,
particularly so in his description of the sun's ability to set and return
(four lines to Catullus's one, whereas the description of human death is
three lines to Catullus's two). The greater expansiveness has the effect
of heightening the pathos of the contrast between the sun's renewal of
itself and the finality of human death.

For me, the most significant aspect of Castiglione's use of Catullus
has to do with the original's genre. Catullus V is an appeal to the poet's
mistress, which begins

Vivamus, mea Lesbia, atque amemus,
rumoresque senum severiorum
omnes unius aestimemus assis.

(My Lesbia, let us live and love and consider as nothing all the opinions of
stern old men; 1–3.)

Although the poem deals specifically with heteroeroticism, it can be
read more universally as a call for sexual libertarianism. The poet and
his mistress are depicted as a couple whose love makes them immune
to 'quis ... inuidere possit' (anyone who might be envious; 12). This
opposition between a couple and a larger and generally hostile group
of observers is one of the staples of heteroerotic love poetry that
homoerotically inclined poets have found useful. Castiglione's use of
this famous love poem written by a poet associated with sexual licence
serves as a way for him to suggest a romantic reading of the relationship between Iolas and Alcon.

Such a reading is even more strongly suggested by Castiglione's
other primary intertext from classical poetry, Virgil's second eclogue.
There are two significant resemblances between 'Alcon' and this eclogue. The first comes near the beginning of the poem, just after the
summary of Iolas's inconsolable grief. After listing the various kinds of

pastoral labour in which Iolas no longer has any interest (18–20), Castiglione says,

> Tantum inter silvas, aut solo in littore secum
> Perditus, et serae oblitus decedere nocti
> Rupibus haec frustra et surdis jactabat arenis.

> (Nevertheless, in the woods or by the lonely shore, lost by himself and forgetting to retire in the late night, he hurled this vain speech to the unhearing rocks and sands; 21–3.)[13]

The wording of this passage is very close to Virgil's introduction to Corydon's speech in the eclogue:

> tantum inter densas, umbrosa cacumina, fagos
> adsidue veniebat. Ibi haec incondita solus
> montibus et silvis studio iactabat inani.

Both passages begin with 'tantum inter,' in both the speaker is concealed by darkness, in both the speaker is said to have hurled ('iactabat') his speech, in both the speaker addresses only nature rather than people, and in both the speech itself is criticized (it is 'frustra' in 'Alcon' and 'incondita' in the second eclogue). There is also a similarity in the function of the passages within their respective poems. In both cases, the monologue that follows these lines occupies the rest of the poem. The effect of this striking resemblance – and it is inconceivable that an educated reader would not notice the closeness of the lines from 'Alcon' to a passage from the beginning of one of the most famous poems in the European tradition – is to indicate that Iolas's speech, like Corydon's, will express a powerful and frustrated homoerotic desire.

The speech that follows can be divided into five sections: a meditation on Alcon's death in a context that is both cosmic and local (24–67); Iolas's memories of their life together (68–82); his regret at his absence (83–104); the plans he had made for their life together (105–31); and his plans to honour Alcon's memory (132–54). In what follows I shall be looking at the last four of these sections. Castiglione heightens our sense of Iolas's grief by making him present his memories negatively (that is, he expresses them only as things he will not be able to do any more): 'Non ... posthac' (not hereafter; 68, 71). The word 'non' also begins lines 73 and 75. Iolas's memories of Alcon begin with a group scene; in this case, competitions among shepherds. Iolas says that he will no longer see Alcon '[v]ictorem ... volucri certare sagitta,/ Aut jaculo' (victor at competing with the swift arrow or dart; 69–70), an ironic echo, earlier in time but later in the poem, of Alcon as the widowed turtle dove whose love has been killed by a stern shepherd. In the next image, Iolas is remembered for his success in wrestling. In both images, Iolas addresses Alcon by saying, 'te ... adstante' (you are standing by; 68). Although Alcon is physically close to Iolas in this remembered scene, the connection between the two at this point appears casual. Iolas is a spectator, someone who watches while other men are together. This is a milder form of the isolation he expresses throughout the poem and especially at the beginning, when he mentions the mourning shepherds, but adds that he mourned him more than anyone else.

The most important difference between these two images of homosocial competition is that in the first the contestants, although part of a group, are separate, while in the second they must touch in order to compete. The movement towards a more sensual form of homosocial competition leads to a shift from Iolas's memories of Alcon as one of a group of shepherds to memories of Alcon and himself alone: 'Non tecum posthac molli resupinus in umbra/ Effugiam longos aestivo tempore soles' (No longer lying on my back with you in the shade will I avoid the long sunny days of summertime; 71–2). The image of the two men lying in the shade, Iolas on his back, has a sexual charge that is emphasized by Castiglione's choice of 'effugiam.' This word means to flee, to shun, to avoid, and while not incorrect in this context it does seem a little strong as an expression for the seeking of shade at noon, which is, after all, the conventional beginning of much pastoral poetry. Perhaps we are intended to think that what they are really avoiding is the group of shepherds, a potentially disapproving group like the stern old men in Catullus V.

Iolas immediately retreats from the intimacy of this scene. After returning to the idea of Alcon as a musician (73–4), he refers to the women loved by Alcon and Iolas respectively: 'non jam simul ambos/ Audierint ambae nostros cantare furores' (both of them will not now hear both of us together sing of our passions; 76–7). My translation is awkward because the original is awkward. Although Iolas appears to be trying to stress the two heteroerotic couples, rather than introduce two male-female couples he adds a female-female couple to the male-male couple that is the poem's subject: 'ambos ... ambae.' Iolas has tried to situate himself and Alcon first in a homosocial context and then in a heteroerotic one. Both these attempts have failed; next, he shifts from speaking of himself and Alcon as two people within larger groups to attempting to summarize his relationship with Alcon:

> Nos etenim a teneris simul usque huc viximus annis,
> Frigora pertulimusque aestus, noctesque, diesque,
> Communique simul sunt parta armenta labore.
> Rura mea haec tecum communia: viximus una.

(Truly we lived together from our tender years to now, and we passed through cold and heat and night and day and the herds were our mutual labour. My fields were shared with you: we lived as one; 78–81.)

The adverb 'simul' (together) in lines 78 and 80, as well as in line 76, the unusual frequency of the enclitic '-que' (counting 'usque,' five times in three lines), and the shift in line 81 from the first-person plural to direct address all movingly emphasize the close connection between Iolas and Alcon.

Iolas does not permit himself to luxuriate in his memories, however, and his former happiness only increases his present sorrow. At this point we learn that not only has the male couple of Iolas and Alcon been disrupted by death, but a new male couple has been formed: Alcon and Leucippus.[14] In fact, Leucippus usurps Iolas's role in three ways:

> Invideo, Leucippe, tibi: suprema dolenti
> Deficiens mandata bonus tibi praebuit Alcon,
> Spectavitque tuos morienti lumine vultus
> Frigida tu moesto imposuisti membra feretro,
> Sparsisti et lacrimis bustum, ingratumque sepulchrum.

(I envy you, Leucippus: as you grieved, good Alcon, dying, gave you his last commands and watched your face with his dying eyes; you placed his cold limbs on the sad bier, and you shed tears on his grave and on the unpleasing tomb; 87–91.)

The first two examples of usurpation are that Leucippus, and not Iolas, was present at Alcon's death and that Leucippus, and not Iolas, carried out the funeral rites and acted as the chief mourner. Apart from Iolas's understandable emotional distress, the issue of who is to be chief mourner is of special concern in cases in which the person who is the obvious choice cannot claim any familial or legal relation. Iolas's absence at the time of Alcon's death gives a tangible reason for his inability to act as chief mourner, but I would add that Iolas would in any case not have been able to be the kind of chief mourner he would have liked to be: the grieving spouse.

Iolas saw himself as having been replaced in three ways. The third is the worst of all:

> et justa peracta,
> Alconem ad manes felix comes usque secutus
> Amisso vitam socio non passus inertem es;
> Et nunc Elysia laetus spatiaris in umbra,
> Alcone et frueris dulci, aeternumque frueris.

> (and after the due rites, you followed Alcon to the underworld as a happy companion and did not endure a pointless life in the absence of your friend. Now you walk happily in the Elysian shades, and you enjoy sweet Alcon, and you will enjoy him forever; 92–6.)

Iolas has been replaced both here and hereafter. To the four kinds of homoerotic space I mentioned earlier Castiglione has added a fifth: the realm of death, here presented as a place of eternal homoerotic pleasure. Our sense of Iolas's grief is naturally increased by the fact that the sad story of young Alcon's death has a happy ending in the underworld from which Iolas is excluded. He even goes so far as to imagine a shepherd who buries Alcon and Leucippus 'sepulchro/ Uno eodemque simul' (together in one and the same grave; 97–8), performs the last rites, and weeps over their tomb (99–100).

In this passage, Castiglione again suggests some sort of reconcilation. The shepherd burying the two men and then mourning them might seem to provide a suitable consolation for an elegy. Iolas's grief for Alcon and Leucippus would then have been acknowledged at a safe distance by the shepherd, whose appearance in the poem could be taken to represent a return to the pastoral community Iolas appeared to have abandoned, and the tomb could stand, like the elegy itself, as a sign of the compensations that art offers for grief. Yet this is not how Castiglione proceeds. The shepherd is hypothetical, and Iolas's refusal to tell us anything about the real burial denies us the closure we might expect. Furthermore, it is only Iolas's imagination that has provided the homoerotic closure of lines 93 to 96. Thus, although the poem seems at first to end suitably – both because of the tomb and because the poem has reached its one hundredth line – we are really as far from closure as before. In fact, at this point Iolas takes us further into his hypothetical world by relating to us the speech he had made to himself when he thought Alcon was still alive, a speech in which Iolas imagines his reunion with Alcon and their lives together.

This speech contains the most explicit presentation of Iolas's feelings for Alcon. His candour here is made possible, I believe, by the fact that the speech is explicitly labelled as pointless: 'Vana mihi incassum fingebam somnia demens' (Senseless, I imagined empty dreams for myself in vain; 104). The fact that five out of the six words in this line stress the fictional nature of what is to follow and the sixth presents his visions as made for himself creates another kind of homoerotic space, as well as stressing that homoerotic space cannot have real public expression. Iolas presents the reunion as beginning with a physical display of affection – 'caris complexibus ora/ Impediam' (I shall cover his face with affectionate embraces; 110–11) – before turning to conversation:

Sic tandem optato laeti sermone fruemur,
Aerumnasque graves, olim et transacta vicissim
Damna referre simul, rursusque audire juvabit:
Tum veteres sensim fando repetemus amores.

(Thus at last we shall enjoy the happy talk I have wished for, and it will be pleasant to talk of the heavy hardships at the same time as the troubles past and to hear the other's in return: then gradually as we speak we shall return to our former love; 112–15.)

The verb 'fruor,' used in line 96 to describe the pleasure of Alcon and Leucippus in the underworld, is now used to describe the joy of Alcon and Iolas as, in imagination at least, the substitution of Leucippus for Iolas is reversed. Iolas finishes the speech by praising the joys of the countryside in which he and Alcon will pass their days. Castiglione's vocabulary in this section recalls the eclogues, and the picture of 'dulcia ruris/ Otia' (sweet leisure of the country; 116–17) indicates that for Iolas pastoral space is homoerotic space.

Yet the spatial aspects of this speech cannot merely be characterized as pastoral. When Iolas imagines himself returning to his own country, Alcon (Iolas is remembering when he thought Alcon was still alive) is envisaged as 'linquens colles, et inhospita saxa,/ Infectasque undas, et pabula dira veneno' (leaving the hills and the inhospitable rocks and the polluted waves and the poisoned plants; 106–7). The pastoral landscape in which the two men spent their lives, the setting, that is, for most of the poem, is revealed to be unhealthy. Iolas's plan is for the two men to start a new life in a new land. This new land (new to Iolas and Alcon, that is) is Rome: 'Hic recolens sacros primaevae gentis honores,/ Perluit antiquas Tiberis decora alta ruinas' (Here, renewing the sacred rites of a youthful people, Tiber washes the ancient beauties and ruins; 122–3). The 'youthful people' are the ancient Romans. Although their buildings and monuments are now in ruins, they are still beautiful and are entering a period of renewal or renaissance. To us, this may well appear to be one of the most fictional moments of the poem. There was a great deal of what we would call archaeological work in Rome in the sixteenth-century, but most people would characterize sixteenth century Rome as a city always threatened by more powerful states like France and threatening less powerful states like Castiglione's own Urbino rather than as a peaceful place with an attitude of reverence for its past. Of course, it could be said that Castiglione, in writing a Latin poem, is himself 'renewing the sacred rites of a youthful people.'

Homoeroticism (if only in poetry) could well be one of these sacred rites, and it is this aspect that Castiglione stresses in his presentation of the Roman countryside:

Hic umbrae nemorum, hic fontes, hic frigida Tempe,
Formosum hic pastor Coridon cantavit Alexin.
Ergo ades, o dilecte puer.

(Here are shady groves, here are fountains, here is cold Tempe, here the shepherd Corydon sang lovely Alexis. Therefore be present, o beloved boy; 124–6.)

This is Castiglione's second use of the second eclogue. What it tells us is that the landscape in which Iolas awaits Alcon is not merely the potentially homoerotic space of the classical countryside but also the specifically homoerotic space in which the eclogue takes place. The explicitness of the intertextuality here may seem surprisingly candid; my point is that by this stage in the poem Castiglione has erected so many barriers about the poem – the pastoral setting, the use of Latin, the stress on this passage as entirely hypothetical even within the world of the poem, and, above all, the fact that the poem is addressed to a dead man – that he can afford to be candid; in any case, Corydon's love is unsuccessful. More than most poems, 'Alcon' shows us just what is necessary in order to achieve homoerotic space.

This homoerotic space is doomed never to exist. The final section of the poem is concerned with a different kind of space altogether: the tomb Iolas proposes to build for Alcon. Just as the picture of Iolas's joyful reunion with Alcon replaces the picture of Alcon and Leucippus in the underworld, so this tomb replaces the tomb that Iolas imagined a shepherd constructing for Alcon and Leucippus. The difference between the tombs is that the one built by Iolas will be empty. In fact, forms of 'inanis' occur three times in the ten lines following Iolas's fantasy of reunion. I think this is a further intertextuality with the second eclogue, although admittedly a rather more concealed one than the others. As I pointed out, when Castiglione introduces the monologue that occupies the rest of the poem (lines 21 to 23) he follows closely Virgil's introduction of Corydon's monologue (lines 3 to 5). There is one significant divergence, however: he provides no equivalent for Virgil's statement that Corydon delivered his speech 'studio ... inani' – or, at least, no equivalent at that point in the poem. This is partly because such a statement would serve no purpose in the narrative of the poem. While there is no obvious reason for Corydon's desire for Alexis to be in vain ('inanis'), Iolas's desire for Alcon is patently in vain from the beginning of the poem as Alcon is dead. The pointlessness of Corydon's desire is the subject of the second eclogue, while the pointlessness of Iolas's desire is part of the background of the poem. When Castiglione does use forms of 'inanis' the word has both the sense of 'vain, pointless' as in the second eclogue and the sense of 'empty.' The suggestion is that Iolas's whole world is pointless because it is empty. As well, while Corydon's disappointment takes place in a world in which homoerotic love is a possibility (even for Corydon, even if not with Alexis), Iolas lives in a world that is altogether empty even of the possibility of homoerotic love. Castiglione's uses of 'inanis' after the idyllic picture of Iolas and Alcon suggests that Iolas's wishes are in vain, not just because of the death of Alcon but also because of the nature of the world in which the poem is set: in fact, the 'ancient rites' of the Romans and of the pastoral world more generally are unfortunately not being renewed.

The first use of 'inanis' in this section comes when Iolas characterizes his vision of his future with Alcon as a delusion: 'Haec ego fingebam miser ab spe ductus inani' (This I imagined, wretched, led by empty hope; 130). In the second eclogue, it is Corydon's desire that is 'inanis,' but Castiglione says that the impetus for Iolas's desire is 'inanis' and thus locates the futility in the larger world rather than merely in the personal situation of the speaker. The second use of a form of 'inanis' occurs when Iolas pleads to the gods: 'Huc saltem, o saltem umbra levi per inania lapsu/ Advolet' (At least, o at least let the shade take its airy flight here through the void; 135–6). This void is both the air through which Alcon's ghost will fly and the world as a whole – void, or empty, because Alcon is dead. As with the first use of 'inanis,' Castiglione stresses the extent of the emptiness. Finally, however, what is empty is the tomb. The fact that Iolas is separate from both the living and the dead body of his beloved underscores our sense of the impossibility of homoeroticism in the world of the poem. Whatever poets may imagine about their lives with other men is ultimately an illusion and real homoerotic space is an empty tomb. Even in death, there is no place for the bond between Iolas and Alcon.

Yet we can perhaps find some hope in the third use of a form of 'inanis.' This occurs in the passage in which Iolas states his plans to build the tomb: 'Ipse meis manibus ripa hac Anienis inanem/ Constituam tumulum' (I shall myself with my own hands build an empty tomb on this bank of the Anio; 139–40). The change from the Tiber to the Anio is significant in itself. The Tiber is the main river of Rome, its name is often used metaphorically to mean Rome, and it is one of the principal symbols of Rome. The Anio, by contrast, is a river with a Sabine name rather than a Latin one, and although it flows very close to Rome it has never been a symbol of the city. I think there are three main reasons for Castiglione's decision to mention the Anio. First, and most obviously, it is a play on words: 'Anienis inanem,' as if 'Aniens' were the positive form, which does not in fact exist but which would mean full, of the adjective 'inanis.' Second, the shift from the Tiber, where Iolas vainly planned to live with Alcon, to the Anio, where Iolas's plans can be carried out, indicates that he has found, if not homoerotic space, then at least a space in which he can operate and in which he can mourn Alcon, and by mourning him continue to testify to the reality of their lives together. Third (and I think this is the most important), although the Tiber is associated with Rome itself, the Anio does flow by one of the most celebrated of all Roman ruins: the Villa Adriana, built by the Emperor Hadrian. In this passage Castiglione sets up a comparison between Iolas and Hadrian. Hadrian was also absent when his lover

Antinous died and Hadrian also constructed a monument by the Anio to his lover, one that, like Iolas's projected tomb for Alcon, does not contain the body of the man it honours. In the absence of any connection between Iolas and the world in which he lives – a world characterized as 'inanis' – Iolas at least gestures to a connection with the past. This homoerotic space exists in the connection between the classical past and the present. It may well be the appeal to Hadrian as a precedent that makes it possible for Iolas to be more explicit than he has been up to this point in the poem: 'Nos Alcon dilexit multum, et dignus amari./ Ipse fuit nobis' (Alcon loved me greatly, and was worthy to be loved. He himself was loved by me; 147–8).

Iolas's declaration of his love for Alcon and of Alcon's for him is the emotional highpoint of the poem and may be as close as the poem can get to a happy ending. What is even more remarkable than the explicitness of that statement, however, is the conclusion to the poem, which takes the form of the inscription Iolas orders to be placed on the tomb:

> Alconem postquam rapuerunt impia fata,
> Collacrimant duri montes, et consitus atra est
> Nocte dies; sunt candida nigra, et dulcia amara.

> (The hard mountains weep exceedingly now that wicked fate has seized Alcon, and day is replaced with dark night; white is black, and sweet is bitter; 152–4.)

As I have already indicated, Iolas refuses the traditional consolations of elegy, such as the cup given as a prize in the first idyll. Although this inscription recalls the one in Virgil's fifth eclogue, the difference between the two can hardly be overstated. While the speaker in the eclogue places the dead Daphnis in a context that includes, in an ordered and benevolent manner, both the earth and the heavens, Iolas continues to presents Alcon's death as a disturbance in natural order. The poem ends with the *adunata* more traditionally found near the beginning of elegies. Wayne A. Rebhorn comments that, '[s]ignificantly, the last word of the epitaph is "bitter,"'[15] and I think the significance lies in the fact that by ending with this word, Iolas signals his intention to continue grieving, to refuse to find substitutes for his beloved Alcon. The empty tomb is now the only homoerotic space left to him.

'So Crewell Prison'

'So crewell prison' was written about thirty years after 'Alcon.' Although we know that Surrey read Castiglione (we have his heavily annotated copy of the 1541 edition of the *Libro del Cortigiano*), I have not been able to discover if he knew 'Alcon.'[16] There are various similarities, although they do not prove that Surrey did know 'Alcon.' The subject of 'So crewell prison' is Henry Fitzroy, Duke of Richmond, the companion of Surrey's youth as Falcone was the companion of Castiglione's, and 'So crewell prison' also moves between pictures of the two young men as part of a larger community and pictures of them alone. Other similarities will become clear and I shall comment on some of them, but given that both poems are elegies, the dissimilarities between them may be more obvious than the similarities. The most noticeable difference is that Surrey writes in the vernacular. As with 'Alcon' and 'Epitaphium Damonis,' the choice of language is part of the poet's larger strategy for the poem. Unlike 'Alcon,' which takes place in a pastoral world that is for the most part not particularly different from the world of the eclogues and that only occasionally seems to become the Italy of Castiglione's own day, Surrey's poem takes place at Windsor Castle – the careful use of the setting is one of the poem's most distinctive features – and moves between the poet's present and the events of a few years earlier. As well, the poetic tradition on which Surrey draws in his poem is not the classical Latin or Greek tradition but rather his native English tradition. Furthermore, while it would certainly be possible to unpack the relation of 'Alcon' to Castiglione's political life, in 'So crewell prison' there is a clear connection between the poem and Surrey's political life.

Finally, while 'Alcon' has always been obscure, 'So crewell prison' has always been quite famous. Indeed, it has been a useful poem for historians of English poetry. Always (and now perhaps primarily) associated with technical innovation, Surrey is said in this poem and in some others to be beginning the tradition of the English elegy. It is certainly true that many of his poems are elegies: there are two ('So crewell prison' and 'When Windesor walles') for the Duke of Richmond,[17] three for Sir Thomas Wyatt, and one for Thomas Clere. This is certainly an important aspect of Surrey's work, much of which centres on remembering, and sometimes innovation and renovation go hand in hand for Surrey, as in his translation of Books II and IV of the *Aeneid*, which is the first use in English of blank verse.[18] There are, however, other possible generic descriptions of 'So crewell prison.' Its classification as an elegy has ruled out the possibility that the poem could be classified in other ways. I want to consider alternative generic contexts for this poem in order to suggest alternative ways to read it. Although 'So crewell prison' is an elegy, it is not just an elegy. My emphasis is on the poem as a love poem and on its relation to other love poems, but I also want to suggest here that we could consider 'So crewell prison' as a kind of translation of the elegiac tradition into an explicitly English setting with explicitly English poetic precedents.

The best way into this subject is to examine the different classification of 'So crewell prison' made by Surrey's two most important editors, Frederick Morgan Padelford (1920) and Emrys Jones (1964). Recent critics have tended to follow Jones's lead; I want to suggest that Padelford's classification is ultimately more interesting (this is not in any sense a negative criticism of the Jones edition as a whole). In Padelford's edition, 'So crewell prison,' which he calls 'The Poets [sic] Lament for His Lost Boyhood,' is classified as an autobiographical poem and, as such, is grouped with the satire on London, the sonnet to Geraldine, 'When Windesor walles,' 'Good ladies, you that have your pleasure in exyle' (a poem whose basis in biography is conjectural), and others, and not with the 'Elegiac Poems,' which includes the three elegies on Sir Thomas Wyatt and the sonnet to Thomas Clere. In Jones's edition, 'So crewell prison' is grouped with the sonnet to Clere, 'When Windesor walles,' and several other poems under the heading of 'Ethical and Elegiac Poems,' while 'Good ladies, you that have your pleasure in exyle' and the sonnet to Geraldine are classified as 'Amatory Poems.'

This examination of the classification of 'So crewell prison' is more than a bibliographic exercise, as the editorial decisions I have mentioned reflect and ultimately help to reinforce ideological considerations. Jones wants to draw a distinction between elegies and love poems, one that is based on gender: a poem with a male speaker and a male subject is for him ipso facto not a love poem. Therefore, he emphasizes the elegiac nature of 'So crewell prison.' In contrast, Padelford divides the poems into translations, poems about the author, poems about the dead, romantic poems, and poems about how we should live ('Moral and Didactic Poems'). I am not suggesting that Padelford's classification is more accurate than Jones's, but I think it is useful that in his edition we approach 'So crewell prison' with the expectation that it will tell us about the poet. The autobiographical element in 'So crewell prison' has usually been taken to be a reference to Surrey's actual imprisonment in Windsor Castle.[19] This is the political context for the poem; the poetic context has always been assumed to be Surrey's elegies and his sonnet 'When Windesor walles.' While acknowledging the importance to 'So crewell prison' of these contexts, I want to suggest a larger poetic context, one that includes both Chaucer's *Troilus and Criseyde* and Surrey's own 'O lothsome place.' The advantage to my project of Padelford's grouping is that it suggests a way of looking at 'So crewell prison' in which the poem can be read simultaneously as an elegy, as a political statement, and as a love poem.

The third of these classifications – 'So crewell prison' as a love poem – is the one that has been discussed least often in studies of Surrey. It is only very recently that critics have been willing to consider the homoerotic aspects of Surrey's verse. Most critics have simply ignored the topic altogether; S.P. Zitner, in his otherwise excellent article on the Clere sonnet, is typical of the attitudes of the very few who have felt obliged to raise the topic even briefly. Commenting on the line 'Thine Earle halfe dead gave in thy Hand his will,'[20] Zitner says,

> The word 'will' acquires overtones of accord and – at a distance – desire. Yet there is no problem here. Despite Surrey's intense friendship with Thomas Clere and, earlier, with Henry VIII's illegitimate son, the Duke of Richmond ... his marriage to Lady Francis Vere seems well placed by Sir Sidney Lee's starchy *DNB* adjective, 'regular.'[21]

It is disingenuous to say that 'will' acquires overtones of accord or desire when the word was a common synonym for desire and even for penis in the sixteenth century. Zitner's use of 'problem' as a synonym for homoeroticism is revealing, but what concerns me most here is the assumption that a man who is married – even in a 'regular' manner – could not also be sexually or romantically interested in other men. Such a view, although by no means uncommon among older scholars even today, is simply untenable now; it makes no sense at all in the sixteenth century.[22]

Given the critical unwillingness to consider the possibility of homoeroticism, the usual assumption is that what Surrey felt for Richmond was friendship rather than love, but the distinction cannot be supported from the poem itself, or at least not in the very modern sense in which critics use it. Surrey depicts his relationship with Richmond as something that transcends other relationships, as a bond that can be compared to the love between Troilus and Criseyde or to love affairs in Surrey's other poems. I think the crucial word in this context is 'fere,' the main term Surrey uses to refer to Richmond. This word was fairly common with Surrey and Chaucer, but fell out of use within a hundred years of Surrey's death. The *Oxford English Dictionary* lists three main definitions: companion, comrade, mate, partner; consort, spouse, husband, wife; equal. These may seem very different now, but if we look at Surrey and Chaucer's use of these terms, it will become apparent that we draw lines where they did not. Chaucer uses 'fere' seven times: once to refer to horses who work together (*Troilus and Criseyde* I.224); three times to refer to a friend or companion (*Legend of Good Women* F.969; *Troilus and Criseyde* I.13 and III.1496); and three times to refer to a mate (*The Parlement of Foules* 410 and 416; *Troilus and Criseyde* IV.791, where the reference is to Eurydice as the 'fere' of Orpheus).[23] Surrey uses the word nine times in his translation of Books II and IV of the *Aeneid* to refer to Aeneas's followers (II.402, 480, 497, 524, 739, 772, 991, 1057; IV.801); twice to mean 'mate' ('When sommer toke in hand the winter to assail' 23; 'An Irate Host' – Jones does not include this poem – 1); once to mean friend (Psalm 55:23); once to refer to people sleeping in each other's arms (Ecclesiastes 4:29); and in 'So crewell prison' to mean the Duke of Richmond, whom I think we should see as Surrey's companion, consort, and equal.

I have given some sense of the range of meanings to show that it is extremely difficult to rule out any possible one. When I gave modern equivalents for 'fere,' I gave only the most likely meaning; the meanings provided by the *OED* are close enough that there is bound to be a certain amount of semantic overlap, and it is not always possible to choose one translation. Perhaps it is better not to choose one translation, either of the word 'fere' into twentieth-century equivalents or of Surrey and Richmond's relationship into its twentieth-century equivalents. In his biographical introduction to his edition of Surrey's poems, Padelford, motivated by a desire to defend Surrey against what he sees as a possible accusation of homosexuality, tries to point out the difference between Renaissance ideas of friendship and our own:

> The sixteenth century was a period when friendships between men were developed with a peculiar lack of restraint and with an ardency that surprises us today. We get some idea of these emotional friendships in the sonnets of Shakespeare, in the correspondence of Sidney and Languet, in

the devotion of Edward II to Gaveston in Marlowe's drama, and in the various episodes of the Legend of Friendship in the *Faerie Queene*.[24]

It may well seem that rather than proving that Surrey and Richmond were 'just good friends,' Padelford has merely managed to state the case for a sexual relationship between the two in the most pointed manner. Although his examples are, for his purpose, hopelessly ill chosen, they do present relationships between men as a continuum that goes from Edward II and Gaveston to the episodes from the *Faerie Queene* (with the sonnets and Languet–Sidney correspondence somewhere, or even anywhere, in between). The relationship depicted in 'So crewell prison' seems impossible to restrict to any one point on that continuum and is better placed in a complex of relationships that includes friendship, companionship, love, and sexuality. For this reason, Padelford's classification of the poem as autobiographical is helpful, because that category in his edition includes political poems and love poems that talk of love between men and women. If we discuss 'So crewell prison' only as an elegy for a friend, we ignore much of the poem. If we follow the implications of Padelford's classification and consider 'So crewell prison' as a poem that tells, among other things, of the romantic love between two young men, we shall finally be in a position to appreciate the poem's complexity.

In order to comment on how the poem works as an elegy and on what distinguishes it from other elegies I want to look first at the conventions of the elegy and then at Surrey's arrangement of his memories. In his article on Surrey's elegies, C.W. Jentoft provides a definition that can be used to separate 'So crewell prison' from the elegies on Wyatt: 'The rhetorical end of praise, whether that praise appears in encomium, epic, or epitaph, is to make men virtuous through the example of the one praised. Lament belongs to tragedy, to the poetry of meditation, or to the pastoral elegy.'[25] Praise and lament can coexist (as they do in Surrey's poems on Wyatt), but I would agree that this is one of the things that makes those poems so different from 'So crewell prison,' in which Surrey is concerned not with men but with one man – Henry Fitzroy, Duke of Richmond – and the aim of the poem is to lament Richmond rather than to encourage other men to be like him. Still, the poem is not simply a personal elegy. Eric Smith defines elegy as 'a particular sort of pastoral, for elegy is specifically about what is missing and also about what is more certainly known to have been formerly possessed.'[26] In this case, what is missing, what was possessed, is not just the Duke of Richmond but also the way of life in which both men were brought up. Ellen Zetzel Lambert sees this double death as an integral feature of the pastoral elegy: 'Death is not only an event *in* the pastoral world; it is also something that happens, or may at any time happen, *to* that world.'[27] In 'So crewell prison,' the two absences – of the man and of the way of life – are represented in the poem and in Surrey's biography by Windsor Castle, still, four hundred and fifty years later, a symbol for royalty. In this respect, the poem conforms to Lambert's definition of the pastoral elegy:

> The pastoral elegy, I would suggest, proposes no one *solution* to the questions raised by death but rather a *setting* in which those questions may be posed, or, better, 'placed' ... [The poems's landscape] remains a concrete, palpable world, a world in which the elegist can place diffuse, intangible feelings of grief and thereby win his release from suffering.[28]

The ways in which 'So crewell prison' differs from most pastoral elegies can best be appreciated by looking at the poem's structure and comparing it to the usual elegiac structure. Peter M. Sacks sees elegies as consisting of procedures or resolutions, each of which

> is essentially defensive, requiring a detachment of affection from a prior object followed by a reattachment of the affection elsewhere. At the core of each procedure is the renunciatory experience of loss and the acceptance, not just of a substitute, but of the very means and practice of substitution.[29]

In 'So crewell prison,' the prior object is both the Duke of Richmond and the place where he and Surrey lived, and the business of the poem is to describe this place; but the poem depicts a situation in which affection cannot be detached from the prior objects: these objects are listed in order to reaffirm the connection between the poet and the places associated with the dead man, rather than to make a reattachment possible. Sacks, who sees elegy as closely connected to the Oedipal conflict, says that 'the elegy clarifies and dramatizes [the] emergence of the true heir,'[30] and it is here that the divergence of 'So crewell prison' from the elegiac tradition is clearest. In Surrey's poem, there is no heir. The death of Richmond and of the way of life he represents is not a death that leads to a renewal: what lies behind 'So crewell prison' is a replacement, and an inferior one at that.

At this point, I want to follow Padelford's lead and consider the autobiographical aspect of the poem. The Duke of Richmond died in the summer of 1536 and Surrey's mourning for him was both protracted and severe. A year after the death, Surrey's father wrote, '[My] son of Surrey is very weak, his nature running from him abundantly. He was in that case a great part of the last year, [which] ... came to him for thought of my lord of Richmond.'[31] At about the time of this letter, Surrey was imprisoned for striking Sir Edward Seymour, the new queen's brother. Seymour is important to the poem as a representative of the new way of life that replaced the traditional life that Surrey and Richmond had led at Windsor in the early 1530s. In the poem, Surrey's imprisonment becomes the opportunity for him to consider the changes in his life and in English society. The upbringing shared by Surrey and Richmond – which can be seen as the centre of the chivalric tradition that informs so much of the poem – has given way to a society in which someone like Seymour, a man of relatively obscure family brought into prominence by the marriage of his sister to the king, can become the equal of Surrey, the heir to a great title, the descendant of several of the most noble families of medieval England, and a close relative of the royal family. One way to read 'So crewell prison' is as a poem constructed on two related antitheses: Richmond and Seymour, and old and new Windsor (by extension, the old court and the new court). Surrey's declaration of his friendship with Richmond is a political statement in this context. Consequently, Surrey is able to align Richmond and old Windsor and declare his allegiance to them while contrasting them implicitly with Seymour and new Windsor. The relations among all four aspects of the antitheses are mediated through Surrey's perspective as a prisoner, and are expressed primarily as a conflict between Surrey's experiences as a prisoner and his expectations of Windsor.

This sort of conflict is quite common in Surrey's poetry. As Walter R. Davis has pointed out, 'The interrelation of the individual human being with his natural context is of extreme importance to Surrey. Frequently, in fact, that nexus calls into question the identity of the self.'[32] In 'So crewell prison,' Surrey reveals to what extent his identity has been constructed by and at Windsor, and demonstrates that the change that has overtaken the castle has overtaken him as well. In the first stanza, for example, just after speaking of Windsor as 'prowde,' Surrey speaks proudly of his friendship with a king's son and of the fact that the two lived in considerable state, and thus introduces the identification between people and places on which so much of the poem depends. By the end of the poem, Surrey's feelings for Richmond can no longer be distinguished from his feelings for Windsor Castle. Surrey structures 'So crewell prison' by presenting the structure of identity as something dependent on architecture in its literal sense; in other words, the identification of a person and a place becomes more than a metaphoric equivalence.

The poem moves from a general lament on the fact of imprisonment in a place associated with a vanished happiness to a particularization of that place and then inward to the state of the poet himself. 'So crewell prison' and 'When Windesor walles' are usually considered together, since this summary could be used for the sonnet also, with the difference that in the sonnet what makes the present sorrow incongruous is not so much past happiness as the beauty of spring. Surrey does not explicitly state in 'When Windesor walles' that he is a prisoner there, nor does he mention his associations with the place. Although both poems move outward to describe the setting, there is nothing about the description in this part of the sonnet that specifically refers to Windsor. I shall discuss thematic connections between the poems later; I want now to look at the structural connections. I believe that the two poems are not merely connected by subject matter: they are versions of the same poem. 'So crewell prison' is a more developed version of the sonnet, but it is still based on sonnet form. In 'When Windesor walles' Surrey employs the sonnet form he invented and that is now irritatingly called a Shakespearean sonnet: there are three quatrains rhyming ababcdcdefef, a final couplet rhyming gg, and usually a volta in the ninth line. 'So crewell prison' has fourteen stanzas, the first thirteen of which are quatrains rhyming abab and the last of which is a rhyming couplet; there is also a volta in the ninth quatrain. Furthermore, in the sonnet, the volta is signalled by the words 'Wherwith, alas.' In the longer poem, the volta comes in the second line of the ninth stanza and is also signalled by 'Wherwith, alas.' The greater length of 'So crewell prison' enables Surrey to turn the setting of 'When Windesor walles' into a more particular place and time, but in both poems the underlying structure is the sonnet with its self-contained but related quatrains leading to a conclusion with a more general application. The rigour of this structure is partly responsible for preventing 'So crewell prison' from being a mere string of images.

I say 'partly' responsible because Surrey's first stanza indicates a way to read the poem, a context to which the poem's images can be related:

So crewell prison howe could betyde, alas,
As prowde Wyndsour, where I in lust and joye
With a kinges soon my childishe yeres did passe,
In greater feast then Priams sonnes of Troye. (1–4)

These pleasant associations have been replaced by sorrow and Windsor is now a place 'Where eche swete place retournes a tast full sowre' (5):

Past pleasure, heightened by the epic allusion whereby Surrey and the King's son approach the status of Priam's sons (and perhaps face their fate, as well), instead of lightening present pain, only intensifies it by the very fact of its irretrievability; the resultant attitude is complex, for we have in this moment combined the pain of disgrace, the possible pleasure afforded by 'eche swete place' in what would normally be a pleasant enough 'prison,' and the denial of that pleasure by the memory of pleasures that are no more.[33]

Surrey and Windsor itself connect the past and the present, while Richmond, youth, freedom, and happiness are confined to the past, and maturity, imprisonment, and sorrow characterize the present.

After establishing this framework, Surrey examines the happy associations of 'eche swete place' until the volta, just as in 'When Windesor walles' he describes the beauty of the scene before exploring the implications of the 'wearied arme' (1) and 'restles hedd' (2). The poem 'moves, not only through an imagined day in time, but spatially away from the "voyd walles" that now form his prison out into the fields and the forest, to end at the end of the day within those walls once more.'[34] After the first stanza, each stanza until the ninth (in which the volta occurs) presents an activity and a place associated with Surrey's life with Richmond. The memories move from the courtyards at the heart of the castle to the rooms around them, the areas around the castle, the grounds beyond, and ultimately the walls. These walls are at once those that separate the castle and its grounds from the surrounding countryside and the walls of the castle itself, which separate inside from outside. Although the 'statelye sales' (9) and the 'graveld ground' (17), for instance, are only important to Surrey now because of their associations, the walls enclose him in the poem's present, just as they did in the past. The two elements of the poem – the enumeration of past pleasures and the mourning over the fact that they are past – are brought together at the end: the 'tast full sowre' finally overwhelms the catalogue of 'eche swete place.' As a result, it is at this point in the poem that the two parts of Surrey's life at Windsor unite: 'the irony of the first term for Windsor, "So crewell prison," is such that by the end of the elegy, in a figure of *peripeteia*, the prison contains a deeper prison, that within the speaker himself.'[35] Surrey identifies Richmond with the positive aspects of Windsor; we see at the poem's conclusion that Surrey himself, to his peril, is now identified with the prison that Windsor has become.

The catalogue is not, however, merely a list of places and of the activities associated with them: the poem also – in fact, primarily – depicts the relationship between the two boys. Their life at Windsor is seen to consist largely of competitions: competitions for women, debates, 'palme play' (13), jousting, wrestling, and hunting. In order to demonstrate how great their love for each other was, Surrey says several times that he and Richmond turned each competition, each possibility for strife and contention, into an occasion to show love, just as he recalls the 'hateles shorte debate' in 'When Windesor walles' (7). Insofar as the boys do compete, they compete on each other's behalf: 'With wordes and lookes that tygers could but rewe,/ Where eche of us did plead the others right' (11–12). When they joust, for instance, they do so 'with swordes and frendlye hertes,/ With chere as thoughe the one should overwhelme' (18–19), and when they play at 'palme playe' they cannot even keep their eyes on the ball (14–15). Surrey and Richmond's aim is to demonstrate their mutual love, and they do so, in what is still an acceptable way for men to show affection for each other, by engaging in physical activities together. Even their pursuit of women, which recalls the rather lacklustre heteroeroticism of Iolas and Alcon, becomes a means for them to communicate their love, as Crewe points out:

> Ostensibly, the 'dased' lovers have their minds on the 'dame' in the tower, whose attentions they solicit; but this dazing follows the description of male stripping for the game, and the 'bayting' of the woman's eyes can also imply their deception. Is the game of handball, like all other other tournaments and competitions to which the poem refers, the pretext and deception under which homoerotic passion flourishes?[36]

As Davis notes, the memories are presented in a temporal context as well as in a visual perspective.[37] The first reference to time occurs when Surrey speaks of morning dew: 'With sylver dropps the meades yet spredd for rewthe' (21). By the time he speaks of the walls (33), night has fallen and the last memory recounted in the poem is of what Surrey and Richmond did at night:

> The swete accord, such slepes as yet delight,
> The pleasaunt dreames, the quyet bedd of rest,
> The secret thoughtes imparted with such trust,
> The wanton talke, the dyvers chaung of playe,
> The frendshipp sworne, eche promyse kept so just,
> Wherewith we past the winter nightes awaye. (35–40)

The change in the memories as the poem progresses is from diurnal contact, which occurs through activities or through other people, to unmediated nocturnal contact. I said earlier that Surrey and Richmond express their love through physical activity; sex, of course, is a physical activity. Whether or not the two boys had sex, Surrey depicts their relationship in the language of love poetry.

The antepenultimate stanza is Surrey's apostrophe to Windsor Castle. I take this stanza and the shift it heralds to be at the centre of the poem's meaning. In his book on Renaissance lyric, Douglas L. Peterson contends that this shift is too abrupt and that the end of the poem is unsatisfactory because of what he sees as too severe a change in tone: 'The sudden shift from a language which is styleless in its simplicity, and therefore fresh, to the diction of eloquence is curious.'[38] Although I do not agree with Peterson's objections – nor with his assessment of the tone of the first part of the poem, which seems to be complimentary in a peculiarly left-handed way – I do agree that the shift is curious, and I think Peterson is correct in drawing our attention to it. Surrey's diction changes here because it is at this point that he wishes to make the poetic context of 'So crewell prison' explicit. I want to show this by looking at the poetic context of the apostrophe and then by doing a close reading of the poem's last three stanzas.

Sessions points out that there are 'very Chaucerian subtexts for these two elegies ['So crewell prison' and 'When Windesor walles']: Palamon's lament in *The Knight's Tale* and Troilus's at the palace of the lost Criseyde.'[39] Surrey's use of *Troilus and Criseyde* – at this time probably the most famous love story in English literature – is especially noticeable. In 'When Windesor walles,' for example, he speaks of 'joily woes' (7). As Alicia Ostriker notes, this 'oxymoron comes from *Troilus*, ii, 1099.'[40] A.C. Spearing points out that the 'easy sighes, such as folke drawe in love' ('So crewell prison' 8) 'recall the "esy sykes" of the lover in *Troilus and Criseyde,'* and he goes on to suggest that Surrey's use of Chaucer in 'So crewell prison' is not limited to the borrowing of expressions:

> It is possible that behind the memories of personal experience lies a literary memory of the passage in Book V of Chaucer's poem, in which Troilus, now abandoned, rides around Troy ... in order to stir up memories of the events and emotions that occurred at each before Criseyde's departure.[41]

Perhaps the most famous part of the passage to which Spearing refers is the *planctum Troili*, in which Troilus apostrophizes the palace in which Criseyde lived:

> O paleis, whilom crowne of houses alle,
> Enlumyned with sonne of alle blisse!
> O ryng, fro which the ruby is outfalle,
> O cause of wo, that cause hast ben of lisse! (V.547–50)

This apostrophe is the main literary model for Surrey's apostrophe in 'So crewell prison.' Davis sees the use of the Chaucerian passage as a way for Surrey to indicate the depth of his attachment to Richmond: 'the death of a friend with whom one has had such intense pleasure may well be seen by the survivor as a kind of unrequited love.'[42] Sessions also sees the use of the erotic mode as an attempt on Surrey's part to suggest the strength of his friendship for Richmond.[43]

While these comments are useful, they do not go far enough. The correspondence between the two poems is much more extensive than either Davis or Sessions sees. 'So crewell prison' begins at this point to resemble a love poem because it has begun to be a love poem. The use of the *planctum Troili* as a model suggests that 'So crewell prison' is not about unrequited love but about requited love and about the effects of death and political disturbance on that love. In Chaucer's poem, a man has been separated from his lover because of the exigencies of wartime diplomacy; in Surrey's, a man's memories are threatened by a disagreeable political situation. Another resemblance between this section of *Troilus and Criseyde* and 'So crewell prison' is the identification between architecture and people. For Troilus, the buildings and stones of Troy are invested with his love for Criseyde, just as for Surrey every aspect of Windsor Castle is a reminder of Richmond and the love they shared. The allusions to a poem set in Troy remind us of the comparison at the beginning of 'So crewell prison' between Surrey and Richmond and 'Priams sonnes of Troy.' Surrey's use of the *planctum Troili* can be seen both as a way to present 'So crewell prison' as a poem about the loss of a lover and as a way to present it as a poem about the loss of a civilization. Finally, if we return to the idea of Surrey's poem as a poem about a double death, *Troilus and Criseyde* is the obvious precursor. Nor is 'So crewell prison' the only poem in which Surrey uses this particular Chaucerian intertext. The poem Padelford calls 'Rueful Associations' also seems to have the *planctum Troili* as a source: 'O lothsome place, where I/ Have sene and herd my dere' (1–2). In this poem, the reason for the lovers' separation is the cruel nature of love itself rather than any external force. Although the speaker addresses a place throughout, rather than love or his lover, the place is never particularized and he ends by deciding to leave. The place is incidental to the love rather than an essential part of it, as it is in *Troilus and Criseyde* and 'So crewell prison.' Surrey's use of Chaucer in this poem is limited and 'Rueful Associations' is interesting not so much for its connections to Chaucer as for its connections to 'So crewell prison.' Along with 'When Windesor walles,' 'Rueful Associations' and the *planctum Troili* form the poetic context that we shall need in order to examine the ending of 'So crewell prison,' and I want to stress that this is the context of love poetry.

The ninth, tenth, and eleventh stanzas introduce the apostrophe and help to set it in the context of love poetry. The poem's volta comes in the ninth stanza when the poet's description of Windsor, which has been getting farther and farther away from the room in which he is confined, comes to the walls: 'The voyd walles eke, that harbourd us eche night' (33). The thought of these walls reminds Surrey of what he and Richmond did each night, and it is this thought that makes him weep. The progression in 'When Windesor walles' is roughly parallel: the poet goes from describing what he can see of the external world to remembering the life he led, a life of 'joily woes' and 'hateles shorte debate' (7), to weeping. In the sonnet, the equivalent of the 'voyd walles' in 'So crewell prison' is 'the weddyd birds so late' (5); seeing a traditional natural image for wedded love reminds the poet of his own love. I say the birds are equivalent to the walls because these walls are both literal, as stone structures that once harboured Surrey and Richmond and that now prevent Surrey from leaving, and metaphoric, in that they suggest the embrace of lovers. The connection between walls and arms is established at the beginning of the sonnet: 'When Windesor walles sustained my wearied arme,/ My hand my chyn, to ease my restles hedd' (1–2). The castle is not merely the setting but also something to which the poet is metaphorically and literally attached. This identification is behind a great deal of 'So crewell prison,' in which both the poet and the castle have been deserted by Richmond: both the walls of Windsor Castle and Surrey's arms are 'voyd' because they no longer contain Richmond. The memory of former happiness is, inevitably, no consolation:

> And with this thought the blood forsakes my face,
> The teares berayne my cheke of dedlye hewe;
> The which, as sone as sobbing sighes, alas,
> Upsupped have, thus I my playnt renewe. (41–4)

G.W. Pigman notes that the word 'playnt' is significant: Surrey 'points to the connection [between 'So crewell prison' and love poetry] by calling his lament "my playnt" only a few lines after writing "Of pleasaunt playnt and of our ladyes prayes."'[44] Furthermore, in the stanza after the apostrophe, Surrey says that the only answer he receives is 'a hollowe sound of playnt' (50). The apostrophe is thus placed in a context of poems that complain of the hardship of love.

The role of Surrey's apostrophe is not merely to present Windsor as a place associated with a former love (which is how Troilus presents Criseyde's palace), but also to establish Surrey as Richmond's chief mourner:

> O place of blys, renewer of my woos,
> Geve me accompt wher is my noble fere,
> Whome in thy walles thou didest eche night enclose,
> To other lief, but unto me most dere. (45–8)

Each line of the apostrophe serves to connect Surrey and Richmond and to present their connection as romantic in nature. The first line, with its obvious Chaucerian echoes, suggests a parallel between Troilus and Surrey. The second draws a parallel between 'So crewell prison' and a similar passage in 'Rueful Associations':

> sins thou, desert place,
> Canst give me no accompt
> Of my desired grace
> That I to have was wont. (33–6)

Here are the same expression and the same situation in what is undeniably a love poem. In the first two lines of the apostrophe, then, Surrey connects 'So crewell prison' to one of his own love poems as well as to what was then the most famous love lament in the English language. In the third line, I think Surrey is making the same metaphoric equivalence that is behind the ninth stanza: both the castle walls and Surrey's arms enclosed Richmond 'eche night.' It is the fourth line that is crucial, however. Here, Surrey declares his rights and implies that his claim to be the chief mourner has a better basis than all other claims, including those of Richmond's father, the king, and Richmond's widow, Surrey's own sister. As in 'Alcon,' the speaker must explicitly assert his right to be chief mourner in a context, but Surrey's task is harder. While Iolas's rivals were his own brother and the hypothetical and unnamed shepherd, Surrey must oppose the claims of blood relationship and marriage. His actions are bold indeed.

Surrey's presentation of himself as Richmond's chief mourner is part of his move from prisoner to grieving lover. The imprisonment, which originally seemed to be the subject of the poem, gives way to the poet's grief for his dead lover, as the final couplet shows: 'And with remembraunce of the greater greif,/ To bannishe the lesse I fynde my chief releif' (53–4). Rather than finding consolation for loss, the poem presents the loss as a consolation in itself. In the last few lines of the poem, Surrey asserts his pre-eminent status as Richmond's chief mourner and Richmond's pre-eminent status – even after his death – as the main focus of emotion and concern in Surrey's life. Surrey's historical and poetical imprisonment in Windsor Castle (I refer both to the incarceration itself and to the way in which the poet's perspective ranges farther and farther from the centre of the castle until checked by the walls) is ultimately presented as a mere metaphor for the poet's imprisonment in his love. By concluding the poem with an assertion of the power of his love, Surrey, like Castiglione, emphatically refuses the traditional *consolatio*.

Sexuality in Milton's 'Epitaphium Damonis'

'Epitaphium Damonis' is a poem that strongly recalls 'Alcon.' There are numerous resemblances in diction and imagery, but perhaps the most immediately apparent resemblance is that in both poems the poet was absent when the man he loved died. Absence has a different role in

'Epitaphium Damonis' than in 'Alcon,' however. While Castiglione ultimately transforms the speaker's absence into the absence of the lover's body from the tomb by the Anio, Milton makes Italy itself, where he was when Diodati died, into something that is absent not just from the poem but from Milton's life. As well as changing much of the emphasis of 'Alcon' and the use it makes of various themes and images, Milton makes a much more explicit use of the details of his life. Yet perhaps the most significant difference between the two is that 'Epitaphium Damonis' includes – indeed, focuses on – the whole issue of a poetic career. In this respect, 'Epitaphium Damonis' recalls the elegies of Theocritus and Virgil, in which there is almost as much discussion of poetry as of the men who are the subjects of the poems. Milton's elegy contains the most explicit statements he ever made about his plans for his poetry, and the few critics who have written on 'Epitaphium Damonis' have concentrated on this aspect of the poem.

We tend to read Milton's Latin elegy for Charles Diodati through 'Lycidas,' his best-known elegy (and possibly the best-known elegy in all of English literature), and also, because of Milton's discussion of his poetic career, through *Paradise Lost* and the other poems Milton wrote after 'Epitaphium Damonis.' To some extent, the poem, with its plans for the great British epic, lends itself to being stretched on the *rota Virgilii* and serving as a transition between early and late Milton. Albert C. Labriola says, for instance, that the poem 'shows Milton at a crucial juncture of his life ... [T]owards the end of the poem, in announcing plans for a *magnum opus*, he brings to a close the early phase of his development and undertakes with uncertainty and anxiety the role of epic poet.'[45] Janet Leslie Knedlik suggests that in 'Epitaphium Damonis' 'we hear a disconsolate shepherd-poet whose pastoral artistry is being cut untimely short.'[46] These points are well taken and are necessary to our understanding of the poem, but any consideration of Milton's plans for himself as a poet as stated in 'Epitaphium Damonis' should also take into account Milton's views on sexuality. 'Epitaphium Damonis' is a poem that talks about sex at least as often as it talks about poetry; indeed, the two aspects of the poem cannot be separated.

One of the few Miltonists to discuss the sexual aspects of the poem is John T. Shawcross, but his account is marred by the odd conclusions he draws, as for instance when he says that Diodati was 'one whose sexual life cannot be described but whose rough personality outlines – his excesses, his fickleness in friendship, his sensual nature, his drifting life – would not deny a rather promiscuous homosexuality.'[47] In order to construct this (not unpleasing) fantasy, Shawcross treats the various poems and letters he discusses primarily as biographical raw material: in other words, he emphasizes the sexual aspects of the poem at the expense of the poetic aspects. More typical is a cautious suggestion that sexuality is a factor in the poem but only as a metaphor. For instance, in his otherwise excellent article Gordon Campbell declares that '[i]n Milton's England active homosexuality was deemed a sin, and it would be wrong to describe Milton's relation with Diodati in these terms. But their friendship was not less passionate for not being physical.'[48] It is clear that Campbell has no basis for his certainty. Common sense suggests that the friendship was physical, since the most obvious reason for using sexual metaphors to describe a relationship is that the relationship is or was sexual. Although we cannot be sure what happened, I propose to give Milton the benefit of the doubt and assume that he and Diodati were lovers. In any case, my argument does not depend on whether or not their relationship was sexual.

Whatever the true history of Milton and Diodati may be, I think Shawcross is correct when he says that Milton appears to find 'a sense of wrongness in human sexual activity.'[49] Milton presents sexuality as something that separates a man from other men and from his true vocation. He approaches the subject with caution, and his technique for talking about sexuality in this poem is allusive rather than declarative. The sexual allusions begin in Milton's invocation: 'Himeridae nymphae – nam vos et Daphnin et Hylan,/ ... meministis' (Nymphs of Himera – for you remember Daphnis and Hylas).[50] The reference to Daphnis signals Milton's modelling of the elegy (at this early point, at any rate) on the first idyll, in which the elegist is also called Thyrsis. The reference to Hylas that follows immediately is also an allusion to Theocritus, although in this case to an explicitly homoerotic idyll.[51] Although the story of Hylas was well known and would have been available to Milton in more than one version, I think that Milton had Theocritus's thirteenth idyll in mind, which I have discussed in chapter 1. At the end of the idyll, 'beautiful Hylas was numbered among the blessed' while 'the heroes mocked Heracles as a deserter.' Theocritus presents Heracles as a man who deserts his duty because of his love for another man. Milton's allusion to Hylas, then, brings together the theme of females as opposed to or indifferent to men's concerns and the theme, which underlies much of Milton's concern in 'Epitaphium Damonis' with his poetic career, of love as an impediment to duty. Milton does not wish to arrive late and in an undignified manner to the main task at hand.

Diodati died in England in August 1638, when Milton was in Italy. His absence is one of his main regrets in the poem, just as Castiglione's absence is one of his main regrets in 'Alcon,' although as Castiglione was apparently in England when Falcone died, Milton's situation is not a repetition but rather a mirror image (I shall return to this point). Near the beginning of the poem, Milton says that two harvests have passed

Ex quo summa dies tulerat Damona sub umbras,
Nec dum aderat Thyrsis; pastorem scilicet illum
Dulcis amor Musae Tusca retinebat in urbe

(Since the last day had taken Damon down to the shades and still Thyrsis was not there, for the love of the sweet Muse detained that shepherd in the Tuscan city; 11–13.)

This is not just the literal reason for Milton's absence, it is also a way for Milton to depict poetry as something that is in competition with Diodati. At this point in the poem, since Diodati died in London and poetry is associated with Tuscany, the comparison is to Diodati's advantage – that is, he is seen as more important than poetry. Nevertheless, I think Milton is setting up a parallel between himself, distracted from his career as an epic poet first by being in Italy and then by mourning for Diodati, and Heracles, who let the Argo sail without him while he searched for his lost lover. Eventually Diodati, like Hylas, will have to be given up.

This defalcation from duty appears in the pastoral context as the shepherd's neglect of his own duties. The most obvious example of this is the refrain – 'Ite domum impasti, domino iam non vacat, agni' (go home unfed, lambs, your master has no time for you), which appears seventeen times in the poem from line 18 to line 179.[52] The importunity of the lambs stresses Thyrsis's failure as a shepherd and serves as a reminder to the reader that mourning too long carried on becomes an indulgence. The repetition of the refrain calls attention to the repetitive nature of agricultural labour (which Marx brilliantly characterized as 'the idiocy of rural life'). The implication is that Milton is growing restive with the pastoral as a genre just as Virgil did. The hungry sheep are not the only sign of Thyrsis's inability to function in the pastoral landscape, however. He tells us that

seges alta fatiscit!
Innuba neglecto marcescit et uva racemo,
Nec myrteta iuvant.

(the tall grain droops. The unwedded grapes wither on their neglected vine and the myrtle-groves do not please; 64–6.)

As Shawcross points out, the 'tall grain' is phallic[53] and its drooping is a sign of phallic impotence. Milton pairs it with the feminine symbol of the 'unwedded' grapes and extends the reference to the myrtle groves, which are a symbol of Venus. Thus, it is not Milton's sexuality alone that is at a standstill: the land itself is sterile. Both human and natural fertility have stopped because of Damon's death. Thyrsis's grief, then, is placed in a larger context in which it appears as a harmful indulgence, since it is not just a problem for him but for nature as well.

Up to this point in the poem, Thyrsis has been in a landscape without humans. Now we hear of human attempts to console Thyrsis and to get him to return to society. Both the references to the blight affecting the landscape around him and to the irruption of human society into his reverie underline the impossibility of being alone with one's grief. The consolers come in two groups: first men and then women. The dominant figure among the men is Mopsus, who says, 'Aut te perdit amor, aut te male fascinat astrum' (Either love destroys you or a star has a bad influence on you; 78). Mopsus appears to favour the latter explanation, but at least he considers that love may be the cause of Thyrsis's grief. The nymphs who follow the men do not even consider this as a possibility and urge him to fall in love as a cure for his melancholy, saying that 'bis ille miser qui serus amavit' (he is twice miserable who fell in love late; 86). Like the nymphs in Theocritus's first idyll and the nymphs who abduct Hylas in Theocritus (although Milton depicts those nymphs as mourning him), these nymphs are fundamentally unsympathetic. Thyrsis's consolers, like Samson's in *Samson Agonistes*, fail to console and succeed in demonstrating the unbridgeable gap between the protagonist of the poem and the society in which he finds himself. Thyrsis's love for Damon is invisible to the men and women who are ostensibly his companions.

As if recognizing the inefficacy of human consolation, Thyrsis turns to contemplating the animals:

quam similes ludunt per prata iuvenci,
Omnes unanimi secum sibi lege sodales,
Nec magis hunc alio quisquam secernit amicum
De grege.

(how similar are the young bulls that play in the fields, all companions to each other according to their law, nor does one especially single out another from the herd as a friend; 94–7.)

Thyrsis then goes on to summarize the similar behaviour of wolves, wild asses, seals, and sparrows. The list has certain sexual overtones. The first is in Milton's use of 'iuvenci.' This term refers to young bulls, that is, bulls that have not yet attained adulthood and been mated with cows. Although the word can refer to castrated bulls, Horace uses it metaphorically to refer to young men still officially under their mothers' control when he wishes to stress that their sexual urges are not controllable.[54] Bulls are traditionally a symbol of brutish urges, and it is probable that Milton wishes the reader to keep this in mind when he speaks of their social behaviour.

To Milton, seals may also have suggested a lack of discrimination in sexual matters. John K. Hale has shown that Milton was interested in the Greek tradition that female seals would on occasion invade human dwellings to have sex with human men. In notes made in 1635 to a Latin translation of Lycophron's *Alexandra*, Milton insisted on the sexual nature of this belief, in opposition to the translator, who considered the passage metaphorical.[55] In the context of 'Epitaphium Damonis,' the female seals who sexually attack human men can be compared to the water nymphs who kidnap Hylas. The most obviously sexual reference in the list of animals is the final one: 'vilisque volucrum/ Passer habet semper quicum sit' (that worthless bird the sparrow always has someone to be with; 100–1). Thyrsis says that when the sparrow's companion is killed, 'Protinus ille alium socio petit inde volatu' (he quickly then looks for another as a companion in his flight; 105). Along with myrtle, the sparrow is one of the symbols of Venus, and many Latin poets, most notably Catullus, use the sparrow to suggest sexual licence.[56] Thyrsis's vision of the animal world has a certain wistful quality. The indiscriminate pairings of animals are what make animals lower than humans, but the animals may be happier.

The passage is based on the section in Theocritus's first idyll where Thyrsis tells how Daphnis was visited by consolers who, like their counterparts in Milton's poem, failed to console. The relevant example is the speech of the ithyphallic god Priapus, who mocks Daphnis's melancholy by comparing him to a goatherd: 'when the goatherd sees how they [the male goats] mount the she-goats, his eyes melt, because he was not himself born a goat'; (I.87–8). Priapus tells Daphnis to look at 'the maidens [and] how they are laughing' (I.90). Theocritus phrases the references to the two female objects of Daphnis's gaze similarly in order to underscore the fact that for Priapus animal and human sexuality are equivalent. Lambert has pointed out this resemblance between Theocritus and Milton: 'Theocritus ... balances the sense of Daphnis's separateness from nature against the sense of his participation in her order,' while in 'Epitaphium Damonis' '[t]he bonds which unite one man with another are not only finer than, they are contrary to the kinds of bonds which unite one creature with another.'[57] Daphnis, of course, shows no interest either in goats or in people and he dies because he can ultimately neither escape nor transcend the natural order. Milton's Thyrsis, however, is more removed from the pastoral world and is consequently able to survive by leaving that world altogether.

At this point in the poem, however, Thyrsis's separation from the pastoral world is seen only as a source of sorrow. Humans, Thyrsis says, are much less fortunate than animals: 'Nos durum genus, et diris exercita fatis/ Gens' (we are a stern species, a breed wearied by cruel fate; 106–7). Human misery comes from the fact that it is rare for a man to find a suitable companion and that if that companion is lost he cannot be replaced:

Aut, si sors dederit tandem non aspera votis,
Illum inopina dies, qua non speraveris hora
Surripit, aeternum linquens in saecula damnum.

(or, if fate finally not opposed to our prayers grants [a companion], a day and hour when we expect nothing seizes him, leaving an eternal loss for the ages; 109–11.)

As the poem has 219 lines, lines 109–11 are at its exact centre. They mark the turning point in the poem between the pastoral and the epic worlds, between, that is, the Thyrsis who grieves in the countryside and the Thyrsis who consecrates himself to the idea of English epic poetry. Although the pastoral machinery – the refrains, the depiction of Thyrsis and Damon as shepherds – remains, the focus of the second half of

Milton's poem is on Italy and England and on the poems Thyrsis intends to write. I see this as being the main structural device in the poem, and I think the crucial words are 'aeternum' and 'saecula' in line 111. The first word means eternal; the second means both age (either lifespan or century) and the people who live in that age. By saying that his grief for Damon will last for ever, Thyrsis puts this grief in a larger temporal context than the procession of harvests that constitutes pastoral time. The same purpose is served by the use of 'genus' and 'gens' earlier in the passage. From now on, Thyrsis will think of Damon in the context of human history as a whole.

As a result, poetry will separate the living man from the dead man. Until this point, Thyrsis's poetic ability, his writing of the elegy, has connected the two despite Damon's death. The process of separation begins with Milton's farewell to Italy:

Quamquam etiam vestri nunquam meminisse pigebit,
Pastores Tusci, Musis operata iuventus,
Hic Charis, atque Lepos; et Tuscus tu quoque Damon.

(Yet it will never displease me to remember you, Tuscan shepherds, youths who labour for the Muses: here was grace and here was charm; and you too were Tuscan, Damon; 125–7.)

This passage marks an important shift in the way Diodati is presented in the poem: from being associated with England, where he was born and where he died, to being associated with Italy, where his family had originated. The stress on Diodati as Italian – and, consequently, on Milton as not Italian – may in part be motivated by the fact that, as the historian Michael Rocke points out, the association of Florence with sodomy was 'a commonplace in the late Middle Ages and Renaissance.'[58] In distancing himself from Italy, Milton is distancing himself from this imputation. Furthermore, Milton's stay in Italy was originally presented as a separation from Diodati. Now Milton speaks of his return to England as a departure from Diodati. Behind these lines is one of the most famous passages from the *Aeneid*: 'nec me meminisse pigebit Elissae/ dum memor ipse mei, dum spiritus hos regit artus' (nor will it displease me to remember Elissa as long as I remember myself, as long as my spirit rules these limbs; IV.335–6).

The allusion to the *Aeneid* has more than one function in 'Epitaphium Damonis.' Perhaps most obviously it emphasizes that the relationships Thyrsis speaks of will soon exist only as memories. The allusion also treats Diodati under the same heading as the contemporary Italian poets Milton mentions, a categorization that is difficult to square with the tone of the poem as we have known it. I think this difficulty is precisely the point here: up to this point, Thyrsis's feelings for Damon have set him apart from people, from animals, and from the landscape itself. By emphasizing Diodati's Italian origins, Milton is able to distance himself from him and to present their love as similar, perhaps even identical, to the friendship and admiration he felt for the Italian scholars and poets he came to know in Italy. This conflation of emotions that may seem very different to us is underlined by Milton's use of 'Charis' and 'Lepos,' words that can suitably be used to describe almost any sort of amicable or romantic relationship. Furthermore (and this is of course the most obvious implication), in making this allusion Milton presents himself as Aeneas and Diodati and the other Italians as Dido – felicitously, an anagram of the first four letters of the dead man's surname. Yet while Aeneas left Dido to fulfil his destiny in Italy, Milton must leave Italy to fulfil his destiny in England. The allusion to the *Aeneid*, particularly when juxtaposed with the allusions to pastoral poetry up to this point, prepares the reader to see Milton as an epic poet and can even be taken to suggest that in imitating Virgil Milton intends to surpass him.

Milton's plans for his epic begin with the arrival of Trojan ships off the Kentish coast (lines 162–3). Here Brutus, the grandson of Aeneas, establishes an empire that will eventually become the kingdom of England. This is one of the standard myths of origin in Renaissance England, but what is remarkable about Milton's version is that he refers to Trojan rather than Italian ships and that he does not mention Brutus. Instead, Milton refers to Brutus's wife Inogen, who was believed to have been Greek, and to Brennus, Arviragus, and Belinus, who were all Celtic chieftains. Of these men, both Brennus and Arviragus fought against the Romans; as Merritt Y. Hughes points out in his note to line 164, 'Brennus sacked Rome in 390 B.C.' After dealing with ancient Britain, Milton plans to tell the story of Arthur. He claims that he will not care if his poems are not read in 'externo ... orbi' (the outside world; 174) as long as he is read in England, which he presents through a brief catalogue of English rivers. In the last line of this catalogue Milton refers first to the Tamar and then to 'extremis ... Orcades undis' (the Orkneys in the outermost seas; 178), thus almost bracketing the kingdom. Farther than this, apparently, he is not prepared to go. All these aspects of this section suggest that Milton is trying simultaneously to use Virgil and the glory of the Roman empire as precedents for his own epic project and to neutralize the foreign threat they represent. Milton seems to be concerned to minimize the Italian element both in his poetic and in his personal life. This is another way in which 'Epitaphium Damonis' can be seen as a mirror image of 'Alcon,' rather than as a repetition. While Castiglione begins the final section of his poem by invoking ancient Rome, Milton begins the final section of his by invoking ancient Britain and by doing so, I would argue, at the expense of ancient Rome. For Castiglione, the Rome of Virgil's time appears as a homerotic space and is thus a suitable setting for the reunion of the two men that he proposes; for Milton, I think, Rome's ability to provide homoerotic space is one of the things that he must leave behind as he moves from Tuscany to England.[59]

Milton is left with some concrete proof of his stay in Italy, however: the cups that he tells us Manso gave him (181–3). The precedent for these is the cup offered by the goatherd to Thyrsis as the prize for singing in Theocritus's first idyll. The goatherd describes the cup at some length: it is covered with depictions of the lives and loves of shepherds, which is to say that it functions as an equivalent, in another artistic medium, of the subject matter of Theocritus's idylls (I.27–61). Theocritus's ecphrasis firmly places the elegy we are about to read in the realm of art. I think Milton's description of the scenes on Manso's cups serves a similar function, and in this context it is noteworthy that the scenes the cups present are not pastoral subjects. Hale says that Milton 'places on the cups many objects exotic to pastoral, and then describes them in a carefully controlled series, so that they accumulate into a Platonic ascent, or ladder of love.'[60] The description goes from the Red Sea, Arabia, and the Phoenix to 'polus omnipatens, et magnus Olympus' (the sky spreading over everything, and great Olympus; 190). Labriola says of Milton's plans for his epic that in 'tracing the lineage of Britons to Graeco-Roman antiquity, [the epic] would have depicted martial heroism and celebrated the role of the poet in reviving that cultural ideal.'[61] I think we are supposed to read the cups in conjunction with the passage to which Labriola refers. In addition to British history, Milton wants to deal with both Christian and pagan mythology. This conflation of traditions prepares us for the linking of the Bible and classical mythology in the last line of the poem.

Before I look at the ending of the poem, I want to consider what Milton finds on Mount Olympus: 'Quis putet? hic quoque Amor' (Who would have thought it? Here also is Cupid; 191). Thyrsis's rather stagy surprise comes from the fact that love, which has been a source of some discomfort, is now enthroned at the highest point of the artistic traditions that the cups depict. That these traditions are artistic suggests that Thyrsis's problems can only be solved in art. The social and moral prohibitions that govern human sexuality can only be transcended in a form like elegy, where the subject is doubly removed – by art and by death – from the poet. The transcendence is emphasized by Milton's characterization of Cupid, who in this poem is not the winged god of vulgar loves but rather an altogether loftier deity: 'Semper in erectum spargit sua tela per orbes/ Impiger, et pronos nunquam collinat ad ictus' (The tireless one always scatters his arrows on high through the spheres, and never aims his shot downwards; 195–6). In 'Epitaphium Damonis,' Cupid is a platonized Priapus. This is in keeping with the trend of the poem's conclusion, which presents the sexuality of the poem's first part in an idealized and distanced way, just as the depiction of Cupid as a figure of inexhaustible phallic potency heals the impotency imaged in the drooping grain of line 64.

Since Milton's Cupid is a celestial deity he inspires celestial love, and for this reason Damon himself is assured a place on Olympus:

Tu quoque in his – nec me fallit spes lubrica, Damon –
Tu quoque in his certe es; nam quo tua dulcis abiret
Sanctaque simplicitas, nam quo tua candida virtus?

(You also – indeed, no unsure hope misleads me, Damon – you are certainly also here; for where would your sweetness, your holy simplicity, your shining virtue have gone?; 198–200.)

This apotheosis has typically been seen as a complete turning away from the pastoral elements that have dominated the poem up to this point, but as Knedlik points out, the shift in tone has been overemphasized and 'some elements of classical pastoral are apotheosized rather than renounced in the elegy's conclusion.'[62] I agree that the pastoral elements do not completely drop out of the poem, but these elements now apply only to Damon. The division between the two men has become apparent as a difference in genre, with Thyrsis moving toward the epic and Damon celebrated in a fusion of styles that is still, despite the biblical overtones, largely pastoral in the Greek and Latin tradition. Knedlik says that 'the adjective "Sion" ... reinforces the imagery of pastoral apotheosis, evocative as it is of the pastoral redemption of Millenial Israel.'[63] In this way, Thyrsis places Damon at the summit of two pastoral traditions, one pagan and one Christian.

The final section of the poem is clearly a great compliment to Damon. It is not, however, entirely congruent with the rest of the poem and it represents Milton's greatest divergence from 'Alcon,' as Estelle Haan has shown:

> Unlike the pagan world of the *Alcon*, however, in which the speaker's only form of consolation is the erection of a monument in his friend's honor, Milton's poem achieves a positive *consolatio* whereby death is seen, not as final in itself, but as a gateway to a happier and fuller existence, since the deceased friend does not dwell in a pagan underworld, but conquers death itself by rising to heaven.[64]

Haan focuses on the undeniably triumphant aspects of the consolation; more cautiously, Michael West has remarked that '[w]hat the *consolatio* curiously fails to provide is any feeling that Damon's capacity for tender friendship and his strongly individualized nature – heavily emphasized, if not dramatized, throughout the poem, can find expression in Heaven.'[65] All traces of the real Damon have been eradicated and all his connections to earth have been severed: 'pluvium pede reppulit arcum' (with his foot he pushes back the rainbow; 204). Milton stresses Damon's scorn by using 'pede,' which is not necessary for the sense of 'reppulit,' but which does alliterate with it, 'pluvium,' and, in the first section of the line, 'purus.'[66] In contrast, the corresponding section in 'Lycidas' reads as follows:

> Now, *Lycidas*, the Shepherds weep no more;
> Henceforth thou art the Genius of the shore,
> In thy large recompense, and shalt be good
> To all that wander in that perilous flood. (182–5)

While Lycidas is able to retain a connection to this world, and to the very sea in which he was drowned, Damon is higher even than the rainbow, which in classical mythology connects earth and heaven and which in Christian mythology is the proof of divine interest in human affairs. The distance between Milton and Diodati, which the latter's death can now be seen merely to have begun, has increased since the insistence on Damon's Tuscan origins.

Somewhat paradoxically, part of the distance between the two men at the end of the poem comes from the fact that Milton drops the poetic mask and gives Damon his real name. West says that 'the apotheosis of

Damon suggests only more strongly his irrevocable detachment from his friends. The assumption of a new true name completes the erasure of Damon as a distinct character.'[67] Milton declares that Diodati will be the name 'cuncti/ Caelicolae norint' (all the celestial inhabitants will know; 210–11), while 'silvisque vocabere Damon' (in the forests you will be called Damon; 211). The poetic fiction of Damon is firmly placed in the realm of art and, in fact, in that part of the realm of art that Milton has already renounced ('vos cedite, silvae' [give way, forests; 160]), while Diodati, the man himself, appears to have been utterly translated. In other words, the Damon whose death has been so bitterly mourned in the poem is revealed to be a figure in an ecphrasis, and it would appear that this pastoral ecphrasis is less promising poetically to Milton than the ecphrasis associated with Manso's cups. The relegation of Damon to the forests completes Milton's distancing of himself from his pastoral subject.

The last eight lines of the poem describe Diodati's position in heaven. Milton begins by establishing Diodati's right to this position:

Quod tibi purpureus pudor, et sine labe iuventus
Grata fuit, quod nulla tori libata voluptas,
En! etiam tibi virginei servantur honores!

(Because blushing modesty and youth without disgrace pleased you, because you did not taste the pleasures of the bed, lo! the rewards of virginity have been kept for you; 212–14.)

The word 'tori,' which I have translated as 'bed,' has a wide range of meanings. The base meaning is a protuberance or bump, and the *Oxford Latin Dictionary* gives the following meanings (among others): a curve or ridge such as a tumulus; a bolster or the pallet on which dead bodies are placed; a bed and, by metaphoric extension, sexual intercourse; a muscle or other fleshy protuberance. It is inconceivable that so careful a reader of classical literature as Milton would not have been aware of these meanings, and I think 'tori' is deliberately polysemous. Milton's use of the word allows him to connect phallic sexuality with the bed in which it is indulged, the platform on which the corpse is displayed, and, finally, the structure of displaced earth that bears the memorial inscription (*epitaphium* from *epi* and *taphos*: upon the grave).

The polysemy in this passage allows Milton to refer to sex while referring to death. As a consequence, the poet is still distanced from the sexuality he explores in his poem. In the lines that follow (and that end the poem), Milton speaks more openly about sexuality, but he is still aware that the fervency of his love and grief for Diodati might suggest to readers that the poet followed Theocritus and Virgil as models rather more closely than ecclesiastical and civil law would permit. By insisting on Diodati's purity, then, Milton seeks to forestall the accusation that their friendship was sexual. Sexuality turns out to be the chief reward of virginity:

> Ipse, caput nitidum cinctus rutilante corona,
> Laetaque frondentis gestans umbracula palmae,
> Aeternum perages immortales hymenaeos,
> Cantus ubi, choreisque furit lyra mista beatis,
> Festa Sionaeo bacchantur et Orgia Thyrso.

> (You yourself, your handsome head bound in a shining crown and carrying shady fronds of joyful palms, will forever conduct the immortal marriages, where song and lyre are passionately joined with blessed dances, and the festal orgy rages under the thyrsus of Sion; 215–19.)

The sexuality that is Diodati's heavenly lot is not like earthly sexuality, just as the heavenly Cupid is not like the earthly one, for both the heavenly Cupid and the heavenly Diodati are characterized by unflagging potency.

In order to write the sexuality that has been covert throughout the poem, Milton has recourse to the ecstatic sexual imagery of both paganism and Christianity. The combination is not usually felt to be a success. Hale aptly says that '[t]he climax of climaxes is here handed over to the startling conjunction of "Sionaeo" with "Thyrso."'[68] The combination, although startling, is still appropriate and it is a very significant combination for Milton's career as a whole. In his discussion of the ending Fred J. Nichols says that

> the pastoral song must cease to be pastoral in order to be efficacious. That the poem must reject the very tradition of which it is a part, shows the extent to which Milton's disenchantment with the Latin language as a means of poetic expression is a part of his more general difficulty in integrating classical, and therefore pagan, literary traditions with his own Christian convictions. This is a problem that Milton will ultimately resolve, in English, with the writing, much later, of Paradise Lost.[69]

Milton did write some Latin poetry later and he continued to use pastoral elements, but it is helpful to see 'Epitaphium Damonis' as a turning point. If 'Epitaphium Damonis' is a sort of poetic autobiography, and I think that this is one important aspect of the poem, then we can see Milton's biblical epics as the happy ending. After all, the fusion of genres previously felt to be mutually exclusive is suggestive of *Paradise Lost*, which is an English poem with a strong Latinate flavour, a biblical tale in a pagan literary framework, and a heroic tale with a largely pastoral setting. In *Paradise Lost*, Milton found a way to unite in a less startling way the various elements that have made the ending of 'Epitaphium Damonis' appear so strange.

He did so, however, at a certain cost. Although *Paradise Lost* is a strongly sexual poem, it is concerned with heterosexuality and, to a much lesser extent, with the sexuality of angels. There is still no place, at least on earth, for sexuality between men and the tension at the end of 'Epitaphium Damonis' has not been resolved. For me, this tension is located in Milton's reference to the thyrsus, a wand carried by Dionysus that was wrapped in vine leaves and topped with a pine cone. The thyrsus is a suitable symbol for the sort of mystical marriage Milton describes, both because of the association of Dionysus with ecstasy and because the thyrsus is undeniably a phallic symbol. As such, it is related to the grain of line 64 and to the arrows of Cupid. More importantly, Milton makes a pun here on thyrsus and Thyrsis. Under his pastoral pseudonym, Milton shares Diodati's sexuality in a way he could not do (or would not admit to doing) on earth. Thyrsis, then, is both a poet and a lover, both the speaking voice and the embodiment of phallic sexuality. In abandoning Thyrsis, his pastoral persona, Milton gives up the sexuality symbolized by the thyrsus. For Milton, the equation of the two can only be a pun, a play on words. We can even take the pun in two ways: from the point of view of Thyrsis, the thyrsus is as a phallic symbol; for Milton, the thyrsus is a symbol of the pen with which he creates his visions of things that cannot come to pass on earth.

Milton's path toward the epics he wrote was long and his poetic career was frequently and famously interrupted. His optimism and his belief in his ability to write the great English epic persisted, however, and are perhaps best illustrated in the frontispiece to the 1645 edition of his poems. I shall use Leah S. Marcus's brilliant description:

[T]he central figure in the frontispiece seems to gesture toward the distant shepherds as toward an earlier, and now superseded, version of himself –

a self, perhaps, that had participated in a prewar world of pastoral mirth that must now be set behind him. The shepherds in the background are making rustic music, but the oldest figure in the foreground is surrounded by four muses in the corners outside the oval. He claims a higher art than the pastoral.[70]

Allowing for the replacement of mirth with grief, the picture is highly suggestive in the context of this chapter. Milton now defines himself poetically in opposition to the pastoral. The pastoral world is presented as homosocial, while the poet is the only man in a group composed of women. Homoerotic space is left behind as the poet moves into the heteroerotic space of the epic.

CHAPTER FOUR

Pastoral and the Shrinking of Homoerotic Space

As I suggested in the last chapter, the pastoral elegy continued to function as a site of homoeroticism throughout the Renaissance.[1] This was not always the case with other pastoral poems such as the collections modelled on Virgil's *Eclogues* that were so popular at this time, even though these collections usually included an elegy. Although pastoral poets continued to think of the pastoral as a genre that permitted a relatively great freedom of expression, this freedom was increasingly used primarily – sometimes exclusively – to comment on political and religious matters. What was true of the poets has, as a rule, been true of the critics as well, and in the last fifty years, critical discussions of Renaissance pastoral have tended to focus on politics and religion rather than on the two interconnected topics that most concern me here: homoeroticism and classical intertextualities. In this chapter I want to look at the ways in which Renaissance poets tried (hoped?) to accommodate the homoeroticism that was such a prominent part of their classical sources. My examples are Edmund Spenser's *The Shepheardes Calender* (I shall also look more briefly at 'Colin Clouts Come Home Againe'), Richard Barnfield's *The Teares of an Affectionate Shepheard* and its sequels, and William Browne's *Britannia's Pastorals*. Of these works, only *The Shepheardes Calender* has continued to be widely read and studied (although Barnfield is currently making something of a comeback), but all three poems were popular at the time and can thus be considered to have been in the poetic mainstream in a way that is not true of 'Alcon' or even of 'Epitaphium Damonis': and although Surrey's elegy for Richmond became a popular poem, it was not written for the public. The very popularity of the pastorals I discuss in this chapter (something that all three poets sought) and the fact that they were aimed at a wide audience were among the factors that dictated the nature of these texts' negotiations with homoeroticism.

For my purposes, both the most obvious and the most significant feature of English Renaissance pastoral is its increasing hetero-sexualization.[2] In classical pastoral, both homoeroticism and hetero-eroticism are discussed, and it is highly unusual for women to appear as characters. In the Renaissance pastoral, by contrast, overt homo-eroticism is rare and there are many female characters. Although the elegy, which is by this time usually pastoral in setting, continues to be homoerotic or at least homosocial, the pastoral itself is less and less likely to offer the possibility of homoerotic space – or, at any rate, it is less and less likely to offer it explicitly: there is some homoeroticism in *The Shepheardes Calender* and *Britannia's Pastorals*. It may well be that Renaissance poets felt that homoeroticism was a feature intrinsic to the pastoral and that to omit it altogether would result in a poem that was inauthentic, which is to say insufficiently Virgilian. Barnfield would appear to be an exception here, as much of his poetry is openly homoerotic (the subject of the poems of his I shall discuss is the male narrator's love for a beautiful man), but even here the pressure of heteroeroticism can be seen in the way that the homoeroticism of the narrator is ultimately presented as merely a stage on the way to a sexual and romantic interest in women. Whereas earlier the turn towards heteroeroticism happens after the pastoral phase of the poetic career is completed, in Barnfield's poem the turn occurs in the pastoral poem itself.

The three poets I discuss in this chapter find very different solutions to what must have appeared to them as a problem (pastoral's homoerotic content and history), but I think that for all of them this homoeroticism would have seemed at least partly an aspect of the foreignness of pastoral, of its origins in another time and place. All three poets to a greater or lesser extent try to make the genre English, and the turn toward heteroeroticism may well be an aspect of this attempt. For all three as well, the pastoral marks the beginning of their own poetic careers. With Spenser, of course, everything is different and his literary career is always uppermost in his mind. In fact, *The Shepheardes Calender* is famous for being one of the most self-conscious poetic debuts ever and the critics have tended to follow his lead by reading it primarily as preparation for the *Faerie Queene*. Spenser is a poet who can clearly be seen to have followed the example of Virgil, and *The Shepheardes Calender* is obviously the first step in his progress toward the epic.[3] In what follows, I shall show the extent to which Spenser's use of Virgil lies behind the homoeroticism of his poem both in terms of a character like Hobbinol and in his negotiations of his relation to the classical and English poetic traditions.[4] After considering *The Shepheardes Calender*, I shall look briefly at 'Colin Clouts Come Home Againe' in order to trace the evolution of Spenser's treatment of the homoerotic aspects of the pastoral. My particular interest is in how Spenser deals with the tendency of the homosociality of the pastoral to turn into homoeroticism.

The Shepheardes Calender

One way to fit the first of the twelve poems that make up *The Shepeardes Calender* into the pastoral tradition is to consider the ways in which Spenser alters the tradition set up by Theocritus's first idyll and Virgil's first eclogue. The idyll begins with a homosocial scene that leads to singing, while the eclogue begins with a man singing about his love for a woman and then turns into a homosocial scene. Spenser's sequence, which also differs from its models in beginning in winter, begins and ends with a solitary speaker. Furthermore, while all three poems deal to some extent with sombre themes, only 'Januarye' does not distance itself from them. Daphnis's death (or, rather, dying) is the subject of the song sung by one of the characters in the idyll, but the idyll begins with a beautiful description of the setting and ends in an affirmation of the bonds between the men. The eclogue also ends this way, and even Meliboeus's grief at having to leave Italy is juxtaposed with Tityrus's happiness at having his land secured. In 'Januarye,' there is little else beside Colin Clout's complaints (his speech takes up 59 of the poem's 78 lines). Spenser makes these complaints even more depressing because Colin is not provided with the male companionship that is a source of comfort in the two classical poems, although admittedly only temporarily so in the eclogue. Colin begins by comparing himself to his rather feeble sheep and to the cold weather; in the ninth stanza, he turns to discussing his romantic problems, which he presents as the result of 'that carefull hower,/ Wherein I longd the neighbour towne to see.'[5] Two lines later, however, he blesses the time 'Wherein I saw so fayre a sight, as shee' (52).

Colin's indecision about whether to curse or bless the hour in which he saw the woman he loves is certainly not unusual in sixteenth-century love poetry. What should strike us is that he is in love with a

town-dweller. Whether male or female, humble or exalted, the love
objects of shepherds in classical poetry lived in the country. The importance of this detail, to which I shall return, has been overshadowed by
the revelation in the next stanza:

> It is not *Hobbinol*, wherefore I plaine,
> Albee my loue he seeke with dayly suit:
> His clownish gifts and curtsies I disdaine,
> His kiddes, his cracknelles, and his early fruit.
> Ah foolish *Hobbinol*, thy gifts bene vayne:
> *Colin* them giues to *Rosalind* again. (55–60)

On the face of it, this declaration is plain, yet it poses numerous problems. The first person to try to explain everything is the tireless commentator E.K., whose note to line 57 reads, 'His clownish gyfts) imitateth
Virgils verse, Rusticus es Corydon, nec munera curat Alexis.' In adducing the classical parallel from the second eclogue, E.K.'s purpose is, I
think, to establish a literary precedent both for the line and for the
homoeroticism behind it. We are perhaps supposed to draw the inference that to present in this context the love of one man for another is not
sexual deviation but rather literary fidelity.

By line 59, however, E.K. has apparently come to feel that merely
adducing parallels is not enough and he attempts to dictate an interpretation of the Hobbinol passage. Fearing that readers may feel the lines
'sauour of disorderly loue,' a fear that is particularly serious as he has
been stressing a reading of the poem as autobiographical and has in fact
told us in his first note that Colin represents Spenser himself, E.K.
launches into a learned disquisition in which he declares that any
suggestion of what

> the learned call paederastice ... is gathered beside [Spenser's] meaning.
> For who that hath red Plato his dialogue called Alcybiades, Xenophon and
> Maximus Tyrius of Socrates opinions, may easily perceiue, that such love
> is muche to be alowed and liked of, specially so meant, as Socrates vsed it:
> who sayth, that in deede he loued Alcybiades extremely, yet not Alcybiades
> person, but hys soule, which is Alcybiades owne selfe. And so is
> paederastice much to be præferred before gynerastice, that is the loue
> which enflameth men with lust toward woman kind. But yet let no man
> thinke, that herein I stand with Lucian or hys deuelish disciple Vnico

Aretino, in defence of execrable and horrible sinnes of forbidden and vnlawful fleshlinesse. Whose abominable errour is fully confuted of Perionius, and others.

It could easily be argued that E.K.'s excessive gloss works against its stated purpose;[6] for one thing, it would be possible to construct a reading course on Greek love from his note alone. Furthermore, as Richard Rambuss points out, the gloss is not entirely successful even on the face of it: '[E]ven as E.K.'s pedantic note unfolds in the direction of a platonization of "paederastice" that appears to disavow male relations that are sexual, it nonetheless affirms the value and primacy of male bonds that are eroticized.'[7]

To me, the most important part of the gloss is the allusion to the second eclogue. Spenser invokes a famous romantic triangle from classical literature in the course of setting up his own rather different romantic triangle. Spenser's two most obvious changes to Virgil's triangle are that he adds a female character and that the person who provides the link between the other two members of the triangle is the speaker rather than the person whom the speaker loves. In other words, while the central figure in Virgil's triangle is Alexis, the lover of one man and the beloved of another, the central figure in Spenser's triangle is the unhappy Colin and there is no sexual relationship to match the relationship between Alexis and Iollas. By making one of the characters in the triangle a woman, Spenser opposes homoeroticism and heteroeroticism. His changes make it difficult to map the correspondences between the triangles, as Goldberg points out: '[I]f Colin is Alexis to Hobbinol's Corydon, is Colin thereby cast as Corydon in relationship to Rosalind's Alexis? How far does the allusion to Virgil's eclogue go? Where does the literary allusion place the erotics of Spenser's texts?'[8] Colin is simultaneously Corydon, insofar as he is a poetic shepherd whose love is unrequited, and Alexis, insofar as he scorns the rural presents that are all that a shepherd can afford. Perhaps more significant, however, is the fact that the only possible equivalent for Iollas in 'Januarye' is Rosalind. Yet although Iollas is rich, there is no suggestion that he is outside the pastoral sphere, while Rosalind, as we recall, lives in a town. The crucial opposition in Virgil is between Corydon's rural gifts and Iollas's wealth; in Spenser the opposition is between Hobbinol's 'clownish gifts and curtsies' and Rosalind's origin in 'the neighbour towne.' Colin's love for her can thus be understood to be a form of social climbing, as something that could lead to social advancement – and to poetic advancement as well: women, as Colin appears to recognize, can provide the way out of pastoral.

As I remarked earlier, Spenser's reconfiguring of the romantic triangle from the second eclogue has the effect of setting up an opposition between homoeroticism and heteroeroticism. To a certain extent, this opposition is built into the Virgilian model of a poetic career as the homoerotic pastoral gives way to the epic, with its dependence on heteroeroticism, but by beginning *The Shepheardes Calender* with this opposition Spenser signals his intention to leave the pastoral genre as soon as possible. Virgil could be said to function as a precedent for Spenser here, as he is also impatient with the pastoral genre, but his impatience, which is first demonstrated in the fourth eclogue, is shown in his desire to write poetry about wars. His farewell to the genre in the tenth eclogue is largely motivated by his desire to write about the soldier Gallus, but he also avows his love for Gallus. Spenser's impatience is shown in the very first poem of his sequence and homoeroticism is a part of the genre that he wishes to leave behind. The homoerotic space of the eclogues, in which a range of sexualities was permitted, has shrunk to the point where homoeroticism, although still present, is clearly linked to a rusticity that is no longer quaint or pleasing. Hobbinol turns out to be quite important in *The Shepheardes Calender* (although he does not even appear in the argument to 'Januarye'), but there is no indication that his love for Colin will be successful nor do there appear to be any other male characters in the poem who are in love with men. Colin's rejection of Hobbinol in favour of Rosalind is part of Spenser's own shift from the homosocial pastoral to the heteroerotic epic.

Hobbinol does not appear as a character in *The Shepheardes Calender* until 'Aprill.' Like Virgil's fourth eclogue, Spenser's fourth pastoral poem deals with a subject that is too grand to be part of the pastoral world. Virgil's eclogue deals with the birth of a child, and thus gestures toward the heterosexuality that is the theme, or at least the goal, of the epic. In contrast, Spenser's version of 'paula maiora' appears to take place in a world that is exclusively female. Colin's poem – Hobbinol's recitation of which occupies most of 'Aprill' – is the famous song to Elisa. The fact that this poem is set in a female world is emphasized by the speaker's addresses to Elisa's companions: 'Ye dayntye Nymphs' (37), 'you Virgins' (41), 'this beuie of Ladies bright' (118), 'Ye shepheards daughters' (127). Spenser's stress on Elisa as virginal and as removed from the world of men is motivated first by the desire to pay tribute to the virgin queen herself and second by the fact that although Spenser wishes to leave the pastoral genre behind, he does not wish the opposition between homoeroticism and heteroeroticism that he set up in 'Januarye' to be resolved just yet. In loving a woman rather than a man, Colin may have made the right choice, but he is still not ready for marriage. Just as Virgil must continue writing pastoral poems even after the fourth eclogue, so Colin must continue in the pastoral world rather than moving to the 'neighbour towne.' 'Aprill' testifies to the presence of women in the pastoral sphere, but at this point the male and female pastorals are not merged.

Hobbinol's recitation of Colin's poem is prefaced by a discussion between him and Thenot, in which Hobbinol's place in the *Shepheardes Calender* is made clear. The argument to the eclogue says that 'Hobbinoll being before mentioned, greatly to have loued Colin, is here set forth more largely, complayning him of that boyes great misaduenture in Loue'; he adds that Colin's love has estranged him from those 'who moste loued him' and from poetry itself. Hobbinol's unhappiness is stressed in the poem's first line when Thenot asks him 'what garres thee greete?' (1). Thenot lists four possible sources of sorrow: the last is sympathy with the rainy month; the first three concern misfortune to Hobbinol as a shepherd, as a poet, or as a lover (a heterosexual one – 'Or art thou of thy loued lass forlorne' [4]). Hobbinol is quick to correct Thenot's misapprehension:

> Nor thys, nor that, so muche doeth make me mourne,
> But for the ladde, whome long I lovd so deare,
> Nowe loues a lasse, that all his loue doth scorne. (9–11)

Hobbinol's assertion of his love for a man is carefully circumscribed by being stated parenthetically, as it were. It seems that he is not unhappy because Colin does not love him but because Colin is unsuccessful in his love for Rosalind. Whatever it may once have been, Hobbinol's love is now primarily altruistic. What Spenser is doing in this passage is crucial to his use of homoerotic space. The restriction of homoeroticism to the pastoral world is not unusual, but in 'Aprill' Spenser takes this restriction further by assigning the homoeroticism to Hobbinol, a secondary character, by making Hobbinol's love decidedly non-sexual, and by devoting most of the eclogue (117 of the poem's 161 lines) to a poem that Hobbinol is required to recite in praise of a woman.

The two shepherds end the eclogue by reproving the absent Colin.

Thenot says, 'Ah foolish boy, that is with loue yblent' (155) and Hobbinol says, 'Sicker I hold him, for a greater fon,/ That loues the thing, he cannot purchase' (158–9). This reproof is a return to Hobbinol's criticism of Colin at the beginning of the eclogue:

> Shepheards delights he dooth them all forsweare,
> Hys pleasaunt Pipe, whych made vs meriment,
> He wylfully hath broke, and doth forbeare
> His wonted songs, wherein he all outwent. (13–16)

Colin's abandonment of pastoral life in favour of the love of a woman from the town is presented primarily as the abandonment of his poetic gift. Yet while Colin's obsessive concentration on his heteroeroticism is censured, the turn towards women of which his love for Rosalind is an example is endorsed by the subject matter of the song as well as by the two emblems ('O quam te memorem virgo' and 'O dea certe'), which come from the scene in the first book of the *Aeneid* in which Aeneas first speaks to his mother Venus. In the first, Aeneas addresses the nymph who has appeared to him; in the second, he recognizes that the nymph is in fact his mother. These emblems are presumably intended to serve as a paradigm for Colin, who should progress from his personal love for a woman to the poetic worship of a goddess, a move that would entail writing an epic, an English *Aeneid*: the parallel scene of recognition for Colin would be his acceptance of this poetic destiny. Thus, while heteroeroticism is preferred to homoeroticism, heteroeroticism itself is only acceptable when it is pressed into the service of the epic.[9] Spenser presents Hobbinol's love for Colin, a love that is purged of sexuality and seems mainly to consist in preserving and disseminating Colin's poetry, as superior to Colin's (premature) desertion of the pastoral world.

It is not until the June eclogue, at the end of the first half of the *Shepheardes Calender*, that Colin and Hobbinol appear together. The argument says that '[t]his Aeglogue is wholly vowed to the complayning of Colins ill successe in his loue,' but it seems to me that the main subject is poetry. As in 'Aprill,' Colin's love is presented as an interruption in his poetic career. Hobbinol begins by pointing out the beauty of the setting in a passage that is closely modelled on the beginning of Theocritus's first idyll; in his answer, Colin describes himself in terms that recall the beginning of the *Aeneid*: 'But I vnhappy man, whom cruell fate,/ And angry Gods pursue from coste to coste' (14–15).[10] This is not to say that Hobbinol is stuck in the pastoral world while Colin wishes to enter the epic world, as Hobbinol himself says that Calliope and other Muses admired Colin's singing and were 'halfe with shame confound,/ Shepheard to see, them in theyr art outgoe' (63–4). Hobbinol's principal point is that Colin should be content with the beautiful dales in which the eclogue takes place rather than seek to live in 'those hilles, where harbrough nis to see' (19). The comparison between high land (ambition) and low land (being content with one's humble lot) also forms the subject of 'Julye'; here, the ambition Hobbinol hints at is Colin's social climbing, his love for a woman from the town.

Colin disclaims any lofty poetic ambitions – 'Of Muses *Hobbinol*, I conne no skill:/ For they bene daughters of the hyghest *Ioue*' (65–6) – and says that he sings only to relieve his sorrow: 'Enough is me to paint out my vnrest' (79). At this point, the eclogue takes a turn as Colin moves from discussing his own feelings to talking about Tityrus (that is, Chaucer), who taught him poetry. While this is not a complete change of subject, as Tityrus is described as 'the soueraigne head/ Of shepheards all, that bene with loue ytake' (83–4), the poem does appear to be turning into an elegy:

Nowe dead he is, and lyeth wrapt in lead,
(O why should death on hym such outrage showe?)
And all hys passing skil with him is fledde,
The fame whereof doth dayly greater growe. (89–92)

The movement toward elegy is qualified by the fact that in the *Shepheardes Calender* Tityrus means Chaucer. As a rule, the name is taken to be Virgil's own pseudonym in his eclogues, and an association with Virgil would entail an association with the homoerotic elegies of the classical tradition. By replacing Virgil with Chaucer, Spenser avoids these associations. Colin characterizes Chaucer as a poet who wrote (heteroerotic) love poems and humorous poems (85–7); the only work of Chaucer's that could be considered an elegy is the *Book of the Duchess*, a lament for a woman. In his presentation of Chaucer as his poetic master, Colin enrols himself in a tradition that is native and heteroerotic rather than foreign and homoerotic. Colin's references to poetic tradition in this eclogue have the effect of removing the elegy from pastoral homoerotic space.

In any case, the eclogue never does develop into an elegy, as Colin mourns Tityrus's death in order to use him for his own purposes. Much of the *Shepheardes Calender* is informed by an implicit narrative of a progression (as Spenser would have thought of it) from the pastoral, which is increasingly seen as a solipsistic genre, to the epic, which is presented as a way for the poet to engage in public affairs. Colin's turn toward a consideration of literary history may initially appear to be an intermediate step in this process, but the revelation that he still thinks only of Rosalind indicates that he has really made no progress at all. The abruptness of the change from the celebration of Tityrus's poetic power to the desire to profit from him is underlined by the peculiarly unpleasant image Colin uses:

> But if on me some little drops would flowe,
> Of that the spring was in his learned hedde,
> I soone would learne these woods, to wayle my woe. (93–5)

Line 95 suggests that what is planned is a melancholy version of the action of the original Tityrus at the beginning of Virgil's first eclogue (when Meliboeus says 'formosam resonare doces Amaryllida siluas'), but Colin goes on to reveal that he has a more personal aim in mind:

> Then should my plaints, causd of discurtesee,
> As messengers of all my painfull plight,
> Flye to my loue, where euer that she bee,
> And pierce her heart. (97–100)

Although Colin's desire is not that Rosalind should repent but rather that she 'well be knowne for such [her] villanee' (104), he still thinks of her as his primary poetic subject. Even in the presence of Hobbinol, Colin cannot conceive of a return to the homosocial world of the classical pastoral.

Spenser emphasizes this point by calling Colin's successful rival Menalcas, a name taken from Virgil's eclogues and often presumed, like Tityrus, to be a self-portrait. Spenser's Menalcas is very different from the Virgilian original who appears in the third and fifth eclogues, in both of which he engages in completely amicable singing matches that end in draws. I think Spenser wishes particularly to invoke the fifth eclogue, which occupies the same position in the *Eclogues* that 'June' does in the *Shepheardes Calender*: each ends the first half of the sequence. The implicit comparison Spenser sets up here is crucial to our sense of his negotiations with the pastoral tradition, especially since in the fifth eclogue, Menalcas and his ostensible rival both sing elegies for Daphnis. Virgil thus completes the first half of his pastoral sequence with a poem that stresses the homosocial cooperation of two shepherds, that gracefully acknowledges his own predecessor in the pastoral tradition, and that mourns the death of a beautiful man. Spenser's allusions to the fifth eclogue serve to draw our attention to his distance from Virgil. The most obvious difference between the poems may be that Chaucer has replaced Virgil as the primary literary forebear, but it is also important that the elegy that we expect from our knowledge of Virgil and that Colin leads us to expect because of his references to Tityrus does not materialize and that the focus on the poem is ultimately on a woman rather than on the male speakers or on the man who is mourned in the course of the poem. Furthermore, while Menalcas and Mopsus move from competition to a display of mutual admiration in which it is impossible to choose one as the victor, Hobbinol is clearly subordinated to Colin even though both are parallel as unsuccessful lovers. In his presentation of Hobbinol in 'June' as well as in his use of the fifth eclogue, Spenser seeks to purge the pastoral of the homoeroticism that has historically been one of its defining features.

Spenser actually does present a singing competition in 'August,' but even here the emphasis is on his difference from Virgil. Like Virgil's song competitions, this one ends in a draw ('Fayth of my soule, I deeme ech haue gayned' [131]), but here Cuddie, who is the judge, proposes to sing a song Colin wrote about Rosalind. This is the second poem that Colin has written about a woman and that is recited by someone else, but while the first poem celebrated the great Elisa, this poem is merely concerned with Colin's private troubles and thus appears as backsliding in the narrative of poetic development that, as I have said, is one of the important aspects of the collection as a whole. The fact that Colin is stuck is emphasized in the poem by his preference for solitude, as opposed to the crowd scenes of the lay to Elisa:

> Resort of people doth my greefs augment,
> The walled townes do worke my greater woe:
> The forest wide is fitter to resound
> The hollow Echo of my carefull cryes. (157–60)

I think that the 'hollow Echo' is not only the natural phenomenon so common in pastoral poetry, but also an allusion to the mythical Echo as a symbol of the consequences of an obsessive and hopeless love. By this, Spenser is able to suggest that heteroeroticism is not the means by which Colin will find it possible to leave the pastoral behind. Rather, just as homoeroticism must lead to heteroeroticism, so heteroeroticism must lead to something greater than, although connected to, itself. This is the veneration of a powerful and royal woman of which we have already seen an example in 'Aprill' and to which Spenser returns in 'Nouember.' Colin's love for Rosalind ultimately appears as a petty (because wholly personal) version of the public virtue demonstrated in the two great poems to Elisa and Dido.

One significant aspect of the elegy to Dido is that Colin recites it himself. We now see him, however briefly, as a model poet publicly performing a publicly important poem. In addition, the fact that 'Nouember' is an elegy resolves two problems from earlier in the sequence. The first is Colin's romantic despair, which has been one of the main subjects of the sequence since the beginning. I do not mean to suggest that by writing the elegy for Dido Colin has ceased to grieve over Rosalind's hard-heartedness ('December' shows otherwise), but rather that his personal sorrow for a woman who does not seem to be important in the grand scheme of things contributes to a poem that expresses public sorrow for a woman who was 'the greate shepehearde his daughter sheene' (38). As Ronald Horton points out, the elegy formalizes 'the traditional turn from the poetry that centers on self ... to public discourse directed toward public recognition and reward.'[11] At least temporarily, Colin is able to function as a public poet, a step that is of course of great importance to Spenser, for whom the public aspect of poetry was crucial. Colin's elegy for Dido can also be seen as the completion of his elegy for Tityrus in 'June,' an elegy that turned into yet another complaint at Rosalind's cruelty. As I pointed out, the swerve away from the elegy, with its homoerotic connotations, towards hetero-erotic love poetry is an important stage in Spenser's general reduction of homoerotic space. Nevertheless, one result of this swerve was that the *Shepheardes Calender* lacked an elegy. In 'Nouember,' then, Spenser is able to give his sequence the elegiac poem that has been an essential feature of the pastoral sequence since the very beginning. Furthermore, he does so in a way that is typical of his handling of the pastoral genre: by including in his sequence an elegy for a woman, Spenser further reduces homoerotic space.[12]

It is no surprise to the reader that Spenser is planning to leave the pastoral genre behind, but even though E.K. has said that Colin stands for Spenser, it will not be possible for Colin himself to write a different kind of poetry. Spenser's use of the calendar as a framework might seem to be a strategy to put movement into the largely static pastoral sequence, but the sequence is tied to the endless repetition of the months. Although Spenser himself will move to other genres, Colin ends the year in the same position in which he began it: once again, he is alone in the landscape. This time, however, he bids farewell to the landscape and all its inhabitants and finally to Hobbinol: 'Adieu good *Hobbinol*, that was so true,/ Tell *Rosalind*, her *Colin* bids her adieu' (155–6). Shore comments that '[t]he days of youthful friendship between Colin and Hobbinol are gone forever, but the value of their friendship can be affirmed even in the final moment of parting.'[13] Leaving aside the fact that the characterization of Hobbinol and Colin's relationship as 'youthful friendship' is rather disingenuous, I would say that what is most important here is not so much Colin's farewell to Hobbinol as his desire, even at the last moment, to employ him in the service of hetero-eroticism. Spenser ends the *Shepheardes Calender* by demonstrating that the bonds between men that are so central a part of the pastoral can be harnessed for the purpose of celebrating bonds between men and women. This represents a diminishment in the status of homoeroticism in the pastoral, and we can see a further diminishment in the fact that the particular bond between a man and a woman that is at issue here is doomed to fail and is of no great importance anyway in Spenser's plans for his poetic career. In order to develop the possibilities adumbrated in Colin's poems in 'Aprill' and 'Nouember,' Spenser must abandon both the pastoral and his pastoral persona.

Spenser does make use of Colin twice more, in 'Colin Clouts Come Home Againe' and in Book VI of the *Faerie Queene*, and these subsequent appearances give us additional insights into Spenser's negotiations with the pastoral and with its homosociality. The title of the first of these poems suggests the same kind of cyclical motion typical of the calendar itself, while the closeness of the poem's opening to the opening of the *Shepheardes Calender* points to a similar lack of progress; where the sequence says, 'A Shepeheards boye (no better doe him call),' 'Colin Clouts Come Home Againe' has 'The shepheards boy (best knowen by that name)' (1). In the former poem, Spenser suggests that Colin occupies a lowly position and the sequence thus begins with a statement of the desire to transcend the pastoral genre. In the later poem, however, there is no longer a disjunction between the pastoral poet and the occupation he holds. This means that Spenser has left Colin behind, but it also means that Colin is now, within the limits of the pastoral frame, a successful poet, whereas one of the subjects of the *Shepheardes Calender* was Colin's abandonment of poetry because of his unsuccessful love. By the time Spenser published 'Colin Clouts Come Home Againe' in 1595, he had established himself as one of the leading poets in England and he had begun to publish his epic. What we can see in both 'Colin Clouts Come Home Againe' and Book VI of the *Faerie Queene* is the realization that, as A. Leigh DeNeef has pointed out, 'the Virgilian progress is a false model of the poet's own choices'[14] – false, that is, in that it implies that the pastoral must be left behind, when in fact what we see in Spenser's later poems is that the pastoral continues to be of use.

In both of Colin's later appearances, his function is to signal the temporary union of court and country. This is not immediately apparent in 'Colin Clouts Come Home Againe,' however, which begins with Colin and Hobbinol – who, the narrator tells us, 'lou'd this shepheard dearest in degree' (14) – in a pastoral setting, but the initial impression that Colin is unchanged is dispelled by Hobbinol's first speech: '*Colin* my liefe, my life, how great a losse/ Had all the shepheards nation by thy lacke' (16–17). In his very affectionate speech, Hobbinol stresses Colin's absence from the pastoral world and when he asks Colin to recount his adventures, it is clear that the tale that ensues will not be a pastoral poem. Colin's reply is almost entirely taken up with the praises of a woman he saw in his travels and he ends his first speech with a sort of invocation:

Wake then my pipe, my sleepie *Muse* awake,
Till I haue told her praises lasting long:
Hobbin desires, thou maist it not forsake,
Harke then ye iolly shepheards to my song. (48–51)

Both the homoeroticism represented by Hobbinol and the homosociality represented by the as yet undifferentiated shepherds are now firmly placed in the service of the glorification of women, and what is true of these men as characters is true of the pastoral setting as a whole: for the remainder of the poem, Spenser employs the setting as a frame for an inset poem (composed of a series of connected poems) that is not essentially pastoral and that has obvious similarities to the *Faerie Queene* itself. Spenser thus creates a tension between the pastoral and the epic. Colin has returned to the pastoral world of shepherds and shepherdesses primarily in order to testify to the existence of a larger world.

Spenser's depiction of the pastoral world itself has changed since Colin's first appearance. The *Shepheardes Calender* dealt with shepherds, but one of the distinctive features of 'Colin Clouts Come Home Againe' is its focus on shepherdesses. Furthermore, these shepherdesses do not merely form part of Colin's audience, they also take an active role in the dramatic setting of the poem. In the *Shepheardes Calender* the frames for the inset poems were sketchy at best and any scene setting was confined to the beginnings and endings of the eclogues, but 'Colin Clouts Come Home Againe' is structured as a frequently interrupted narrative. Although Colin is the main speaker, his recitation is directed and shaped by the questions he is asked. The first question comes from Hobbinol, who is followed by Cuddy. Both of these characters are familiar from the *Shepheardes Calender* and their return might be taken to suggest a return to homosociality; we might even think that the return of Hobbinol will lead to developments in the story of his love for Colin. The next speaker is a woman, however, and in total five out of the ten speakers who ask questions of Colin are women. The presence of female characters is an obvious indication that Spenser has moved from the classical pastoral, which tends to be exclusively male, to the Renaissance pastoral, in which shepherdesses are frequent. As well, the female characters in 'Colin Clouts Come Home Againe' are not merely presences, nor do they function merely or even primarily as love objects. Like the shepherds, the women ask questions that help to shape the poem. In other words, the women contribute to our sense of poetry as communal. This is an important change from the *Shepheardes Calender* and from the pastoral in general, in which poetry arises out of solitude or out of small all-male groups. The shift towards a communal kind of poetry is related to the Virgilian model of the poet's progression from the pastoral, which deals primarily with individuals or small groups, to the epic, which deals with society as a whole. By depicting a community that has both male and female members, Spenser goes beyond Virgil's depictions of essentially all-male communities.

I would like to examine more closely some of the poem's female speakers. The first woman to speak is Thestylis (she is introduced at line 156), who interrupts Colin's account of Irish rivers to make a request: '[R]ead now eke of friendship I thee pray,/ What dittie did that other shepheard sing?' (159–60).[15] Both Hobbinol and Cuddy have asked to hear specific songs, but Colin's granting of Thestylis's request is our first indication that women also have the power to dictate the poet's repertoire. Not only does the poet not sing solely for himself, he sings for an audience that includes both men and women. This point is made clear by the fact that four other women speak in the poem; in fact, Thestylis herself has two more speeches and the second elegy in 'Astrophel' is called '*The mourning* Muse *of* Thestylis.' The third woman to speak is Lucida, and her intervention is especially interesting:

> Shepheard, enough of shepheards thou hast told,
> Which fauour thee, and honour *Cynthia*:
> But of so many Nymphs which she doth hold
> In her retinew, thou hast nothing sayd. (457–60)

Lucida's reproving comment is seconded by Melissa, and as a result Colin launches into an enumeration of women at the court. The patterning of this part of the poem is highly significant. The speeches of the two shepherdesses come almost exactly halfway through the poem, just after the catalogue of courtiers, all of whom are male. The two catalogues are connected by the fact that the list of poets ends with Astrophel and the list of women begins with '*Vrania*, sister vnto *Astrofell*' (487). The two catalogues are not entirely balanced, however, as Colin mentions 11 men in 80 lines, but 12 women in 99 lines (the ratio is roughly the same) – to say nothing of the fact that the main figure behind both catalogues is Cynthia herself.

There is a certain balance between the lists, however, as Colin also speaks of the shepherd of the ocean and thus tells his pastoral audience about twelve men and twelve women. On the other hand, as two of the men (Amyntas and Astrophel) are dead and the central figure is Cynthia herself, women predominate numerically in the inset narrative. In the pastoral frame, there are five women and five men, not counting Colin himself. The emphasis on women in 'Colin Clouts Come Home Againe' is one of the ways in which Spenser signals the turn toward the epic, and specifically toward the sort of epic that he wants to write – one that is largely concerned with heterosexuality – at least in the form of dynastic marriages.[16] We can also see signs of this turn in Spenser's strategies for dealing with the pastoral's tendency to be homosocial. The first example of this tendency is the presence of Hobbinol and his affectionate greeting of Colin, which I have already mentioned. The second comes at the very beginning of Colin's narrative. He says of his meeting with the shepherd of the ocean,

He pip'd, I sung; and when he sung, I piped,
By chaunge of tunes, each making other mery,
Neither enuying other, nor enuied. (76–8)

This passage recalls the amicable singing matches of the *Shepheardes Calender*, but the homosociality is qualified, I think, by the way in which Spenser presents their musical collaboration. The two men are like parallel lines that can never meet: Spenser's emphasis is on the separate nature of their contributions rather than on their union. Furthermore, the connection between Colin and the shepherd of the ocean, like the connection between Colin and Hobbinol at the beginning of the poem, leads to a poem whose subject is a woman. It is the woman who is the focus of their music-making. Spenser demonstrates that both the pastoral genre and the homosociality which is one of its salient features are useful in the composition of the larger-scale poems that he saw as his chief work.

The third feature of 'Colin Clouts Come Home Againe' that might seem to signal a return to the homosocial pastoral is the poem's progression towards elegy. The first sign of this comes with Colin's elegy for Amyntas, one of the poets he met in his travels, and continues with his reference to Astrophel's death and with the elegies to Astrophel that followed 'Colin Clouts Come Home Againe' in the 1595 volume. In keeping with the poem's general transformation of the pastoral, however, the elegies that emerge from this volume are firmly heterosexualized. For example, Colin says that

Amyntas quite is gone and lies full low,
Hauing his *Amaryllis* left to mone.
Helpe, O ye shepheards helpe ye all in this,
Helpe *Amaryllis* this her losse to mourne. (434–7)

Whatever Amyntas's importance may have been as a poet (or as Colin's friend), the description of him takes his love for Amaryllis as its starting point and stresses that she is the chief mourner. The elegy for Amyntas leads directly into the first mention of Astrophel, whose death is the subject of the various poems that, as I have said, completed the 1595 volume. The fact that Astrophel is Sidney clears these elegies of any suspicion of homoeroticism, since mourning Sidney is more obviously an obligation, whether poetic or political or religious or all three, rather than an expression of personal feeling, although personal feeling may well be an element in many of the elegies that were written about him. Here as in 'Nouember,' Spenser includes the requisite elegy, but he does so in such a way that he is able to remove homoerotic or even homosocial connotations from it. Although both Dido and Astrophel belong to the pastoral world, they are presented as existing on a higher plane and as being altogether more important. Instead of providing a means for men to express their love for each other, elegy is now a means for the poet to transcend the limitations of the pastoral.

As in the conclusion of the *Shepheardes Calender*, however, Colin is not included in this transcendence. At the end of 'Colin Clouts Come Home Againe,' the shepherdess Melissa praises Colin for his skill in talking about love and adds, 'But most, all wemen are thy debtors found, / That doest their bountie still so much commend' (901–2). Melissa suggests that Colin is primarily a poet of love rather than (strictly speaking) a pastoral poet and that his particular talent is in writing about women; to a certain extent, then, she moves Colin, as a poet, beyond the pastoral genre. Unfortunately, her comment leads to a return to the subject of Colin's romantic failure:

That ill (said *Hobbinol*) they him requite,
For hauing loued euer one most deare:
He is repayd with scorne and foule despite. (903–5)

The poem ends very much as 'December' does, as Colin calls upon his fellow shepherds to witness 'That hers I die, nought to the world denying, / This simple trophe of her great conquest' (950–1). Yet while in 'December' Colin compared his life to the progression of the year and consequently made his death seem like a submission to the laws of nature, here he submits himself to a woman who is described in line 951 in terms that make her seem like one of the female warriors typical of Renaissance epics. Colin's submission is a part of Spenser's subsuming of the pastoral to the heterosexual epic, a process that is complete by Book VI of the *Faerie Queene*. In this book, Colin appears only briefly, still singing the praises of women. The focus is on the knight Calidore, and to him the pastoral landscape is merely a holiday (as Spenser pointedly remarks: 'Who now does follow the foule *Blatant Beast*, / While *Calidore* does follow that faire Mayd' [X.1.1–2]). That the 'faire Mayd,' the shepherdess Pastorella, turns out to be of noble birth, only emphasizes the extent to which the pastoral is now wholly contained by the epic; that is, it is always the epic – patriotic, violent, heterosexual – that is really the subject. Homoerotic space has disappeared altogether and even pastoral space has shrunk.

The Affectionate Shepherd

In a few years in the last decade of the sixteenth century, Richard Barnfield made a name for himself as a poet and then stopped writing poetry altogether, or stopped publishing it at any rate.[17] He has the distinction of being the only English poet before the twentieth century to be famous for poetry that is universally recognized to be homoerotic; part of this fame is due to the obvious comparison between Barnfield's sonnets and Shakespeare's. That is, the existence of Barnfield's sequence of love sonnets to a man is used to make Shakespeare's similar sequence seem less strange. In fact, Barnfield's homoerotic poems form a relatively small part of what is in any case a rather meagre output: four short books and seven short poems classed by his most recent editor as Dubia.[18] I believe that his homoerotic poems (by which I mean 'The Teares of an affectionate Shepheard,' 'The Second Dayes Lamentation,' 'The Shepherds Content,' 'Certain Sonnets,' and 'An Ode') are best read as a narrative. The story these poems tells is of the extinction of the homosexual, if not of homosexuality itself, and they can thus be compared to Spenser's pastoral poems, which also present a steadily shrinking homoerotic space. Yet although the *Shepheardes Calender* and 'Colin Clouts Come Home Againe' are clearly Barnfield's models in many ways, there are two important differences: Barnfield never gives the impression that he will leave the pastoral genre in order to write an epic; furthermore (and, for my purposes, more importantly), Barnfield is ultimately unable to endorse either homosexual or heterosexual desire. Both the vividly presented sexuality of his poems and the ambiguity of the ending of the narrative in 'An Ode' work against a reading of these poems as unequivocally opposed to homoeroticism.[19]

The Affectionate Shepheard was published in 1594, when Barnfield was only twenty. The second line of the title ('Containing the Complaint of *Daphnis* for the love of *Ganymede*') emphasizes the homoerotic nature of the poetry, although the book contains other poems, like 'Hellens Rape. Or A Light Lanthorne of Light Ladies,' that are not homoerotic at all. Barnfield may have felt (correctly, I think) that 'The Affectionate Shepheard' was the best piece in the book, but the fact that homoerotic poetry is considered to be the draw and that it is given the power to authorize other kinds of poetry cannot help but assume some significance in the dynamic between heteroeroticism and homoeroticism in the poems I discuss. As Kenneth Borris suggests, 'The organization and content of the volume constitute an implicit argument that male same-sex love is not, per se, on any different moral or religious level from that of heteroerotic experience.'[20] Despite – or rather because of – the prominent advertisement of the poems' content, however, Barnfield emphasizes the limits of homoerotic space. To begin with, the poems are presented as pastoral (they concern a shepherd) and as classical imitations (they concern characters called Daphnis and Ganymede). As well, the reference to the poems as a complaint suggests that in Daphnis we may be intended to recall the dying Daphnis of the first idyll, in which case the poems would have an elegiac quality. The reduction of homoerotic space is familiar, but other features of the title page work against this reduction. The first is Barnfield's Latin epigraph, *Amor plus mellis, quam fellis, est* (love has more honey than gall). This sentiment will be reversed at the end of the first poem in the book, but here it could be taken to indicate that what starts as a complaint may end up as a triumphant narrative. A further indication of the possibility of a triumphant narrative is the name Barnfield gives to the man Daphnis loves. While Ganymede is certainly a common name for a beautiful youth – and, by this point, a slang term for a young man who had sex with other men – we can also read this name as an allusion to a tradition that is diametrically opposed to the one represented by Daphnis; that is, the young man whose beauty leads Jupiter to grant him immortality as opposed to the young man whose death because of love inaugurates the pastoral genre. I think we should understand the oscillation between the mournful and triumphant narratives of homoerotic love as paradigmatic for Barnfield's homoerotic poems as a whole.

   The use of these highly evocative classical names might suggest that the poems will be close to Theocritus and Virgil, but although Barnfield clearly knew and used this tradition (especially, as one would expect, the second eclogue), his poetry is remarkable for its Englishness, an important part of which is his reliance on Marlowe and, to a lesser extent, Shakespeare and Spenser.[21] The poems as a whole demonstrate Barnfield's close reading of 'The Passionate Shepherd,' *Dido Queene of Carthage*, and *Hero and Leander*, and there is even one direct quotation. Line 104 of 'Teares' ('Crownets of Pearle about thy naked Armes') reproduces almost exactly *Edward II* I.i.162 ('Crownets of pearle about his naked armes').[22] In making this reference, Barnfield alludes to what must have been the high point of homoeroticism in English literature up to that point. For Barnfield, Marlowe represents a homoerotic tradition that is native and contemporary rather than classical and foreign. His use of Marlowe is analogous to Spenser's use of Chaucer in the *Shepheardes Calender*, but with the crucial difference that citing Chaucer as a literary predecessor establishes the poet's affiliation to a heteroerotic tradition, whereas in his poems Barnfield seeks to present himself as belonging to a homoerotic tradition that includes Virgil and to demonstrate that this tradition has contemporary followers beside himself. Renaissance poets invoke the classics to talk about homoeroticism and to make an implicit contrast between the earlier era's relative frankness and a more constrained contemporary discourse; in positioning himself and Marlowe as contemporary poets of homoeroticism (and in making his pastorals recognizably English), Barnfield can be taken to suggest that homoerotic space could even include England.

The first poem in the book does not maintain this optimistic note, since Barnfield begins by returning to the plaintive tone:

> I began to rue th'unhappy sight
> Of that faire Boy that had my hart intangled;
> Cursing the Time, the Place, the sense, the sin;
> I came, I saw, I viewd, I slipped in. (3–6)

This passage recalls the first eclogue of the *Shepheardes Calender*, in which Colin says, 'A thousand sithes I curse that carefull hower,/ Wherein I longd the neighbour towne to see' ('Januarye' 49–50). One difference between Spenser and Barnfield is the latter's reference to sin, which might lead us to believe that he is referring to Christian prohibitions against sexual activity between men; however, Barnfield's other allusion in this passage works against the idea that religious ideas about sexual morality are going to be important: 'I came, I saw, I viewd, I slipped in' recalls Julius Caesar's famous saying.[23] Barnfield translates 'veni' and 'vidi' literally, but then his translation diverges from the original. First he adds 'I viewd,' which transforms his action from simply seeing to what seems like an amorous gaze, and then he translates 'vici' (I have conquered) as 'I slipped in.' With its obvious reference to sodomy, 'I slipped in' makes the conquest specifically sexual. Barnfield suggests that although Daphnis's love is unhappy, as one would expect, it was once reciprocated. This makes the poem very different, not only from those Renaissance poems that only hint at sexual activity, but even from Virgil's second eclogue, its closest source, in which Corydon has apparently never had any success with Alexis (in fact, I think it was largely his frustration that permitted the popularity of the second eclogue in Christian Europe). It is hardly conceivable that a Renaissance poet could write a narrative of male love that ends happily, but at least Barnfield has given his narrator happy memories.

In the second stanza, the reference to sin is developed, although here again the Christian disapproval of homoeroticism is invoked only to be set aside:

> If it be sinne to love a sweet-fac'd Boy,
> (Whose amber locks trust up in golden tramels
> Dangle adowne his lovely cheekes with ioy,
> When pearle and flowers his faire haire enamels)
> If it be sinne to love a lovely Lad;
> Oh then sinne I, for whom my soule is sad. (7–12)

In his book on Barnfield (the first book-length study of Barnfield ever published), Harry Morris attempts to link this stanza to E.K.'s gloss on Hobbinol in 'Januarye,' for instance, 'Let no man thinke, that herein I stand ... in defence of execrable and horrible sinnes of forbidden and unlawful fleshlinesse.'[24] The connection between homoeroticism and sin is hardly so recherché that Barnfield's use of it requires a precedent, but Morris, whose homophobia is at odds with his admiration for Barnfield's poetry throughout his book, wishes to stress the connection. Nevertheless, he has to admit the much closer resemblance to the end of the fourteenth sonnet of *Astrophil and Stella*. This sonnet is Astrophil's response to a friend who has told him that love is sinful; Astrophil begins by claiming that his love has made him a better person and ends by declaring, 'Then Love is sinne, and let me sinfull be.'[25] The mood invoked by Barnfield's allusion is thus defiance rather than contrition and his use of this sonnet could indicate that he means that romantic love in general is sinful (an idea that was a commonplace in the Renaissance) rather than that the romantic love of one man for another is sinful.

In the fourth stanza, Daphnis reveals that he has a rival for Ganymede's affections. Following the second eclogue, which so much in the poem's title and set-up has encouraged us to see as Barnfield's model, we might expect a male rival like the prosperous Iollas; we are instead given a female rival. Daphnis tells us that the nymphs sought Ganymede's love and then says that he rejected them all except for

> the faire Queene *Guendolen*,
> Her he embrac'd, of her was beloved,
> With plaints he proved, and with teares he moved. (22–4)

The 'teares' with which he moves Guendolen are clearly more effective than the 'teares' of the poem's title. Predictably, Daphnis will go on to resent her interference ('Oh would shee would forsake my *Ganimede'*; 85) and to contrast his virtuous love for Ganymede with her lust: 'I love thee for thy gifts, She for hir pleasure;/ I for thy Vertue, She for Beauties treasure'; 209–10). Guendolen's presence in the poem allows Daphnis to launch into an inset narrative. Barnfield tells a story about Death and Cupid meeting, getting drunk, quarrelling, and inadvertently exchanging arrows. The result is that the beautiful young man Guendolen loves dies, while an unappetizing old man, whom Daphnis describes with great unkindness, falls in love with her and will not leave her alone.[26] Gregory W. Bredbeck has aptly said that '[t]he passion of Daphnis may be *contra naturam*, but it certainly makes more sense than the hetereoerotic love in the poem, which is expressed in terms of slapstick mishaps, deathly misfires, and divine mistakes.'[27] Daphnis may be unhappy or even unnatural, but at least he is dignified. Instead of bringing in hetereoeroticism as a tacit reproof to homoeroticism, Barnfield contrasts it unfavourably with homoeroticism. It seems clear that Ganymede would be better off with Daphnis than featuring in Guendolen's rather squalid love life.

After the inset narrative, Daphnis spends the remainder of the poem (85–234) attempting to seduce Ganymede, although he does return to the subject of Guendolen in order to contrast his love with hers. Her role in the poem is solely that of a foil: she is accused of being 'light in behaviour' and insincere in her affections and of loving Ganymede only for his looks. As Daphnis points out in one of the poem's most memorable lines, these will fade: 'But sometime Nature will denie those dimples' (212). In this passage Daphnis makes the comparison I quoted above: 'I love thee for thy gifts, She for hir pleasure;/ I for thy Vertue, She for Beauties treasure.' Barnfield's distinction will remind readers of Shakespeare's twentieth sonnet and especially of its conclusion: 'But since she pricked thee out for women's pleasure,/ Mine be thy love and thy love's use their treasure.'[28] This sonnet is usually understood to mean that the speaker's love is not sexual, but such an interpretation is untenable in the case of Barnfield's poem:

O would to God (so I might have my fee)
My lips were honey, and thy mouth a Bee.
Then shouldst thou sucke my sweete and my faire flower
That now is ripe, and full of honey-berries:
Then would I leade thee to my pleasant Bower

Fild full of Grapes, of Mulberries, and Cherries;
Then shouldst thou be my Waspe or else my Bee,
I would thy hive, and thou my honey bee. (95–102)

With its unmistakable references to fellatio, to semen, and to penises, this passage demonstrates that the homoeroticism of the poem cannot be reduced to friendship, that favourite device of squeamish critics. The sexual nature of the passage would not, of course, rule out the possibility of friendship in the more expansive sixteenth-century sense.

There are several other erotic passages in Barnfield's poetry, especially in 'The Affectionate Shepheard.' I have chosen this one because it leads to a passage that reads like an extension of the 'Passionate Shepherd' – a passage beginning, moreover, with the quotation from *Edward II* mentioned above. In the play, the line occurs in Gaveston's speech about the shows he will stage to titillate the king. The man wearing the jewels will be a lovely boy dressed as the goddess Diana: 'And in his sportfull hands an Olive tree,/ To hide those parts which men delight to see' (I.i.64–5). Gaveston creates a scenario in which what might at first appear to be a goddess famous for virginity is actually a man with considerable erotic allure and in which the parts men delight to see are actually male genitals. In 'The Affectionate Shepheard,' lines 95–102 and the use of this intertextuality with its strongly homoerotic connotations mark the whole section as being explicitly sexual. What would probably have appealed to Barnfield is Marlowe's presentation of male beauty as something generally appreciated (especially when presented in classical disguise). In fact, Marlowe presents homoeroticism as the truth behind literary representation, just as on the Renaissance stage the truth behind the representation of femininity was a male actor. Barnfield adopts Marlowe's tone and the persuasions of his speaker, but Barnfield's speaker is addressing a man and Barnfield has sexualized Marlowe's pastoral imagery. In this respect, he could be said to have surpassed in boldness the poet whom, as I have suggested, he saw as his predecessor in English homoerotic verse. More importantly for my purposes here, 'Teares' demonstrates that pastoral space is still, at the end of the sixteenth century, a potentially homoerotic space.

Unfortunately, the potential is not realized and 'Teares' ends with an inversion of the Latin tag that began it: Daphnis now says, 'Plus fellis quam mellis Amor.' When the next poem begins ('The Second Dayes Lamentation of the *Affectionate Shepheard*'), the mood is sombre and the poem is now the complaint advertised on the book's title page. Daphnis

switches from promising Ganymede sexual pleasure in a pastoral landscape to promising him immortality through poetry: 'Ile grave thy
name in Beauties golden Booke,/ And shrowd thee under *Hellicons*
protection' (33–4). By 1594, the promise of poetic immortality had already become a standard feature of much English poetry, in which it
usually functions as an inducement to love; in the context of the *Affectionate Shepheard*, however, Daphnis's offer signals a turn away from the
sexuality of 'Teares.' Although 'The Second Dayes Lamentation' is not
without attempts at seduction (most notably in lines 103–8), the focus is
on moral advice, including an attack on long hair for men (109–36) and
an extended comparison of dark and fair things (217–312).[29] This passage begins with the line 'O faire Boy trust not to thy Beauties wings'
(211), which recalls the famous line from the second eclogue: 'O formose
puer, nimium ne crede colori' (2.17). The similar phrasing emphasizes
the differences between the poems: Virgil's Corydon uses the contrast
between dark and fair in his attempt to seduce Alexis, while Daphnis,
at least in 'The Second Dayes Lamentation' is all too easily distracted
from seduction by the siren song of sententiousness. All this advising
gives Daphnis a rather avuncular quality. While in 'Teares' there was no
reason to think that Daphnis and Ganymede were not coevals,[30] here
Daphnis appears much older than Ganymede, as, in fact, he ends up
being: 'But now I finde it too-too true (my Sonne),/ When my Age-
withered Spring is almost done' (413–14).

Daphnis's stress on his age and on the age difference between him
and Ganymede at the end of 'The Second Dayes Lamentation' leads to a
renunciation of love as unsuitable for one so old. At the very end of the
poem he tells us, 'I hy'd me homeward by the Moone-shine light;/
Forswearing Love, and all his fond delight' (443–4). His renunciation is
emphasized by the poem that follows, 'The Shepherds Content or the
Happines of a Harmles Life.' The subtitle ('Written Upon Occasion of
the *Former Subiect*') links this poem with the two that precede it. Klawitter
points out this connection in his note on line 4 ('His thoughts are pure
from all impure intent'): 'Barnfield's insistence here on a pure intent is a
far cry from his earliest sentiments in "The Affectionate Shepheard."
There his narrator is selfishly aggressive; here he assumes the role of a
kindly, disinterested guide.' I agree that the poems should be read
together and that the speaker in 'The Shepherds Content' should be
identified with the new, sententious Daphnis, although I think 'selfishly aggressive' is going a little far. The poem he delivers is a conventional paean to the simple joys of the pastoral life that includes elegies

for Astrophel (115–25) and Amyntas (126–32) and references to contemporary poets (224–7). Spenser, who appears as Collin in 'The Shepherds Content,' seems to have taken this poem as his model for 'Colin Clouts Come Home Againe,' which was published the year after Barnfield's book and also includes elegies for Astrophel and Amyntas. In both poems, although admittedly to a much greater extent in 'Colin Clouts Come Home Againe,' the standard features of the pastoral are stripped of their homoeroticism and the genre is used primarily to criticize the corruption of the court and to discuss poetry itself. The pastoral world is no longer an idyllic space separate from the larger world; it is now entirely dependent. As I pointed out at the beginning of this chapter, the use of the pastoral genre for social and literary critiques means a general subsuming of the pastoral world to the social realities of the time, and this leads to the foreclosure of the possibility that it could be a homoerotic space.

The turn from homoeroticism to heteroeroticism in Barnfield's book is obvious in his treatment of love in 'The Shepherds Content,' in which courting a woman is presented as one of the joys of the shepherd's life:

Another while he wooes his Country Wench,
(With Chaplets crownd, and gaudy girlonds dight)
Whose burning Lust her modest eye doth quench,
Standing amazed at her heavenly sight. (189–92)

This love is apparently to be preferred to the love in the book's first two poems both because it is directed toward a woman and because the shepherd's lust is under control; in other words, we are invited to admire this kind of love precisely because it is diametrically opposed to the love that was the subject of the first two poems in the book. In Barnfield's formulation, heteroeroticism appears to be less powerful than homoeroticism. At the end of the poem, Daphnis begins to speak of the cruelty of love – 'How happie were a harmles Shepheards life,/ If he had never knowen that Love did meane' (259–60) – but even this theme, which might seem to offer Daphnis an opportunity to return to the situation of 'Teares' and 'The Second Dayes Lamentation,' is presented (with a particularly memorable example of internal rhyme in line 267) in heteroerotic terms:

There are so manie *Danaes* nowadayes,
That love for lucre; paine for gaine is sold:

No true affection can their fancie please,
Except it be a *Iove*, to raine downe gold
Into their laps, which they wyde open hold. (266–70)

It is depressing, if not perhaps surprising, that one of the concomitants of the speaker's turn toward heteroeroticism is a greater misogyny.

In discussing the happy life of shepherds, Daphnis does speak of his romantic problems. At the beginning of the poem, for example, after one and a half stanzas about the happiness of shepherds, Daphnis begins to complain:

No Briefes nor Semi-Briefes are in my Songs,
Because (alas) my griefe is seldome short;
My Prick-Song's alwayes full of Largues and Longs,
(Because I never can obtaine the Port
Of my desires: Hope is a happie Fort). (15–19)

With their familiar pun on 'Prick-Song' and their reference to the pain of prolonged tumescence, these lines are strongly sexual, but there is nothing in them to indicate the gender of the person who is causing him all this pain.[31] Similarly, even in his long excursus on the pain of love (213–72) Daphnis does not name Ganymede or use male pronouns to refer to him. His treatment of love's cruelty is as general as his treatment of pastoral life: a specific homoerotic attachment has given way to a generalized heteroeroticism. Only at the very end of 'The Shepherds Content' is the gender of the person whom the speaker loves revealed: 'Now I must leave (awhile) my rurall noate,/ To thinke on him whom my soule loveth best' (296–7). The poems that follow 'The Shepherds Content' in the book are a sonnet that reads like an imitation of Samuel Daniel and that, like 'The Shepherds Content,' avoids revealing pronouns about the 'cruell tyrant Eyes' (2) of the speaker's beloved and two poems about women, one about a virtuous one (Matilda Fitzwalter) and one about a sinful one (Helen of Troy). The speaker's admission that he loves a man is thus a momentary lapse in the shift from homoeroticism to heteroeroticism, a shift emphasized by the change from a 'rurall noate' to poems about history and mythology, which is itself a change from poetry with a male subject to poetry with a female subject.

These shifts would seem to signal Barnfield's adherence to the Virgilian model of a poetic career, if it were not for the parenthetical 'awhile,' which turned out to mean only one year. In 1595, Barnfield published *Cynthia. With Certaine Sonnets, and the Legend of Cassandra.* The beginning of this book (an address 'To the curteous Gentlemen Readers') appears to demonstrate Barnfield's detachment from the pastoral and from homoeroticism. In this address, Barnfield deals with the success of *The Affectionate Shepheard* but also with its homoeroticism:

> Some there were, that did interpret *The affectionate Shepheard*, otherwise then (in truth) I meant, touching the subiect thereof, to wit, the love of a Shepheard to a boy; a fault, the which I will not excuse, because I never made. Onely this, I will unshaddow my conceit: being nothing else, but an imitation of *Virgill*, in the second Eglogue of *Alexis.*[32]

Barnfield is his own E.K. in this epistle and, as with E.K.'s defensive note about Hobbinol in 'Januarye,' the prose exculpation raises more questions than it settles. Barnfield admits that the subject of his earlier poem was 'the love of a Shepheard to a boy,' but it is not clear what the interpretation he never meant is. When he speaks of 'a fault, the which I will not excuse, because I never made,' he presumably wishes to be understood to say that he has not personally loved a boy. This seems like a standard disclaimer and the laudable 'imitation of Virgill' like a standard rationalization for his choice of theme, but Barnfield does not take the opportunity, as E.K. does, to condemn homoeroticism. He merely says that as he has not made this fault himself he is not obliged to excuse it, which is a different thing altogether. To a certain extent, this passage removes homoeroticism from the sphere of moral judgment and presents it as a matter of taste, as something that might perhaps form part of a man's experience, if only to be rejected. In his epistle, Barnfield does nothing to rule out the possibility that a man might try sex with another man and like it and, as we shall see, the presentation of homoeroticism as a possible part of a man's maturation is precisely the situation that obtains in the narrative Barnfield presents in part of the 1595 volume.

As a narrative poem about goddesses, the first poem, 'Cynthia,' follows the last two poems in *The Affectionate Shepheard* in concentrating on femininity. Since 'Cynthia' is a version of the judgment of Paris, there is a pastoral setting, but the focus on the poem is on feminine beauty and excellence (especially Elizabeth's). The last poem in the book also focuses on women, as it tells the story of Cassandra. In these poems, then, Barnfield would seem to have turned from homoerotic pastoral to the world of epic, a world in which women are central, at least in his version of it. Between these poems, however, Barnfield returns to homoeroticism in a sequence of twenty sonnets and in the ode that follows the sequence. In his inimitable way, Morris comments that 'the appearance in the sonnet sequence ... of an aberrant love more extreme than any in *The Affectionate Shepheard* discounts completely the poet's defense' (in the epistle to his readers).[33] These remarks might lead readers to expect pornography, but Barnfield's sonnets are decorous enough for the most part. Nevertheless, Morris is correct in indicating that the return to a homoerotic theme (a return that is emphasized by the use of the characteristic images of the earlier poems) undermines Barnfield's stance in the epistle. Since the book begins and ends with poems celebrating women and the ode that follows the sequence presents homoeroticism as a phase in the progression to heteroeroticism, the incongruity of the sequence and the epistle can be seen as a sign of an incongruity between Daphnis and Barnfield – between, that is, the speaker and the poet. After all, the tendency of the 1595 volume as a whole is to contain homoeroticism, to emphasize it as poetic rather than actual practice, as imitation rather than life.

Still, there are aspects of the sequence that cannot be neutralized by the poet's turn toward female subjects. One of these has to do with imitation itself. If, as Barnfield says in the epistle, the homoeroticism of the poems is to be taken as an imitation of Virgil, what are we to make of the homoeroticism of the sequence? If we see these sonnets as imitation, then they are most obviously imitations of other sonnet sequences and all the sonnet sequences to which contemporary readers could have compared Barnfield's concern a man's love for a woman. This literary context cannot be used to excuse homoeroticism. In other words, the homoeroticism of Barnfield's sonnets is actually emphasized by their literary context, a neat reversal of the usual strategy of de-emphasizing or at least containing homoeroticism by pointing to a literary context. In fact, Barnfield ends his sequence by mentioning two famous sonneteers:

Ah had great *Colin* chiefe of shepheards all,
Or gentle *Rowland*, my professed friend,
Had they thy beautie, or my pennance pend,
Greater had beene thy fame, and lesse my fall. (9–12)

What is most notable about the allusion to Spenser and Drayton is the suggestion that either of those poets, who wrote their sonnets to women, might well have written about Ganymede. It would appear that men and women are both suitable topics for male sonneteers. Even if we are to consider the difference between writing to Elizabeth Boyle or to Idea and writing to Ganymede as purely a question of subject matter and not a question of subject matter that reflects sexual practice, the implication is still that in literary terms homoeroticism and heteroeroticism are equal. Within the sonnet sequence itself, at least, Barnfield presents the turn toward women as merely one literary option, rather than as a poetic or moral imperative.

The argument that the sonnets can be read as to some extent resisting the heteroeroticism they appear to promote has been taken further by Daniel F. Pigg. In a short but densely written essay that focuses on the eighth sonnet, he suggests that 'Barnfield ... attempts a critique of the normative, heterosexual sonnet tradition by refashioning and reappropriating that discourse to represent same-sex attraction under the guise of sublimation and transferred desire.'[34] Pigg refers to Daphnis's change from loving Ganymede to loving a woman. After saying, 'Him I thought the fairest creature,/ Him the quintessence of Nature' (53–4), Daphnis tells us that he has found a new love:

> For since then I saw a Lasse
> (Lasse) that did in beauty passe,
> (Passe) faire *Ganymede* as farre
> As *Phoebus* doth the smallest starre. (57–60)

It was, apparently, just a phase, although Barnfield undermines his praise of female beauty by citing a male god, just as Marlowe does in the famous address to Helen of Troy in *Doctor Faustus*. The comparison is especially significant, as Phoebus is often associated with homoeroticism. Some readers may take Daphnis's change from loving a man to loving a woman as a sign of a change in his identity or even as moral amelioration, but Barnfield really presents it as amelioration of Daphnis's aesthetic judgment. What Daphnis says is that he was wrong to think that Ganymede was the most beautiful person in the world: 'But yet (alas) I was deceiv'd,/ (Love of reason is bereav'd)' (55–6). Rather than conforming to the dictates of a homophobic society, Daphnis recalls Virgil's Corydon who, when he realizes that he has no chance with the man he loves, considers loving either a woman or a man. In a way that may seem paradoxical, the turn from a male to a female love object is really a return to a pre-Christian morality. Daphnis's hetero-eroticism should not be taken as heterosexuality and poses no threat to homoeroticism.

I think that in some ways Pigg's comment is really more pertinent to the ode that follows the sonnets, a feature of the sequence that recalls Daniel's *Delia*, first published in 1592.[35] Both odes contrast the poet's misery with the beauty of the vernal landscape, but while the poet in *Delia* merely resolves to die – 'But her will must be obaide,/ And well he ends for loue who dies' (23–4) – Daphnis actually does die. At this point it is revealed that his lament has been overheard by a shepherd who ends his recitation by saying that he must go home to tend to his sheep (the revelation that the poem has been overheard and thus has two speakers may have influenced Milton in 'Lycidas'). While Daniel's ode is essentially a love lament, Barnfield's is an elegy and, what is more, an elegy for the speaker himself. In ending his homoerotic, pastoral sequence with a character called Daphnis who recites his own elegy as he dies for love, Barnfield alludes to Theocritus's first idyll, the very beginning of the homoerotic, pastoral genre. Dying for love is a standard ending for a love poem, and I think Barnfield wants us to think both of Theocritus and of Daniel and the whole Petrarchan tradition behind him, but even here we can see the poet attempting what Pigg calls 'a critique of the normative, heterosexual sonnet tradition.' What is significant about the ode as an ending to these poems as a whole is not that Daphnis loves a woman but that he does not die until he loves a woman or, to put it with reference to poetry, he does not die until entering a genre that focuses on heteroeroticism. Renaissance poets tended to demonstrate that the pastoral could no longer function as homoerotic space and in many ways Barnfield is no exception. Still, he refuses to find a replacement that is, in the literal sense of the word, viable. In the address to the readers, Barnfield characterized homo-eroticism as a fault, but the heteroeroticism to which Daphnis turns does not appear as an improvement. Homoeroticism may be unfortunate, but heteroeroticism is positively fatal.

Britannia's Pastorals

Like Barnfield, William Browne began his literary career young and achieved success instantly. In 1613, at the age of twenty-three, he published an elegy on the Prince of Wales and, later that year, the first book of *Britannia's Pastorals* (which included a revised version of the elegy);

the poem's second book came out in 1616. In between, he contributed poems to *The Shepherd's Pipe* (1614). Unfortunately, Browne was also like Barnfield in giving up his poetic career at an early age. His last publication in his own life was a reissue of the first two books of *Britannia's Pastorals* in 1625;[36] the third book was not published until 1852. Although Browne was for many years a popular poet whose influence can be detected not only in other seventeenth-century poets like Milton, but even as late as Keats and Elizabeth Barrett Browning, he is now known almost exclusively for the frequently anthologized epitaph for the Countess of Pembroke, beginning 'Underneath this sable herse/ Lies the subject of all verse.'[37] The neglect of Browne is partly due to the generally low opinion of the pastoral poets who followed Spenser and partly to the fact that the narrative of *Britannia's Pastorals* clearly demonstrates Browne's lack of interest in narrative.[38] It is as a descriptive poet that he excels, and even if his great pastoral is not successful as a cohesive narrative – in this respect it certainly resembles the *Faerie Queene* – it is interesting both as an attempt to make the pastoral completely English (for instance, the books of the poem consist of songs, not cantos) and as an attempt to blend the pastoral with the native and medieval tradition of romance.[39] For my purposes it is also interesting for its relation to the homoerotic tradition of pastoral and, especially, of pastoral elegy. In fact, *Britannia's Pastorals* as a whole is remarkably elegiac in tone, particularly so in Book II. Browne's use of elegy serves to contain his poem's marked emphasis on male beauty and on strong emotional attachments between men. I shall concentrate on these aspects of the poem.

The first beautiful man to be introduced is Remond, a poet – 'young Remond, who full well could sing,/ And tune his pipe at Pan's birth carolling' (I.1.476–7) – who will turn out to be one of the poem's major characters.[40] Browne's description of him is both erotic and allusive:

> Whose locks (ensnaring nets) were like the rays
> Wherewith the sun doth diaper the seas,
> Which, if they had been cut and hung upon
> The snow-white cliffs of fertile Albion,
> Would have allured more to be their winner,
> Than all the diamonds that are hidden in her. (I.1.481–6)

Browne underlines the eroticism of the passage by referring to Remond's hair as 'ensnaring nets.' The image is a commonplace in Renaissance love poetry, but it is always women's hair that ensnares men's hearts. This stress on Remond's power to attract men is bolstered by allusion to a passage from the famous description of Leander in Marlowe's *Hero and Leander*:

> His dangling tresses that were never shorne,
> Had they beene cut, and unto *Colchos* borne,
> Would have allur'd the vent'rous youth of *Greece*,
> To hazard more, than for the golden Fleece. (55–8)[41]

Both as an allusion to Marlowe (the use of feminine rhyme in lines 485 and 486 also recalls *Hero and Leander*) and as an allusion to a passage remarkable for its celebration of male beauty, Browne's intertextuality strengthens the eroticism of the passage and the fact that Remond, like Leander, appeals to other men. In the descriptions of both Remond and Leander, the emphasis is not so much on a man's beauty as aesthetically pleasing in an abstract sense but as something that will drive other men to action.

As is the case with Leander, however, Remond is interested in women: he loves the shepherdess Fida steadily, although by no means energetically, throughout the poem. Still, his main interest appears to be in Doridon, who is also a poet and also an exceptionally beautiful man. Like Remond, Doridon is interested in women and languidly pursues Marina, the poem's extraordinarily hapless heroine. Doridon is introduced in the second song of the first book and, as Gayley remarks, he 'is described at a length not at all necessary to the narrative.'[42] The description of Doridon, who is introduced as 'a lovely swain' (I.2.405), is characterized by excess, particularly in that it even exceeds the description of Remond in elaboration and in length. While Remond first appears on a bank, Doridon is sitting on a hill. Browne says that it was as if Nature, which 'did hold him/ Her chiefest work' (I.2.408–9), 'thought it fit/ That with inferiors he should never sit' (409–10). Up to this point, it might be assumed that Doridon is set apart from other shepherds because of his poetic excellence, but Browne goes on to say that

> Narcissus' change sure Ovid clean mistook,
> He died not looking in a crystal brook,
> But (as those which in emulation gaze)
> He pin'd to death by looking on this face. (I.2.411–14)

Unlike many commentators on the story of Ovid, Browne clearly understands that Narcissus is not in love with himself but rather with a beautiful man; the myth deals with homoeroticism, not self-love.[43] Browne's change is to suggest that Doridon was the object of Narcissus's love.

Nor is Narcissus alone in his love for Doridon. While Remond is also described as favoured by Nature – 'In framing of whose hand Dame Nature swore/ There never was his like, nor should be more' (I.1.479–80) – and while he is also an object of desire, Doridon is more favoured by Nature and is the object of more desire. Rather than offering a specific description of Doridon's looks, Browne stresses his powers of attraction, which are considerable and impressively wide-ranging. After the reference to Narcissus, Browne cites fish, an eagle, satyrs, fawns, Venus, and Cynthia as all taken by his beauty. Eventually it turns out that

> Lucina at his birth for midwife stuck;
> And Cytherea nurs'd and gave him suck,
> Who to that end, once dove-drawn from the sea,
> Her full paps dropp'd, whence came the milky-way. (I.2.435–8)

Once weaned, Doridon was fed by bees (Browne remarks, 'I know not whether/ They brought, or from his lips did honey gather' [I.2.441–2]), and then by wood nymphs. The profusion of images and the collocation of humans, animals, and immortals make the passage stand out from the rest of the poem. Although much of Britannia's Pastorals is quite elaborate and Browne makes frequent use of classical mythology, the poem as a whole is characterized by a concentration on realistic (given the conventions of early-seventeenth-century pastoral poetry) descriptions of people, places, and emotional states. In this context, the description is striking because of its somewhat self-consciously artistic quality; to use a metaphor in keeping with Britannia's Pastorals, Browne's work is normally about springs and rivers: the description of Doridon is like a baroque fountain.

Browne's allusion to Venus might seem to emphasize Doridon's appeal to women were it not that Venus is presented as his wet nurse, rather than as, for instance, the first of many women who will fall in love with him. Venus usually represents and embodies heteroeroticism, but here she is stripped of her sexuality and represents maternal love. Browne's depiction of Venus creates a notable contrast with Marlowe's presentation of the sole woman in his list of Leander's admirers: 'Faire Cintia wisht, his armes might be her spheare;/ Greefe makes her pale, because she mooves not there' (59–60). Leander's beauty is able to make the virgin goddess lustful, while Doridon's beauty is able to make the goddess of love maternal. Because of this, Doridon appears less like one of the human men Venus was famous for having loved and more like Cupid, Venus's son. Browne is thus able to use Venus in order to stress Doridon's beauty and his erotic appeal without placing him in an explicitly heteroerotic context. Indeed, at the end of the description, Doridon appears to have replaced Venus altogether:

> In brief, if any man were able
> To finish up Apelles's half-done table,
> This boy (the man left out) were fittest sure
> To be the pattern of that portraiture. (I.2.455–8)

The 'half-done table' is a picture of Venus. Browne's strategy in this description is ultimately to emphasize Doridon's beauty and sexuality – and, significantly, his suitability as a subject for art – at Venus's expense: it is now he, rather than Venus, who will be the example of all that is desirable. In a move that is typical of *Britannia's Pastorals* as a whole, masculine beauty is preferred to feminine beauty.

The power of masculine beauty is first demonstrated in Browne's reference to Narcissus; he returns to this theme immediately following this allusion when he tells us that '[t]he eagle, highest bred,/ Was taking him once up for Ganymede' (I.2.417–18). The replacement of Ganymede with Doridon serves to connect him to the most famous example of homoerotic beauty in the classical tradition. Even more sexual is Browne's presentation of Apollo as Doridon's admirer, a reference that is at least as excessive as the reference to Venus, although it is significant that the reference to Apollo is not sexual in a celebratory manner:

> The chiefest cause the sun did condescend
> To Phaeton's request was to this end
> That whilst the other did his horses rein,
> He might slide from his sphere and court this swain. (I.2.449–52)

It is surely significant that Browne balances the allusion to a goddess with one to a god: his stress here is on Doridon's appeal as universal. Apart from the gender balance, however, the two allusions are very different, as is the nature of Doridon's appeal to each of the deities. As was the case with the story about the origin of the Milky Way, this passage presents Doridon as a figure of cosmic importance, but while Venus's love for Doridon makes her maternal, Apollo's love almost leads to the destruction of the world. It is not just that Apollo's love for Doridon lead to Phaeton's disastrous career, but also that in general his loves for men, the most famous of which are for Hyacinth and for Cyparissus, tend to lead to elegies. Browne's pastoral poem also leads to elegies. Although the first elegy in *Britannia's Pastorals* comes at the beginning of the last song of the first book (this is the long elegy, which Browne adapted from his first published poem, for Henry, Prince of Wales, who had died the year before the publication of Book I, at I.5.163–306), as Moorman notes, the second book is characterized by a 'quiet pastoral tone, tinged with a subdued melancholy.'[44]

After a proem in which Browne expresses his hopes for his poem, Book II returns to the story of the unfortunate Marina, who has been stranded at sea and ends up on the shores of the island of Mona. The first thing she sees when she looks around is an inscription on a rock:

> She, on a marble rock at hand beheld,
> In characters deep cut with iron stroke,
> A shepherd's moan, which read by her, thus spoke. (II.1.239–41)

What follows is an elegy in five eight-line stanzas for a man who died at sea. This is the second elegy in *Britannia's Pastorals* (the first, as I pointed out earlier, comes in the fifth song of the first book); what is remarkable is not the presence of elegies but the fact that both are spoken by women. Yet while the first one appears to be a spontaneous utterance on the part of the grieving Idya, the second is a performance of a piece written in stone. To some extent, Browne appears to be trying to remove the pastoral elegy from its homosocial context, something paradoxically clearer in this case than in the earlier one, because although the second elegy is by a man and for a man, it only finds expression when read by a woman. This is the point of line 241: what is originally a 'moan' becomes speech only because of female agency. A little later, Marina reads another inscription for the dead man but is interrupted when she hears 'a woman cry: "Ah well-a-day,/ What shall I do? Go home, or fly, or stay"' (321–2). In this scene, Browne presents the traditional elegy – that is, a man's expression of a grief for the death of another man – in a remarkably distanced way. The reader is distanced from the elegy in two ways: the inscriptions are read by a woman who has no personal connection to the dead man and there is a contrast, implicit but unavoidable, between the grief of an unknown man for another unknown man and the very real and immediate danger faced by two women in the poem's narrative present. The second way is perhaps the more important, as Browne could be understood as saying that female concerns are of more poetic consequence than male ones.

The man who expresses his grief is not really unknown. The first stanza of the elegy ends 'But silence on each dale and mountain dwell,/ Whilst Willy bids his friend and joy farewell' (247–8). Each of the succeeding stanzas also ends with a line naming Willy as the dead man's chief mourner. Willy is William Browne. He had already used this name in the *Shepherd's Pipe* and the character makes an appearance in the third song of the second book. The name can hardly be said to count as a pseudonym; more importantly, it is not really a conventional pastoral name even in English pastoral. The emergence of William Browne as a character within the narrative seems to signal a more personal note, one that, like his name, cannot quite be integrated into the pastoral framework. Neither can the grief: when Willy appears as a character there is no reference to his grief and no explanation of who Alexis is, although Gayley identifies him as 'Browne's favourite companion, William Ferrar, the Alexis of the pastoral circle.'[45] While Spenser's depiction of a heteroerotic Corydon in the sixth book of the *Faerie Queene* demonstrates that even names famous for their homoerotic associations can be heterosexualized, Browne does nothing to make the reader forget the associations with the beloved young man of the second eclogue. The name Alexis does not occur in the elegy, however; only in the six-line epitaph that is also carved into a rock. Conversely, the name Willy does not occur in the epitaph, which stresses the general character of the grief for Alexis's death: he is mourned by 'men' (316), 'each mermaid' (317), and 'the clouds' and 'the Earth' (318). There is thus a contrast between the elegy, which concentrates almost exclusively on Willy's grief, and the more impersonal elegy. The fact that the two men are not named together further distinguishes the two. An elegy is an attempt to turn grief into art; the epitaph represents a further step into art (as the fact that the epitaph is 'inlaid with gold' [311] suggests) and away from the potentially disturbing story of Alexis and Willy.

The melancholy that Moorman characterized as subdued could also be said to subdue in that it ultimately replaces almost all of the narrative momentum in *Britannia's Pastorals* (never particularly brisk in any case). Remond and Doridon are perhaps the two most obvious casual-

ties here, as they never assume the prominence which the elaboration
of the passages that introduce them would seem to indicate. In fact, to
the educated reader, the introduction in adjacent passages of two beautiful male characters would seem to signal a love affair or at least a story
of male friendship reminiscent of Book IV of the *Faerie Queene*. Browne's
presentation of these characters gestures towards this sort of homoerotic
(or at least homosocial) space, but he never quite provides it, and
Remond and Doridon remain just good friends, perhaps, as Gayley
suggests, on the model of Beaumont and Fletcher, of whom John Aubrey
memorably said:

> There was a wonderfull consimility of phansey between him and Mr John
> Fletcher, which caused that dearnesse of friendship between them ... They
> lived together in the Banke side, not far from the Play-House, both batchelors;
> lay together; had one Wench in the house between them, which they did so
> admire; the same cloathes and cloake, &c.; between them.[46]

Remond and Doridon do not share a Wench, but their tepid heteroeroticism is certainly subordinated to their 'consimility' and they tend
to appear in the poem together rather than alone or with the women
they love. Indeed, *Britannia's Pastorals* tends to alternate between scenes
in which the male characters are prominent and scenes in which the
female ones are, as if Browne were unable to write the truly heteroerotic
pastoral that the beginning of the poem leads readers to expect. This
narrative situation recalls the *Shepheardes Calender*'s opposition of the
all-male pastoral setting and the world of women just beyond its borders.

Remond and Doridon's most interesting appearance in the second
book comes when they happen upon a beautiful young man who is,
predictably enough, weeping. The scene occurs in the second song of
the book, much of which is concerned with the wanderings of Remond
and Doridon, who have been brought together by their shared misery:

> Love-wounded Doridon entreats him then
> That he might be his partner, since no men
> Had cases liker; he with him would go,
> Weep when he wept, and sigh when he did so.
> I, quoth the boy, will sing thee songs of love. (II.2.469–73)

These lines – and much of the rest of this passage – gesture towards
homoerotic space, just as the content and placement of the introduc-

tions of these characters do. Doridon's invitation appears at first to be romantic in nature. At the end of the first section of this invitation, however, he says that Remond should sing too: 'when thou plain'st thy Fida's loss, will I/ Echo the same, and with mine own supply' (483–4). The picture of two men each singing songs of love recalls the singing and piping of Colin and the shepherd of the ocean in 'Colin Clouts Come Home Againe.'[47] As was the case with Spenser's characters, Browne's shepherds are also like parallel lines that can never meet rather than like the shepherds of classical pastoral, who are engaged with each other whether in love or in competition or both. The lines I have just cited also draw our attention to the process of substitution. While the obvious meaning in the context is that once Remond has sung about his woman, Doridon will sing about his, the substitution can also be understood as the substitution of female love objects for male ones in the narrative of *Britannia's Pastorals* as a whole and, more generally, as the substitution of heteroeroticism for homoeroticism in Renaissance pastoral.

The two shepherds wander until they enter a beautiful valley and hear a human sound: 'A deep-fetch'd sigh (which seem'd of power to kill/ The breast that held it) pierc'd the list'ning wood' (584–5). When they explore, they find a beautiful youth:

> Here sat the lad, of whom I think of old
> Virgil's prophetic spirit had foretold,
> Who whilst Dame Nature for her cunning's sake
> A male or female doubted which to make,
> And to adorn him more than all assay'd,
> This pretty youth was almost made a maid. (599–604)

The reference is to an epigram no longer believed to be by Virgil: 'Dum dubitat Natura marem faciatne puellam,/ Factus es, O pulcher, paene puella puer' (While Nature hesitated to make a boy or a girl, you almost became a girl, o beautiful boy).[48] The second line of the epigram could also be translated 'you became, o beautiful one, a boy who is almost a girl.' Browne situates the youth between masculine and feminine and goes on to compare him to Amphion and Orpheus and finally to Adonis in a passage that begins with an allusion to Ovid. While the second book of *Britannia's Pastorals* is more Ovidian than the first in any case, in this passage, as in the descriptions of Remond and Doridon, Browne uses allusions to classical literature and mythology to heighten the eroticism of the passage. Given that in the narrative two men are looking for two women, I feel the youth is intended to remind the reader of the myth of the origin of heteroeroticism propounded by Aristophanes in the *Symposium*, in which heteroerotic coupling is caused by the separation of beings originally composed of one man and one woman fused together. In this reading, the androgynous youth could be an emblem of the nature of Remond and Doridon's quest, or a warning about the effeminizing nature of heteroeroticism, or even the thing for which they should really be searching.

These considerations do not appear to occur to the two shepherds. Remond begins by asking the youth what the matter is, in a passage that recalls the questions posed to the dying Daphnis in the first idyll. Like those questions, these are beside the mark. Remond seems incapable of believing that someone as prosperous as the youth appears to be could have any real trouble and he launches into a long and irritatingly sententious speech that recalls Daphnis's turn from seduction to advice in 'The Second Dayes Lamentation.' He does ask one interesting question, however:

> Or have the Parcae with unpartial knife
> Left some friend's body tenantless of life,
> And thou bemoan'st that Fate in his youth's morn
> O'ercast with clouds his light but newly born. (677–80)

The youth does not respond to this or any of the other questions, and after a few pious reflections about death Remond concludes his speech with a long denunciation of avarice (687–732). Almost all of his speech is concerned with material possessions, even though it seems highly unlikely that these could be the source of the youth's sorrow. The suggestion that the youth is mourning a friend is abandoned, but this is the only possibility in keeping with the tenor of Book II as a whole and, as even a slight knowledge of pastoral poetry will indicate, the one that is most likely to be true. It does not occur to Remond that the youth might be grieving over an unhappy love affair with a woman, even though this is the case with him and Doridon. The point of Remond's speech – a speech that is completely unexpected from what we have seen of him until this point in the poem – is to demonstrate his difference from this beautiful and lachrymose young man, a description that would in fact suit either Remond or Doridon perfectly. Remond's refusal to make common cause with the youth is especially marked since it comes so soon after his joining with Doridon. The idea, as I take it, is to minimize the sort of homosocial identification that has traditionally been the basis of pastoral.

The youth does not respond to Remond except to shake his head and then weep again. Next, Doridon tries to draw him out and his speech is markedly different from his friend's. He begins by commenting on the youth's beauty:

Tell us (quoth Doridon), thou fairer far
Than he whose chastity made him a star,
More fit to throw the wounding shafts of Love
Than follow sheep, and pine here in a grove. (739–42)

Remond also comments, although more briefly, on the youth's beauty at the beginning of his speech – 'let no tear/ Cloud those sweet beauties in thy face' (655–6) – but Doridon's introduction is interesting because of the contrast between the reference to Hippolytus, who exemplifies chastity, and the recognition of the power of the youth's beauty. Doridon urges the youth to speak because '[h]e oft finds aid that doth disclose his grief' (744). Unlike Remond, he is concerned to stress the connection between himself and the youth:

Believe me, shepherd, we are men no less
Free from the killing throes of heaviness
Than thou art here, and but this diff'rence sure,
That use hath made us apter to endure. (751–4)

Although his presentation of himself and Remond as more experienced than the youth recalls the sententiousness of Remond's speech, Doridon explicitly presents their wisdom as the only difference. He is thus closer to the pastoral tradition of homosociality among shepherds, although even here the age difference, which is not eroticized, functions as a way to limit, if not to refuse utterly, any homosocial solidarity.

Doridon's speech is interrupted by the sound of a horn, which is followed by a galloping stag and then by 'a gallant dame, fair as the morn' (787). As she runs by she reaches out and rips a branch from a tree near the three men without slowing down. The youth runs towards her, but she is too fast and he is forced to content himself with

the bough the huntress tore,
He suck'd it with his mouth, and kiss'd it o'er
A hundred times. (827–9)

Then he once again bursts into the tears that are, as he refuses to speak, his only means of communication throughout the scene. In conjunction with his sucking of the branch, his muteness makes him appear infantile as he appears to be a pre-verbal creature with purely oral pleasures. His infantilization is heightened by the contrast between him and the woman, who is not only active, but who is a hunter, a pursuit that is traditionally masculine, as Browne's use of the adjective 'gallant' suggests. The episode seems intended to recall the story of Belphoebe and Timias in the *Faerie Queene*, but the difference in context changes our understanding of the scene. Timias is undone by his love for Belphoebe, but he is still Arthur's squire and, in any case, their story is part of a larger story in which both the male and female characters tend to do things appropriate to their gender and even women like Belphoebe and Britomart are clearly marked as exceptions to a very strong rule. In *Britannia's Pastorals*, however, no such situation obtains and there is no male heroism with which to contrast the youth's behaviour. The world of the poem is one in which men are purely reactive. Browne presents activities normally considered typical of women or children as typical of men. Thus, the mute and weeping youth is not unusual, as he may at first appear, but rather typical of the male characters in the poem.

This point is underlined by what happens next in the scene. As the youth continues to weep and to embrace the tree, Remond and Doridon also abandon speech:

> the shepherds by
> Forgot to help him, and lay down to cry:
> 'For 'tis impossible a man should be
> Griev'd to himself, or fail of company.' (833–6)

The three men are now finally united in the sort of homosocial solidarity that both Remond and Doridon were earlier concerned to rule out, or at least to limit. There is even a certain homoeroticism in the lines that follow. Browne describes the youth as having

> all his body bare,
> Save that a wreath of ivy twist did hide
> Those parts which Nature would not have descried,
> And the long hair that curled from his head
> A grassy garland rudely covered –
> But shepherds, I have wrong'd you; 'tis now late,

For see our maid stands hollowing on yond gate.
'Tis supper-time withal. (II.2.844–51)

Narrative necessity, here presented as a woman who represents the domestic sphere (like Thestylis in the second ecologue), interrupts the tantalizing description of the youth. Given that Browne wants to end the second song so that he can return to the story of Marina, the interruption is a further demonstration (like the fact that women deliver the poem's elegies) that the pastoral is primarily concerned with heteroeroticism. This demonstration is somewhat undercut by the fact that Browne's interruption of himself is modelled on the passage in *Hero and Leander* in which the speaker interrupts his increasingly breathless description of Leander's beauty by saying 'but my rude pen, / Can hardly blazon foorth the loves of men' (I.69–70); but in the remainder of *Britannia's Pastorals* (including the third book, which was lost for over 200 years), Browne presents a pastoral world that resembles 'Colin Clout's Come Home Againe' in its balancing of the genders.

By this point in *Britannia's Pastorals* and in English pastoral as a whole, mourning is all that is left of the homosociality and homoeroticism of classical pastoral. Although mourning always formed part of the pastoral, the mourning here is inarticulate: when Browne described Willy's elegy as a 'shepherd's moan' he was using a common metaphor, but the metaphor becomes literal. Conversely, we could say that the literal collapse of Remond and Doridon suggests the metaphorical collapse of the tradition of homoerotic pastoral. In that tradition, mourning marked the end of homoerotic space. In *Britannia's Pastorals*, homoerotic space disappears altogether, leaving only the mourning. This mourning is increasingly likely to be without a clear referent, a grief that dare not speak its name. The elegy and epitaph for Alexis that can only be known because Marina reads them and the inarticulate distress of the youth that is explained, it would appear, by the 'gallant dame' point to the diminution of pastoral homosociality and its replacement by a situation in which women are essential both to narrative movement and to understanding that movement.

CHAPTER FIVE

Idylls and Kings

Up to this point, my focus in discussing Renaissance literature has been on its use of the classical pastoral. I want to turn now to Renaissance responses to the issues posed by the end of the *Aeneid*. Of course, the influence of the *Aeneid* can be detected almost everywhere in Renaissance literature, but my interest in this chapter is not on specific versions of scenes, characters, or even turns of phrases from Virgil's epic but rather on how his depiction of the place of homoeroticism was influential. In my reading of the *Aeneid*, its ending could be taken to suggest that while homoeroticism is perhaps necessary for a band of men struggling to establish a kingdom, the kingdom itself depends on bonds between men and women. Heteroeroticism would then be the mode of kingship and of courts and, in a larger sense, of the civil society toward which the *Aeneid* moves. The great Renaissance epics such as the *Faerie Queene* or *Orlando Furioso* or *Gerusalemme Liberata* are all carefully situated in the world of the court and heterosexual romance is an important aspect of these poems. Even the military sphere is made more heteroerotic by the presence of female warriors like Britomart, Bradamante, and Clorinda, who fight like men but who are destined to love men (unlike Camilla, their predecessor in the *Aeneid*). The literary settings I have discussed up to this point are presented as temporary: they exist as places to which the heroes and heroines may go – indeed, must go – and that may be ideal in some sense, but that are increasingly remote from the centre of action.

An example of this development is the role of the pastoral world in Book VI of the *Faerie Queene*. In the proem, Spenser laments the decline of courtesy, which is the book's subject:

But in the triall of true curtesie,
Is now so farre from that, which then it was,
That it indeed is nought but forgerie. (5.1–3)

Spenser's appeal to an earlier and better time is a conventional part of this sort of poem. Later in Book VI, Sir Calidore finds himself in a pastoral world and stays with the old shepherd Meliboe. The contrast between Calidore, a name that suggests medieval courtly romance, and Meliboe, a version of the name of the shepherd in Virgil's first eclogue, helps to make the point that the pastoral is now associated with the margins of the world. Enchanted with the peace of the pastoral world (and with the beauty of Meliboe's supposed daughter Pastorella), the knight expresses a desire to stay in this idyllic setting:

That euen I which daily doe behold
The glorie of the great, mongst whom I won,
And haue prou'd, what happinesse ye hold
In this small plot of your dominion,
Now loath great Lordship and ambition;
And wish the heauens so much had graced mee,
As graunt me liue in like condition;
Or that my fortunes might transposed bee
From pitch of higher place, vnto this low degree. (IX.28.1–9)

In response, Meliboe stresses the wisdom of the heavens and tells Calidore to be content with his lot: 'But fittest is, that all contented rest/ With that they hold' (IX.29.8–9). Meliboe's faith in the divine ordering of human affairs works to limit pastoral space further. Calidore is slow to learn the lesson, however, and he lingers in the pastoral world until he is forced to return to his knightly duties by the raid of a band of thieves in which 'Old *Meliboe* is slaine' (XI.18.4) and Pastorella is kidnapped. Calidore sets out to rescue her with another shepherd:

Both clad in shepheards weeds agreeably,
And both with shepheards hookes: But *Calidore*
Had vnderneath, him armed priuily. (XI.36.2–4)

The things by which we recognize a shepherd are now only a disguise, a fact that parallels the increasing allegorical use of pastoral in the Renaissance. Just as Calidore is really prepared to fight, so the pastoral is said to be really about politics or church government. His foray is successful, and almost as soon as Pastorella has been rescued she learns that she is not a shepherdess at all but a noblewoman. Her restoration to her proper status means that she is now a suitable wife for Calidore and there will be no need for him to return to the pastoral world.

I believe that the lesson Calidore learns is intended to be learned by everyone and that it is not only the pastoral world that is marginal, but also the military world. Although the episode demonstrates the need for knights, even this need is temporary. The fighting in Book VI is necessary, as the rescue of Pastorella demonstrates, but this fighting takes place on the margins of the courtly sphere that is the real centre of the *Faerie Queene* as well as its logical conclusion; likewise, the pastoral world is necessary to the economy of the court, and, in real life, to the economy of Renaissance England, but it exists on the margins. The court – a place devoted to heteroerotic narratives, unlike the all-male world of the army or of the (traditional) pastoral, and which in Spenser's time was presided over by a woman – is the real story. Spenser's version of pastoral reaffirms the centrality of the court, and although the proem to Book VI hints at problems in the court, the story told in the book itself upholds the court as the place to which all stories (both the narrative of the *Faerie Queene* as a whole and the stories of Calidore and Pastorella) must be referred. The genres of the pastoral and the epic, which were in any case becoming increasingly likely throughout the Renaissance to give prominence to female characters, are firmly subordinated to genres that are inherently focused on both men and women.

This, at least, is how things are supposed to work. In this chapter, my interest is on texts that show the breakdown of this order. Beaumont and Fletcher's *The Maid's Tragedy* and Shakespeare's *The Winter's Tale* both dramatize challenges to the accepted order. In these plays, the presence of elements and characters that recall the all-male world of classical pastoral and epic appears as the return of the repressed. In *The Maid's Tragedy*, Melantius, the representative of the all-male army that maintains the peace upon which civil society depends, returns to court and refuses to be controlled by the laws that govern this society. In *The Winter's Tale*, the danger to civil order comes from the traces of the all-male pastoral and the interference of those traces with the reproductive imperative. To some extent, both plays link social instability at the very highest level with generic disturbances: *The Maid's Tragedy* tends to turn into a play about war, as the people who rule the court of Rhodes become unable to prevent war from overwhelming them; Leontes's pastoral memories threaten to turn *The Winter's Tale* into a pastoral drama permanently. While the ending of Beaumont and Fletcher's play is ambiguous and the order that is restored at the end of the play seems unlikely to last (partly because Melantius is still alive), Shakespeare is ultimately able to present a pastoral that has been largely purged of homoeroticism.

The Maid's Tragedy

In his discussion of *Troilus and Cressida*, Mario DiGangi remarked that 'the most sustained dramatic representations of military homoeroticism appear not in this one play by Shakespeare but in the less frequently discussed body of works by John Fletcher and his collaborators.'[1] Although he does not go on to analyse *The Maid's Tragedy*, his comment is relevant to my discussion. Beaumont and Fletcher's focus in this play is on the collision between military and civilian life. The passage from military to political rule (which is also a passage from a society structured by homosocial bonds to one structured by heterosocial bonds between men and women) is usually understood to be a decisive moment in the history of a people, the moment at which the tribe or clan becomes a nation. Graham L. Hammill has recently said that

> this passage is not one that happens between epochs. There is not an epoch of the battlefield and an epoch of its internalization ... [W]ar bears an 'extimate' relation to civility that is constitutive of civilized psychic space: war appears to be intimate to the civilized subject because it is what the state wants most to exteriorize in its monopolization of violence.[2]

When the soldier Melantius returns to Rhodes at the beginning of *The Maid's Tragedy*, he brings with him a vision of society as rooted in passionate attachments between men; he also serves as a reminder (both to the other characters in the play and to the audience) that civil society depends on this 'monopolization of violence.' Both these things will turn out to be inimical to the maintenance of the status quo in Rhodes.

The play begins with a speech that simultaneously acknowledges the existence of the state-sponsored violence on which the state depends and seeks to contain the threat potentially (and soon actually) posed by that violence. When Lysippus, the king's brother, welcomes Melantius at the beginning, he clearly separates the political and military spheres:

> Noble *Melantius*, the land by me
> Welcomes thy vertues home to *Rhodes*,
> Thou that with blood abroad buyest us our peace.[3]

The remarkably heavy use of first- and second-person pronouns (me / thy / Thou / us) in opposition in these lines emphasizes the distinction Lysippus wishes to make between abroad and at home – this is what Hammill refers to as the exteriorization of war. Furthermore, in using the verb 'buyest' Lysippus presents warfare as if it were a kind of international trade. In these ways, he seeks to neutralize the threat represented by the return of the soldier, of that which has been repressed so that an essentially violent society can represent itself as an essentially pacific one. The fact that Rhodes's enemy is never specified is a telling omission: the warfare that has been keeping Melantius busy thus appears not as an extraordinary circumstance but rather as the natural state of affairs. The action of *The Maid's Tragedy* shows that the separation Lysippus is trying to make cannot be maintained, as John F. Danby points out in his characterization of the play: '[Beaumont] is interested in *situations* – in those situations of conflict which rival loyalties bring along with them, which circumstances alone can manoeuvre into existence, and which choices can only perpetuate or aggravate.'[4] The world of the play is, it appears, a permanently fractured one, and I shall argue that Beaumont and Fletcher are pessimistic about the possibility of a solution.[5] As Danby suggests, the situation will continue and it may even get worse, but it will not get better.

The first example of one of these 'situations of conflict' comes in the very first scene when Melantius reproaches his brother:

> thou art faultie,
> I sent for thee to exercise thine armes
> With me at *Patria*, thou camst not *Diphilus*:
> Twas ill. (I.28–31)

Diphilus responds, '[M]y excuse/ Is my Kings strict command' (I.i.31–2). As Eileen Allman remarks, the king's overruling of Melantius 'clearly usurps the elder brother's rights,'[6] and the usurpation is perhaps even more serious since the place in which they were to meet has as its name the Latin word for 'fatherland.' The situation in this passage is a development of the issue raised by Lysippus's speech: while that passage enforced a distinction between the army and the court, this passage shows that the distinction is hierarchical and that the court is dominant. As Allman points out, the primary conflict here is between the obligations of a brother and the obligation of a subject, but the fact that Diphilus was ordered to remain in Rhodes to attend a wedding is also important, as this sets up a contrast between the military world, which is all male, and the world of court, in which alliances between men and women are celebrated, as well as a further contrast between Melantius's ideas of duty and the king's use of his power to serve his sexual needs. In her discussion of Renaissance political drama, Rebecca Bushnell says that 'the equation of the tyrant's sexual will with his political power represents his private desire as political acts.'[7] *The Maid's Tragedy* is concerned with precisely this conflation (or confusion) between the private and the political. The resulting mingling of private and public selves is crucial to Melantius and to the other characters as well, since it creates a space in which bonds between men that might as a rule be relegated to the military (exteriorization) or to the private spheres (interiorization) can determine actions that will affect the kingdom as a whole.

Melantius states his belief about the basis for connections among men in his response to Lysippus's courtly speech. This response, which contrasts strongly with the passage only a few lines earlier in which Strato characterizes masques as 'tied to rules/ Of flatterie' (I.i.10–11), reveals the philosophy by which he acts:

> My Lord, my thankes, but these scratcht limbes of mine,
> Have spoke my love and truth unto my friends,
> More then my tongue ere could, my mind's the same
> It ever was to you; where I finde worth
> I love the keeper, till he let it goe,
> And then I follow it. (I.i.20–5)

Both the preference of deeds to words and, especially, the idea that love and, by extension, loyalty are elective will turn out to be inimical to the ordered hierarchy of Rhodes. In Melantius's system, 'worth' and all the things implied by that word must not only be earned but also repeatedly demonstrated. One of the important implications of Melantius's speech is that it reveals a preference for elective bonds over established and codified bonds like the one between a king and a subject. As Shullenberger remarks, 'Melantius claims the right to choose, at any time, whom he will fight for.'[8] This claim is a logical extension of the sentiments espoused in the passage I have just quoted and, as the events of the rest of this first scene reveal, it will increasingly bring Melantius into conflict with the king and the society he is supposed to serve. Rather than being a man who has a clearly defined place in a hierarchical society, Melantius is in many ways a free agent.

It is Amintor who is the object of Melantius's love, as he reveals in his speech praising him and giving the history of their friendship:

> when he was a boy,
> As oft as I return'd (as without boast,
> I brought home conquest) he would gaze upon me,
> And view me round, to finde in what one limbe
> The vertue lay to doe those things he heard:
> Then would he wish to see my sword, and feele
> The quicknesse of the edge, and in his hand
> Weigh it. (I.i.49–56)

The erotically charged nature of this passage is not diminished either by the fact that he began talking about Amintor by asking if he had been married yet, or by the entry of Aspatia, whom he believes to be Amintor's wife, right after this speech.[9] Aspatia is the maid whose tragedy Beaumont and Fletcher tell, but as Philip J. Finkelpearl points out, the title can be considered to be ambiguous: '[S]ome have suggested that there are really two maids, ironically including Evadne with Aspatia. And I would suggest the presence of a third maid, the innocent, virginal husband Amintor.'[10] That is, not only could the word 'maid' refer to a female character who is not a virgin, it could even refer to a male character. Thinking of the title in this way allows us to see that gender roles are more fluid in *The Maid's Tragedy* than might be expected; in this respect they resemble the fluidity of relationships adumbrated by Melantius in his response to Lysippus. To a certain extent, then, Beaumont and Fletcher present both positions in the gender system and positions in the political hierarchy as labile. As Lisa Hopkins remarks, '[T]he text's attempts to separate masculinity from femininity are compromised at every turn'[11] – so much so, in fact, that much of the play's ending is concerned with attempting to restore conventional gender roles.

We are now accustomed to see this sort of flexibility in social arrangements in a positive light, but that this is not the case here is made sufficiently clear by the complications that follow on Aspatia's entrance, which I shall briefly go over. When Melantius congratulates Aspatia on her marriage, she thinks he is being sarcastic and says,

> My hard fortunes
> Deserve not scorne, for I was never proud
> When they were good. (I.i.63–4)

After this she leaves the stage. Once Melantius is made to understand that it is Evadne who has just been married to Amintor, he worries that since Aspatia's father, Calianax, already dislikes him he may think

> that I would take
> So base revenges as to scorne the state
> Of his neglected daughter: holds he still
> His greatnesse with the King? (I.i.83–6)

After Lysippus says that he does, Melantius ends this exchange by saying, 'She has a brother under my command/ Like her, a face as womanish as hers' (I.i.105–6). Not surprisingly, the information given in this passage turns out to be essential to the development of the plot and, in particular, to the ending of the play, but it also serves to emphasize the connections among characters: Aspatia may be like Amintor, as Finkelpearl suggests, but she is also like her brother, who serves Melantius – a further sign of the interpenetration of the court and the army; her father is both Melantius's enemy and, like him, one of the king's most trusted servants; and finally (and crucially for the purposes of the plot), Melantius's sister is Aspatia's rival. *The Maid's Tragedy* takes place in a world in which the connections among people that might be presumed to create interdependence actually promote conflict, since there is, it appears, no fixed structure into which the characters and their relationships can be placed and since to injure one person is to offend all those who are connected to that person.

The first example of the military homoeroticism DiGangi mentioned comes in Melantius's speech at Amintor's entrance: 'I might run fiercely, not more hastily/ Upon my foe: I love thee well *Amintor*' (I.i.109–10).[12] When Melantius tries to define his love he falters: 'Thou art my friend, – but my disordred speech/ Cuts off my love' (I.i.113–14). In an interesting feminist analysis of the play, Cristina Leòn Alfar says that this scene is 'significant ... because Melantius's speech about his friend is charged with tension which suggests that an erotic homosocial bond between men acts as a foundation for the patrilineal order.'[13] Although erotic homosociality may indeed serve the patrilineal order, here I think Beaumont and Fletcher's emphasis is on the threat of disorder posed by this bond. In fact, the word 'disordred' is significant. It seems that Melantius has the same problem faced by historians and literary critics today in that he is unable to find a suitable term to describe a strongly emotional relationship between men, although his characterization of his speech may represent one solution to this problem, since 'disordred speech' recalls E.K.'s famous reference, which I discussed in the previous chapter, to 'disorderly love, which the learned call pæderastice.' The disorderly nature of Melantius's speech is a sign of the disorderly nature of his love for Amintor – disorderly both in that it goes against Christian ideas about sexuality (which is what E.K. meant) and in that it threatens the order of the world of *The Maid's Tragedy*. In the context of the play, however, I would agree with Leòn Alfar that homoeroticism is not in itself a sign of disorder; rather, it is the conjunction of homoeroticism with Melantius's unwillingness to remain part of a hierarchical social order that does not meet his ideas of worth which produces the disorder that ultimately overwhelms the world of the play. This conjunction makes it impossible for Melantius to find a word – other than friendship, which is obviously inadequate – to express his love. An emotion that cannot be named by a society is, as the events of the play demonstrate, one that cannot be used by that society. Given Melantius's love for Amintor, his theories about worth, and the special circumstances of the plot, this 'erotic homosocial bond' undermines patrilineal order rather than serving as its foundation.

In the scene that follows, the masque that celebrates Amintor and Evadne's wedding turns out to be preoccupied with questions of disorder. As most commentators on *The Maid's Tragedy* have pointed out, the masque is highly unsuitable for a wedding.[14] Before the masque even begins, there is a heated quarrel between Melantius and Calianax. The fact that the former predicted this quarrel in the first scene of the play suggests that the potential for violence in the complex interrelationships of the play is already being realized, although at this point the violence is only threatened and is, I think, essentially comic since Calianax is primarily a figure of fun. Nevertheless, when the king enters with Evadne and Aspatia he comments on the unsuitability of fighting at a wedding celebration:

> *King.   Melantius* thou art welcome, and my love
> Is with thee still, but this is not a place
> To brable in, – *Calianax*, joyne hands.
> *Calianax.*   He shall not have mine hand.

King.   This is no time
To force you too't, I doe love you both,
Calianax you looke well to your office,
And you *Melantius* are welcome home, –
Begin the maske. (I.ii.99–106)

It is obviously significant that when we first see the king, the central figure in the society of *The Maid's Tragedy* and the person whose presence is supposed to ensure stability, we see him reacting to the animosity of his subjects. Furthermore, the exchange reveals that he is not even able to control that animosity: he quickly gives up his attempt to enforce cordiality and, in an action that recalls Lysippus's first speech to Melantius, resorts to reminding the two men of their function.

The conclusion of the king's speech suggests that one of the purposes of the masque is to cover up the dissensions of the court, and the content of the masque itself would seem to support this view. Although it is ostensibly about the marriage, the masque is primarily concerned with Boreas's interruption of the festivities planned by Cinthia and Night. Cinthia orders Neptune to summon the winds, with the exception of Boreas:

Too foule for our intensions as he was,
Still keepe him fast chain'd, we must have none here
But vernall blasts and gentle winds appeare. (I.ii.175–7)

Boreas does escape, however, and Cinthia is forced to summon Neptune's aid. At the conclusion of the masque, Boreas is presumably still at large, since the story ends when the returning day puts Night and Cinthia to flight. In the masque, as in the king's speech to Melantius and Calianax before it, authority seems to be ineffectual. If we read the masque allegorically we can substitute Melantius, who will also 'swell .../ And win upon the Iland' (I.ii.261–2), for Boreas, the rude north wind too harsh for a wedding. There is another kind of substitution in this scene as well, one we can see in the words with which Melantius greets Evadne before the masque: 'Sister I joy to see you, and your choyce,/ You lookt with my eies when you tooke that man' (I.ii.107–8). The marriage of Evadne and Amintor could then be seen as a substitute for the impossible marriage of Melantius and Amintor. Here, a brother makes way for a sister; as Hopkins suggests, this action is reversed near the end of the masque, when Cinthia sees the approach of day and says, 'I must downe/ And give my brother place' (I.ii.264–5).[15] Alternatively, Cinthia's speech may signal not a reversal, but rather an indication that Evadne's new position as the most important person in her husband's life will not last long and that Melantius will regain his primacy in Amintor's affections.

The next scene demonstrates that Evadne certainly has no desire to play a part in her husband's emotional life or, indeed, in his sexual life either. When Amintor learns that she has vowed never to have sex with him, he bursts out into a condemnation of marriage. After saying to Hymen, '[W]e will scorne thy lawes' (II.i.218), Amintor angrily proposes a new way of living:

> If we doe lust, we'le take the next we meet,
> Serving our selves as other creatures doe,
> And never take note of the female more,
> Nor of her issue. (II.i.224–7)

Kathleen McLuskie has said of this passage that 'Amintor quite clearly acknowledges the political connection between the sexual control of women and the maintenance of social order,'[16] and this is certainly true, but what is more at issue here is Evadne's sexual control of herself and of him and – for me at any rate – Amintor's ideas about what will replace the sort of marriage he had expected. He says that men will find sexual satisfaction with whomever is closest and that they will 'never take note of the female more.' As far as I know, no one has pointed out that he does not just propose a world without marriage, but also one in which heterosexuality and even heterosociality are replaced by homosexuality and homosociality: 'the next we meet' must be a male. In other words, Amintor signals, however temporarily, a move from the world represented by Evadne to the world represented by Melantius – precisely the move suggested by the substitutions in the preceding scene. Furthermore, his statement about adoption – 'we will adopt us sonnes,/ Then vertue shall inherit and not blood' (II.i.222–3) – is a variation of the doctrine Melantius proposed at the beginning of the play:

> where I finde worth
> I love the keeper, till he let it goe,
> And then I follow it.

Both men see social relations such as marriage or authority as forms that are meaningless without the content provided by virtue.

The corollary of McLuskie's comment is that a woman whose sexuality cannot be controlled will threaten the social order, and what we see in the play from this point on is a stress on Evadne's subversive power. In her scene with the king the next day, for instance, she reveals that she thinks in much the same way as her brother, although to very different effect. The king is worried that she has actually had sex with her husband and says, 'They that breake word with heaven, will breake agen/ With all the world, and so doest thou with me' (III.i.163–4). The king naively feels that although this marriage is only a façade, a woman should still be true to her man: he does not realize that his undermining of one of the foundations of his society has begun to destabilize everything. Evadne points out that she never promised to love him forever:

> I swore indeed that I would never love
> A man of lower place, but if your fortune
> Should throw you from this hight, I bad you trust
> I would forsake you. (III.i.171–4)

The radical nature of her ideas is underscored by the reference to fortune: in her view of the world, kingship is held by fortune rather than by right. In her discussion of the marriage, Leòn Alfar takes the conventional view of woman as the object of exchange between men,[17] but as Allman points out, 'Evadne's femaleness is a tool of power rather than a connective force.'[18] In what can be seen as a parody of Melantius's own function in the society of the play, Evadne uses her body to serve the king for profit. In very different ways, both she and her brother represent an individualistic philosophy in which one's position in a hierarchy is chosen rather than assigned; they both serve to indicate that the relations of king and subject or man and woman are not fixed in the world of the play.

Hopkins has suggested that Beaumont and Fletcher's desire to undermine gender norms may even have been behind their choice of Rhodes as the play's setting. As she felicitously remarks, 'Rhodes is famous primarily as the location of the Colossus, a gigantic, celebratory image of manhood that was toppled soon after its erection.'[19] The image of the toppled colossus is important to The Maid's Tragedy both as a sign of the instability of gender – the subject that is Hopkins's main concern – and as a sign of the insecurity of monarchy, and I think that in order to emphasize both aspects of the play, Beaumont and Fletcher have recourse to classical literature. While in the first half of the play the chief sign of the instability of gender is Evadne, in the second half the playwrights increasingly concentrate on Melantius and Amintor as evidence of this insecurity of monarchy. In his 1916 article 'On the Sources of *The Maid's Tragedy*' (he concluded that none existed), William Dinsmore Briggs suggested that the two men were based on Harmodius and Aristogeiton.[20] These men were the two famous Athenian lovers, immortalized in a celebrated statue, who plotted to kill the tyrant Hippias and his younger brother Hipparchus, although they only succeeded in killing the latter and were then put to death.[21] Beaumont and Fletcher may have been reminded of the story by the publication in 1603 of Philemon Holland's translation of twenty of Plutarch's essays, a volume that includes 'Of Brotherly Love or Amity' and two essays that refer to the story of Harmodius and Aristogeiton.[22] Both in the setting of their play and in the development of its two principal male characters, then, Beaumont and Fletcher may have intended to draw on classical stories that feature masculine and political insecurity.

In order to show why the story of Harmodius and Aristogeiton is significant for an understanding of *The Maid's Tragedy*, I want to look at the story more closely. Although there was already a great deal of opposition to the tyrant Hippias among the Athenian upper classes, the story begins when Harmodius rejects Hipparchus's advances and Hipparchus plans to insult Harmodius's sister publicly in retaliation. It is this that moves Harmodius and Aristogeiton to take action. The incident highlights various issues that are of importance to Beaumont and Fletcher's play. In the Greek story, political action arises from causes (the pique of a rejected lover, a brother's concern for his sister) that we would be more inclined to classify as personal. Thus, the episode demonstrates the linking of political and personal (and specifically sexual) concerns that is such a prominent feature of *The Maid's Tragedy*. In adapting the story for the purposes of their play, as I believe they did, Beaumont and Fletcher make a number of changes. First of all, they remove the king's brother from the action. Although Lysippus appears throughout the play, he never has much of a role in the development of the plot. By involving the king in the part of the story concerned with sexuality, Beaumont and Fletcher emphasize the connection between politics and sexuality. Second, they make the figure of the sister more prominent. Although her marriage to Amintor does give him and Melantius an official relationship, Evadne's role in the play is not merely that of a conduit for relations between men, as was the case with the shadowy figure of Harmodius's sister, and her own actions dictate the development of the story. This change in the sister's role is connected to a third change: the playwrights remove the overt homoeroticism of the relationship between their two protagonists and thus bring their play into line with the moral strictures of their own period. Nevertheless, although Beaumont and Fletcher emphasize the familial connection of the conspirators, I think it is clear that what was homoeroticism in the original is still present in the play, if only in a covert form.

Perhaps the biggest difference between the historical episode and Beaumont and Fletcher's recension of it is that while Harmodius appears to have found no difficulty in combining his love for Aristogeiton with his duty to his sister, once Evadne's true relation to the king is known, Melantius's love for Amintor and his duty as her brother are presented as being irreconcilable. Indeed, the crucial question throughout the middle of the play is precisely the relative importance of elective and familial relationships, particularly since Amintor's marriage to Evadne has made Melantius his brother-in-law. Because Evadne is a willing participant in the sexual relationship with the king that is Beaumont and Fletcher's equivalent to the insult that was to be offered to Harmodius's sister, Melantius's choice between his sister and his friend and Amintor's choice between his wife and his friend become choices between homosociality and heterosociality, whereas Harmodius's duty as a brother and his duty as a lover were not in conflict and actually reinforced each other. In *The Maid's Tragedy*, these choices first become an issue in the scene in which Melantius tries to find out what is disturbing Amintor. At the beginning of this scene, he says, 'Ile know the cause of all *Amintors* griefes,/ Or friendship shall be idle' (III.ii.1–2), and when Amintor refuses to tell him what is wrong, Melantius says,

> world? what doe I here? a friend
> Is nothing: heaven? I would ha told that man
> My secret sinnes: ile search an unknowne land,
> And there plant friendship, all is withered here. (III.ii.92–5)

Melantius's 'disordred speech' emphasizes how profoundly Amintor's unwillingness to confide in him has shaken him and how much he depends on his ideal of friendship.

Amintor's reluctance to tell Melantius that his sister is the king's mistress is entirely understandable, of course, and when he does tell him it seems at first that it will put a violent end to their friendship. The furious Melantius responds by asking a question that foregrounds the conflict between elective and familial bonds –

>   shall the name of friend
> Blot all our family, and strike the brand
> Of whore upon my sister unreveng'd. (III.ii.135–7) –

but he ultimately chooses Amintor over Evadne: 'The name of friend, is more then familie,/ Or all the world besides' (III.ii.167–9). His choice of his elective bond with Amintor is forcefully underlined when he says, '[B]ehold the power thou hast in me,/ I doe beleeve my sister is a whore' (III.ii.177–8). Nevertheless, it is important to note that Melantius does not altogether renounce familial bonds in this scene. When Amintor asks, 'What is it then to me,/ If it be wrong to you,' Melantius answers, 'Why not so much,/ The credit of our house is throwne away' (III.ii.187–9). At this point in the play, Melantius still believes that elective and familial bonds can be combined, although as we would expect from Melantius's statement in the first scene that he serves people because of their worth rather than their rank, elective bonds predominate. In any case, the decision to support Amintor is a pivotal moment in *The Maid's Tragedy* as it immediately leads Melantius to plot against the king's life: 'ile waken death,/ And hurle him on this King' (III.ii.190–1). The decision to kill the man whose existence is supposed to give meaning to the nation he rules is the clearest indication that the hierarchy in which everyone is supposed to have a place and over which the king presides is threatened. It could even be argued that from this point on the play's narrative interest comes from discovering which bond will be dissolved next and what will survive this reassessment of the bonds that structure the world of the play.

Amintor's objection to Melantius's plan is that 'it will fixe the name/ Of fearefull cuckold' on him (III.ii.227–8), although in the scene before this he told the king that

>   there is
> Divinitie about you, that strikes dead
> My rising passions. (III.i.239–41)

The change from acknowledging the sanctity of a king to being concerned for one's own reputation is still more evidence of what Shullenberger calls 'the pattern of disintegration enacted in *The Maid's Tragedy*;[23] here, we see the disintegration of loyalty to the king and of Amintor's masculine identity. First, we see him responding to Melantius in a way that suggests that the replacement of a sister by a brother hinted at in the masque is beginning to take place:

> Oh my soft temper,
> So many sweete words from thy sisters mouth,
> I am afraid would make me take her,
> To embrace and pardon her. (III.ii.240–3)

For the rest of the play, Amintor is increasingly feminized and is presented as completely dependent upon Melantius both physically and emotionally:

> *Melantius*.   I warrant you, looke up, weele walke together,
> Put thine arme here, all shall be well agen.
> *Amintor*.   Thy love, o wretched I, thy love *Melantius*,
> Why I have nothing else.
> *Melantius*.   Be merry then. (III.ii.256–9)

Melantius's final statement is meant as reassurance, but in context it also indicates that the intense emotional bond between them will be the only thing left once more conventional bonds such as those between members of a family, between husband and wife, and between a subject and his king have ceased to operate.

Shortly after this, Melantius confronts his sister. This is the first time we see the two alone together and, in fact, the first time that we see family members together apart from scenes like the masque, in which almost all the characters are on stage, or brief exchanges between Melantius and Diphilus. Evadne initially refuses to deal with his accusations:

> *Evadne*.   Begon, you are my brother, thats your safty.
> *Melantius*.   Ile be a woulfe first, tis to be thy brother
> An infamy below the sin of coward,
> I am as far from being part of thee,

As thou art from thy vertue, seeke a kindred
Mongst sensuall beasts, and make a goate thy brother. (IV.i.59–64)

Melantius wants to force Evadne to play a role in his plot and some of
what he says can be dismissed as inflated rhetoric used to make a point,
but it is significant that he, like Amintor on his wedding night, does not
see Evadne's transgression as a private matter, but as something that
undermines the stability of society and reduces humans to a state of
nature in which blood relations no longer matter. In the play, Rhodes is
a society whose primary sources of stability may be presumed to be
kinship, kingship, the gender system, and marriage. Although all of
these have been undermined to some extent since the beginning of the
play, as I have shown, they begin to disintegrate in this scene; and
although kinship still seems to be important, as we see Melantius first
with his brother and then with his sister, it is clear that his primary
concern is for his own honour and for his beloved Amintor rather than
for either of his siblings.

Melantius, who began the play as a loyal soldier whose efforts helped
to maintain civil order, is now presented as the primary threat to that
order. In fact, at one point in this scene with Evadne he uses an analogy
that demonstrates how much things have changed. In speaking of the
king, Melantius compares himself to 'the angry North' (IV.i.73) or Boreas,
who was the agent of disorder in the masque. Like Boreas, Melantius is
now a force that cannot be contained and that threatens to destroy
Rhodes altogether. By the end of this scene, Melantius has forced Evadne
to promise to kill the king and has ordered her not to tell her husband
(IV.i.165–71). The first promise will negate the bond between the subject
and her king and force a woman to do something unwomanly; less
obviously, perhaps, the second will undermine the bond between a
woman and her husband. When Amintor enters, just after Melantius
has left, the gender reversals of the play continue. As in the scene with
Melantius, Amintor is feminized, but here his feminization is contrasted with Evadne's behaviour:

Since I can doe no good because a woman,
Reach constantly at something that is neere it;
I will redeeme one minute of my age,
Or like another *Niobe* ile weepe
Til I am water.

Amintor. I am now dissolved.
My frozen soule melts. (IV.i.253–8)

Evadne uses conventionally feminine rhetoric and goes so far as to suggest that she will be a traditionally passive and mourning woman and to invoke the classical example of such a woman, but it is Amintor who speaks of himself as 'dissolved' and who thus takes the female role, while it is Evadne who prepares to act in a traditionally masculine manner. The femininity of Amintor's speech and behaviour in this scene are especially marked since, as Gail Kern Paster has argued, images of melting and of incontinence were very strongly associated with women and specifically with feminine transgression.[24]

In the fifth act, first Evadne and then Aspatia, who up to this point has actually been a traditionally passive and mourning woman, take action in masculine ways. At the beginning of the act, Evadne uses her femininity and her status as the king's mistress to gain access to his room and to tie his arms to the bed. He takes her actions to be part of a new sex game: 'What prettie new device is this?' (V.i.47). At this point, she berates him, announces her intention to kill him, and stabs him to death. When the king appeals to her by calling her name, Evadne says, 'I am not she, nor beare I in this breast/ So much cold spirit to be cald a woman' (V.i.64–5) – and this comment is emphasized by one of the men who finds the king's corpse and who says, 'Who can beleeve a woman could doe this' (V.i.126), and also by Cleon when he enters: 'Her act! a woman!' (V.i.129). This scene instructs us that conventional ideas of feminine behaviour include being a man's mistress and marrying another man under false pretences, but not avenging oneself. It would appear that women are not supposed to act, with the exception, of course, of sexual action, as we see when the king is titillated by being tied up. Evadne's use of her femininity in this scene suggests that for her, and perhaps by extension for women in general, femininity is not an essence but rather a role that may be performed for a certain purpose. It could even be said that Amintor acts as a woman in Act III, scene ii so that he will not be implicated in the plot to kill the king. Although neither Evadne nor Amintor is especially conventional as regards gender, it is Melantius who leads them to forsake their conventional gender roles altogether.

As she has been so conventionally feminine in the play, Aspatia's adoption of masculine behaviour is more dramatic than Evadne's. In fact, Aspatia has been the very picture of a jilted woman. When she appears in act five, however, she is in man's clothes and is actively seeking death at Amintor's hands. At first, his servant refuses to let her see him, but Aspatia is able to bribe him. The servant's prevarication calls forth the bitter comment that 'all the men I meet/ Appeare thus to me, are harsh and rude' (V.iii.25–6) while women '[h]arbour the easiest and the smoothest thoughts' (V.iii.29), and the even more bitter conclusion that 'it is unjust/ That men and women should be matcht together' (V.iii.30–1). I think that we are probably intended to agree with Aspatia's assessment – *The Maid's Tragedy* does seem to be at least sceptical about the possibility of peaceful cohabitation between the sexes. It should also be noted that while Aspatia's disguise is made plausible by Melantius's reference in the first scene of the play to her brother as being very much like her (I.i.105–8), our memory of this comment as well as the fact that Aspatia's father has been very much in evidence throughout the play should lead us to wonder why her brother and her father – that is, the men who are supposed to protect her – have done nothing for her. Aspatia's actions in the final act could be taken to indicate that women may behave like men if men do not. To some extent, this is the case with Evadne as well, since her husband is clearly unable or unwilling (or both) to avenge her. Since the king is supposed to protect and care for his subjects, I would argue that his use of his power for private gratification represents the most serious example of a man's neglect of his masculine duty in the play as a whole. It is his anomalous behaviour that creates the disorder in Rhodes, a disorder whose most salient feature may well be the disruptions in gender behaviour so prominent in the second half of the play. It is typical of the play that the most telling sign of these disruptions is the assertion of a conventional idea about gender, as for instance when the disguised Aspatia has finally succeeded in provoking Amintor to fight and he makes a statement remarkable for its dramatic irony: 'A man can beare/ No more and keepe his flesh' (V.iii.97–8).

As soon as Amintor has succeeded in wounding Aspatia, Evadne rushes in, '*her hands bloudy with a knife*' (V.iii.107, s.d.). The tableau set up by her entrance is of great importance to Beaumont and Fletcher's resolution (if that is what it is) of the gender issues raised by the play. Aspatia, a woman dressed as a man, lies bleeding to death on the ground, while two people, both with blood-stained weapons, stand over her. All three of the characters have transgressed against the rules of gender, the women by bearing and using weapons and the man by fighting with a woman. Furthermore, and it is this aspect that concerns me most, the three members of the love triangle are together on stage for the first time since the masque. This is a crucial shift in our sense of what the play is really about. The romantic triangle in *The Maid's Tragedy* was revealed to the audience in the first scene, but Beaumont and Fletcher gave it very little treatment, preferring to keep Aspatia separate from the main narrative movement of the play and to avoid confrontation among the three characters involved.[25] Most of the play is concerned with the relationship between Amintor and Melantius; the effect of the authors' return to the romantic triangle is to give the play a more conventional ending than it would have if the final scene focused on the two men. Once Aspatia dies of her wounds and Evadne and Amintor kill themselves, the three form a tableau that I think Beaumont and Fletcher intend us to read as a synopsis of the play, one in which the main intrigue concerns a jilted woman, the man she loves, and the woman he married instead of her. The gender irregularities so apparent in the beginning of the scene are resolved by the tableau's provision of visual proof that the marriage plot has been restored and that *The Maid's Tragedy* is not, despite all the appearances to the contrary, a play about the love between two men. I do not mean to suggest by this that I find Beaumont and Fletcher's handling of the conclusion excessively neat; in fact, I would argue that much of the power of the conclusion is due to their insistence on the cost of the marriage plot.

The character left behind in all this is Melantius, who joins the ranks of the odd men out, those characters like Jaques in *As You Like It* and the Antonios in *Twelfth Night* and *The Merchant of Venice* who are left behind by the relentless forward motion of the heteroerotic imperative, but while Shakespeare does not generally draw attention to the exclusion of these characters from the happy endings, Beaumont and Fletcher give Melantius several important speeches at the very end of the play. When he enters with Lysippus, Calianax, Diphilus, and others, Melantius rushes to Amintor, ignoring Evadne and Aspatia, and cries, '[G]ive a word / To call me to thee' (V.iii.255–6). The only words Amintor says in response to this appeal are 'Oh' and 'What?' (V.iii.257, 261), but Melantius declares, 'That little word was worth all the sounds / That ever I shall heare againe' (V.iii.261–2). His actions would not be unusual for a male character whose beloved is dying, but in that case the beloved would of course be expected to be female. Diphilus comments on the strangeness of this behaviour:

Diphilus.   Oh brother
Here lies your sister slaine, you loose your selfe

In sorrow there.
Melantius.   Why *Diphilus* it is
A thing to laugh at in respect of this,
Here was my Sister, Father, Brother, Sonne,
All that I had. (V.iii.262–7)

Shullenberger says of this scene that 'Melantius now discards "family"
into the pile of outworn ideals which love and honor occupy.'[26] With
the death of Amintor there is nothing to connect Melantius to the
society in which he lives. The homosociality that is supposed to cement
the ties among men and to connect them to their king has ultimately led
to his complete estrangement from the world around him. We can
interpret this aspect of the conclusion as a tragic form of the exteriorization of war under which Melantius has always operated.

In a Renaissance drama, the logical action for a character whose
beloved has died to take is to commit suicide and this is precisely what
Melantius decides to do: 'I am a Pratler, but no more [*Offers to kill him
selfe.*]' (V.iii.276). Beaumont and Fletcher must stop this, however, if
sexual decorum is to be maintained, since if Melantius were to kill
himself, he would form part of the tableau of people who died for love.
His life must be preserved so that he does not appear as a lover at all,
but rather as someone whose concern for his sister's honour led him to
kill his king. Although Melantius presents his desire for suicide as part
of his heroism – saying when the king orders his guards to restrain him,
that 'His spirit is but poore, that can be kept/ From death for want of
weapons' (284–5) – Diphilus calls this desire 'unmanly' (V.ii.278), as
indeed it is according to the standards of Renaissance drama. Hopkins
has commented on the curiously feminine nature of the speech he
makes once he has been restrained:

> There seems something almost luxurious about the quality of Melantius's
> death wish, as he virtually suggests to those around him that they should
> tie down his hands, and then resolves on self-starvation – a method of
> suicide that elsewhere in Renaissance drama is the exclusive preserve of
> female characters. With Melantius's actions the inversion is complete.[27]

Hopkins refers to gender inversion and this is obviously an important
aspect of *The Maid's Tragedy* as a whole and in particular of its final
scene, but I would add that the inversion demonstrated by Melantius in

this scene also indicates what would come to be called sexual inversion and that the main concern for Beaumont and Fletcher at the end of the play is how to represent this inversion.

As the new king, Lysippus is given the play's final speech and he attempts, rather unconvincingly, to pronounce a suitable moral:

> May this a faire example be to me,
> To rule with temper, for on lustfull Kings
> Unlookt for suddaine deaths from God are sent,
> But curst is he that is their instrument. (V.iii.292–5)

The play ends with a restatement of the moral impasse that was so important a part of *The Maid's Tragedy*'s political relevance and an issue frequently raised in the drama of this period: God will punish a wicked king, but it is a crime for a subject to do so. With these lines, a different kind of inversion is completed. When the king's corpse is discovered, Lysippus proposes to pursue Evadne, but Strato says, 'Never follow her,/ For she alas was but the instrument' (V.i.136–7) and adds that it is Melantius who is really responsible for the murder. In the play's final line, Lysippus's repetition of the word 'instrument' and his use of the male pronoun suggests that he has accepted Strato's reading of the situation, a reading that is in harmony with gender norms. In this interpretation, it is Melantius who is the instrument of the king's violent death, while Evadne is merely the instrument of an instrument. The conclusion is not in keeping with the play itself, however, in which Evadne is distinguished by her capacity for all sorts of action. In denying her agency and thus tacitly affirming a view in which men act and women follow them, Lysippus imposes an interpretation of the events of the play that fits with the title's foregrounding of female concerns. *The Maid's Tragedy* is now to be understood as a story about the romantic troubles of women, as the title would indicate. As Finkelpearl suggested in a passage I cited earlier, the maid of the title could be Aspatia or Evadne or even Amintor; it could never be Melantius, however, and this is precisely the point. Beaumont and Fletcher use Melantius's love for Amintor to move the plot along and to bring about the final catastrophe, just as kingdoms such as Rhodes use military homosociality to ensure their peace (or to buy it, as Lysippus says at the beginning of the play). In the end, however, literary texts, like kingdoms, must focus on connections between the sexes.

The Winter's Tale

Much of the most interesting recent criticism of *The Winter's Tale* has concentrated on its linguistic difficulties and especially on Shakespeare's use of what David Laird has called competing discourses,[28] that is, the presence in the play of multiple ways of speaking and multiple versions of the truth. Throughout the play, and perhaps most noticeably in Act V, scene ii, Shakespeare forces us to concentrate on the relation of dramatic incidents, or on what is narrated by one or more of the characters, as much as on the representation of dramatic incidents, or on what is shown to us. My work represents a variation on this line of inquiry, as for my purposes the discourses in competition are generic ones. *The Winter's Tale* resembles *The Maid's Tragedy* in that both deal with the conflict between homosociality and the marriage plot, but while Beaumont and Fletcher do this at the level of narrative, Shakespeare does it primarily at the level of genre – specifically, the pastoral.[29] I see the confusion of genres in the play as a version of Melantius's 'disordered speech,' a kind of speech that, as I have said, may indicate what Renaissance writers sometimes called disorderly love. As in the case of *The Maid's Tragedy*, the disorder spreads from the man who feels disorderly love to the society around him.

I want to look at two sets of competing discourses in *The Winter's Tale*. The first to appear is the competition between the marriage plot and the all-male pastoral. The second, which is in effect a version of the first, is the competition between this traditional masculine pastoral, exemplified in the play by the boyhood of Leontes and Polixenes, and the heterosexualized pastoral exemplified by Perdita and Florizel in the second half of the play. As the first version is related rather than represented and the second is represented rather than related, Shakespeare presents the homoerotic pastoral as literary, insofar as it exists only in language, and the heteroerotic pastoral as real within the terms of dramatic representation, as it takes place before our eyes. The second pastoral is heteroerotic not only in its celebration of romantic attachments between the sexes but also, and perhaps even primarily, because of its emphasis on reproduction. Peter Lindenbaum points out that it is unusual for one work to offer two pastoral environments, especially two such different ones; as he goes on to point out, the crucial difference is that one of these environments 'accommodates the conception of time moving relentlessly forward.'[30] *The Winter's Tale* is concerned with two kinds of time: traditional pastoral time, in which the temporal unit is the day or, at most, the year, and a time frame more familiar from the epic, in which the temporal unit is a generation and it is always clear that the purpose of the present generation is to produce the next generation.

In her fascinating article on *The Winter's Tale*, Nora Johnson comments that the play 'is centrally concerned ... with legitimating theatrical practice'; later in her essay she describes the world of *The Winter's Tale* as 'a realm that welcomes and ultimately makes use of heterosexual fertility as a way of legitimating the scandalous stage.'[31] Johnson's emphasis is on Shakespeare's attempts to deal with the increasingly notorious homoeroticism of the Renaissance stage. In my analysis, I concentrate on the pastoral, which was, like the stage, a relatively privileged site for homoeroticism: as I see it, *The Winter's Tale* demonstrates Shakespeare's desire to bring both the stage and the pastoral under the rule of heterosexuality. In this context, however, the principal manifestation of the heterosexuality towards which the play moves is not the love between a young man and a woman that is the goal both of the *Shepheardes Calender* (even if that goal is never attained) and, in its very different way, of Barnfield's pastoral poetry, but rather the reproduction that follows from that love. Shakespeare's legitimation of the pastoral is thus focused on human fertility. His emphasis on fertility is noticeable throughout the play, and the first sign of it can be seen in his decision to reverse the settings of his source, Robert Greene's *Pandosto*, a work that in its epigram – *Temporis filia veritas* (truth, the daughter of time) – and in its subtitle – *The Triumph of Time* – already gestures toward the idea of reproduction that will turn out to be the central concern of *The Winter's Tale* (although not of Greene's narrative). Greene begins to tell his story by saying that '[i]n the Countrey of *Bohemia* there raygned a King called *Pandosto*';[32] the corresponding character in *The Winter's Tale* is Leontes, who is king of Sicilia. Shakespeare's decision to reverse Greene's choice of settings means that the triumphantly heterosexual ending takes place in Sicily, the traditional setting for pastoral poetry, and can thus be understood as a correction or reformulation of the pastoral genre.[33]

In employing pastoral imagery while stressing the passage of time, the first scene of *The Winter's Tale* highlights precisely the juxtaposition of pastorals I have been discussing. In this scene, the Sicilian lord Camillo talks to the Bohemian lord Archidamus about the friendship between their kings:

Sicilia cannot show himself over-kind to Bohemia. They were trained together in their childhoods; and there rooted betwixt them such an affection as cannot choose but branch now. Since their more mature dignities and royal necessities made separation of their society, their encounters (though not personal) hath been royally attorney'd with interchange of gifts, letters, loving embassies, that they have seem'd to be together, though absent; shook hands as over a vast; and embrac'd, as it were, from the ends of oppos'd winds. The heavens continue their loves! (I.i.21–32)

Camillo uses pastoral imagery in describing the love between the kings as a natural growth and his emphasis on that love is echoed by the homosociality of this opening scene, which consists of two men speaking affectionately to each other. As David McCandless points out, our first glimpse of the world of the play is of an all-male world: 'The opening scene sets up the image of Hermione as female intruder: two men ... make no mention of her but speak exclusively of the long-standing friendship between Leontes and Polixenes and of the great hopes residing in the gallant child Mamillius.'[34] Shakespeare is careful to downplay the homoerotic potential, however, and the echo is a very faint one, given the difference between two best friends and two polite courtiers. Perhaps the correct term in this context is not echo but rather mediation, and the mediation is increased because the love in question is related rather than represented. Our sense of our distance from Leontes and Polixenes is further increased by Camillo's emphasis on the fact that the two men have not seen each other in years. They now communicate solely by proxy and at a great distance. In effect, Camillo's speech serves to limit both homoerotic and pastoral space.

The crucial distance in the passage is not geographical but chronological. In a metaphor that recalls Virgil's statement that his love for Gallus 'crescit in horas/ quantum uere nouo uiridus se subicit alnus,' Camillo uses the word 'branch' as a synonym for 'increase,' but it also suggests the idea of division and separation, both in a hostile sense and in the more neutral sense of 'growing apart.' His speech thus performs what is perhaps the basic function of ideology: something that is brought about by humans – the physical separation of Leontes and Polixenes and, more generally, the turn from homosociality to heterosociality that we can see as the cause for that effect – is presented as a naturally occurring phenomenon. Time, we are told, will inevitably produce heterosexuality (we are still told this). Kay Stockholder says that '[t]he concluding episodes of The Winter's Tale replace the tortured sexuality of the first part with an ideological fairy tale.'[35] Without wishing to deny the fantastic aspects of the play's conclusion, I want to stress that heterosexuality is always presented as an ideological fairy tale in the play. At this early point in the play, however (and this will turn out to be typical of *The Winter's Tale* as a whole), the emphasis is not so much on the workings of heterosexuality as on its products, and the two men begin to speak of Leontes's heir, Mamillius, a little boy of great promise. The stress on Mamillius's glorious future is both important foreshadowing and another way to talk about the passage of time. Camillo says that '[t]hey that went on crutches ere he was born desire yet their life to see him a man (I.ii.39–41). At the very beginning of the play, then, the narrative of *The Winter's Tale* – at least insofar as it is the story of Leontes and Polixenes – is placed in a context of time as measured by human generations: from the boyhood of a character who is a man in the narrative present to the adulthood of a man who is a boy in the narrative present.

What is not immediately clear, I think (at least I have found no critical discussions of it), is how significant it is that Florizel is omitted from this scene (he is first mentioned, by Hermione, at I.ii.34). It might seem natural to talk about him in the context of talking about the two kings and what their adult lives are like, especially once Mamillius has been mentioned, but if either Camillo or Archidamus were to mention him, there would be a parallel between the two kings and their two sons. To some extent, this scene is characterized by its stress on homosocial reciprocity, but this is the limit of that reciprocity. The passionate attachment between Leontes and Polixenes that provides the impetus for the play's narrative can only result in branching, in separation and distance, rather than in the union that is the goal of most narratives and certainly of Shakespeare's romances. The first scene sets up the relationship between Leontes and Polixenes as the play's central issue and therefore, for the purposes of tying up the strands of the narrative, the men must be united, but they must be united in the mediated way that Camillo has presented as typical of their adulthood. To invoke yet another male couple (Mamillius and Florizel) would merely continue the narrative deadlock or, to put it another way, it would turn *The Winter's Tale* into precisely the sort of male homosocial pastoral that I believe it is Shakespeare's intention to rewrite. What is more, a narrative that continued the love between the two men in their sons would present a state of affairs in which homoeroticism was what is reproduced. The only way to give the play an ending that can be recognized as one is to marry the two men by proxy. As a consequence, a daughter is required and one of the sons is superfluous and therefore (in a way that recalls the grim sexual arithmetic of the *Knight's Tale*) will have to be eliminated.

The speech of Polixenes that begins the second scene of the play concentrates on reproduction and sets up the opposition between the all-male pastoral of stasis and the heteroerotic pastoral:

> Nine changes of the wat'ry star hath been
> The shepherd's note since we have left our throne
> Without a burthen. (I.ii.1–3)

The reference to nine months suggests pregnancy – a reference that would be even clearer to an audience because of the presence on stage of the heavily pregnant Hermione – and the allusion is underlined when Polixenes says,

>   And therefore, like a cipher
> (Yet standing in rich place), I multiply
> With one 'We thank you' many thousands moe. (I.ii.6–8)[36]

This is an allusion not only to reproduction but also to sexual activity, since the phrase 'standing in rich place' has a strong sexual connotation.[37] For my purposes, however, what is most significant about Polixenes' speech is that it presents time as measured by '[t]he shepherd's note' (that is, by pastoral poetry) and the unit of that time is not precisely the month, as it is in the *Shepheardes Calender*, but rather the phases of the moon. The distinction may seem trivial, but I believe that it is actually crucial, since the months are part of the cycle of the year, the years are part of the cycle of the century, and so on, while there is really not much difference between, for example, one full moon and the next. Polixenes measures time as shepherds do (at least in pastoral poetry), as a recurring cycle rather than as a narrative progression, even though Hermione's distended belly bears witness to what will turn out to be the most important narrative progression in *The Winter's Tale*.

I want to look now at Polixenes' account of his boyhood, which is one of the most discussed passages in the entire play. In response to what is apparently idle curiosity on Hermione's part, he describes himself and Leontes when young as

Two lads that thought there was no more behind
But such a day to-morrow as to-day,
And to be boy eternal. (I.ii.63–5)

Once again, Polixenes invokes the stasis of pastoral time. Hermione attempts to get him to distinguish himself and Leontes, but he insists on total homosocial solidarity:

We were as twinn'd lambs that did frisk i'th'sun,
And bleat the one at th'other. What we chang'd
Was innocence for innocence; we knew not
The doctrine of ill-doing, nor dream'd
That any did. Had we pursu'd that life,
And our weak spirits ne'er been higher rear'd
With stronger blood, we should have answer'd heaven
Boldly, 'Not guilty,' the imposition clear'd
Hereditary ours. (I.ii.67–75)

I have quoted Polixenes' response in full because it has usually been assumed that he is describing a pre-sexual existence and I want to make the point that there is nothing in the passage itself to rule out sexuality.[38] Polixenes does not say that he and Leontes never did anything that might be considered wrong, but merely that they did not know the 'doctrine of ill-doing,' a phrase that denotes a set of beliefs about sinful behaviour rather than the behaviour itself. It is obviously possible – and, I think, reasonable – to take Polixenes' speech as suggesting that one consequence of adulthood was that he and Leontes realized their sexual activity was classified as 'ill-doing.'

The boyhood of Polixenes and Leontes does not function merely as a happy memory or as an obstacle to the smooth progression of the narrative, but is also an acknowledgment of homoerotic space. William R. Morse remarks that '[t]he power of Polixenes' edenic recollection ... grows not only from its asexuality, but from its evocation of unending constancy.'[39] It may well be that this 'unending constancy' is what bothers critics most. To judge from the criticism of the play, most Shakespeareans appear to be committed to a narrative of male sexual development in which married life is the desired goal. A certain homoeroticism may be permitted in adolescence, but it must be renounced by the fully grown man and, of course, adult homosexuality is characterized by inconstancy. So ingrained are these beliefs and so successful is Shakespeare's use of ideology that virtually all critics of *The Winter's Tale*, even today, take as a given that heterosexuality is the natural result of adulthood for all except the truly obdurate. The result of this unexamined and unstated assumption is that the alternative glimpsed in Polixenes' speech is not taken seriously even by critics who are in no sense conservative. In an influential psychoanalytic analysis of the play, Coppélia Kahn provides a typical assessment: 'The homosexual implications of this nostalgic fantasy are less important than what it suggests about Leontes' attitude toward his mature sexuality.'[40] In characterizing Leontes' vision of himself as fantasy, in depicting married life as mature, and in saying that homoeroticism is less important than heteroeroticism, Kahn's statement serves to contain homoerotic space and even to foreclose the possibility of its existence. For a critic to say that a passage has homosexual implications but that these are not as important to the text as its views on heterosexuality is a typical example of the sort of grudging admission that has replaced the outright refusal to discuss homoeroticism in Renaissance texts. What surprises me more is Kahn's use of the word fantasy. As there is no textual support for doubting Polixenes' word here or elsewhere in *The Winter's Tale*, it should be clear that it is Kahn's reading of the passage that is the fantasy and, to me at least, a troubling one. Finally, as the comments are made by Polixenes, it seems somewhat risky to see them as giving us information about Leontes' thoughts and feelings. It is not my intention to accuse Kahn and all the other critics who rely on a distinction between simple and unrealistic homoeroticism and complex and realistic heteroeroticism of homophobia or to claim that Shakespeare is anything other than conservative, but at least he wishes to gesture toward homoerotic space at the same time that he relegates it to the past.

In a brief but intriguing discussion of *The Winter's Tale*, Paul Hammond states that '[t]he idea that men might be able to inhabit an all-male world, an Eden without Eve, is a recurring dream in Shakespeare's plays.'[41] This all-male world is often military, as in *Troilus and Cressida* or *Coriolanus*. Polixenes' comparison of himself and Leontes to lambs demonstrates that his version of this world, this homoerotic space, is pastoral. This is not surprising in itself, but what distinguishes this aspect of *The Winter's Tale* (its first version of pastoral) from such Renaissance pastorals as the *Shepheardes Calender* or *As You Like It* is that the presence of the feminine is not something that can be accommodated in the pastoral world, but rather is something that puts an end to it. The possibilities opened up by Polixenes' glimpse of this space are contained by the status of his speech as the narration of a distant recollection as well as by the distance between the pastoral world and the court (and Shakespeare increases the distance because in his version of the narrative there is also a contrast between the Sicily of the play and the Sicily familiar from pastoral literature). Still, I would argue that he suggests that things could be different when he says, 'Had we pursued that life.' The subjunctive mood circumscribes this possibility as soon as it is mentioned, but the homoerotic space opened up by this thought continues to resonate, at least with unprejudiced readers. It is important to note that Polixenes is suggesting, if only for a moment, that a passionate attachment between males in an all-male environment could come to pass; furthermore, I think that the use of the verb 'pursued' hints at the possibility that such a life is to be understood as both a goal and a process and not merely as the stasis that the play as a whole is concerned to avoid. For an instant, pastoral homoeroticism appears to have the same status as a possible way of life for an adult male as the heteroeroticism strongly focused on reproduction that it is one of *The Winter's Tale*'s functions to promote.

For several decades now, critics have linked Polixenes' relation of his boyhood with Leontes to Leontes' sudden jealousy and argued that the jealousy can best be explained as a defence mechanism. To my knowledge, the first critic to make this point was J.I.M. Stewart, who said in 1949 that 'Leontes projects upon his wife the desires he has to repudiate in himself.'[42] I would locate the catalyst for his jealousy quite early in the scene. When he refuses to be persuaded to stay, Polixenes says to Leontes, 'There is no tongue that moves, none, none i'th'world,/ So soon as yours could win me' (I.ii.20–1). The idea of a moving tongue, which we could take literally, gives the lines an erotic charge, especially in conjunction with the ambiguity of the verb 'win,' so often used in the love poetry of the time. When Leontes says, as soon as Polixenes has stopped speaking, 'Tongue-tied our queen? Speak you' (I.ii.27), the repetition of 'tongue' is in itself a defence mechanism. Leontes is shifting the erotic implications of Polixenes' appeal on to Hermione, a move which suggests that the transition from homoeroticism to heteroeroticism cannot simply be made once but is always to be done again. It seems to me that when Hermione does succeed in persuading Polixenes to stay, jealousy is the only possible result, and it is important to realize that Leontes' love and lust are not directed solely at either of them. For

Leontes, jealousy is twofold: he is jealous of his wife because he thinks she has sex with his friend and of his friend because he thinks he has sex with his wife. Leontes is ultimately unable either to make the transition from homoeroticism or not to make it, at least in his own person. Only the marriage of his child to Polixenes' child can break the stalemate.

Johnson notes that '[a]s Leontes and Polixenes abandon physical immediacy for "mature dignity," they begin to employ others as go-betweens, as expressions of their relationship.'[43] This aspect of their relationship has already been noted by Camillo, although he spoke mainly of objects rather than of people as mediators. For Leontes, trapped between homoeroticism and heteroeroticism, expressing his love for Polixenes through other people is not a strategy that works. The most important go-betweens – Hermione and Mamillius – exacerbate his panic by appearing to him as reminders of his love for Polixenes. In Hermione's case, this is demonstrated by his projection of his love for Polixenes on to her. Similarly, when he asks Mamillius, 'Art thou my boy' (120), he means both 'are you my son' and 'are you a replacement for Polixenes, the boy I have lost.'[44] Shortly after this question, Leontes blames his emotion, which has become obvious to those around him, on a vision of himself at Mamillius's age,

> unbreech'd,
> In my green velvet coat, my dagger muzzled,
> Lest it should bite its master and so prove
> (As ornament oft does) too dangerous. (155–8)

Most critics have argued that the dagger is to be understood as a phallic symbol and that the passage as a whole depicts a pre-sexual state, but although I also read the dagger as phallic, it is not clear to me why the characterization of it as an ornament should also mean that it is not useful. Many things are both ornamental and useful, as were, for instance, the daggers boys wore at their belts. Furthermore, green is the colour both of jealousy and of sexuality (and particularly of a natural or pastoral sexuality), and the word 'unbreeched' could mean both that the young Leontes was not wearing adult clothing and that he was not wearing clothing at all. I would argue that the passage depicts a homoerotic sexuality that is not dangerous, in contrast with what Leontes sees as the pains and perils of his adult life.

No one could deny that Leontes' speeches and actions in the first three acts are misogynistic: they are clearly not only misogynistic but even fatally so. I merely want to point out that what we see in him in the first half of the play is in effect a sort of false consciousness and that the real enemy is not the woman to whom he is married but the system that subsumes sexuality under the sign of reproduction. As I suggested earlier, most critics, even ones who are not in other respects defenders of the status quo, do not see this and instead condemn Leontes and deny altogether the existence of any alternative. Leontes himself does not see any alternative: to choose either homoeroticism or heteroeroticism entails a painful loss and it is impossible to combine the two. His identification of himself and his son clearly indicates that the latter must die, since it means that Mamillius has come to represent not the hope for the future expressed by Camillo and Archidamus in the first scene of *The Winter's Tale*, but rather a repetition of the past in which, to rephrase Polixenes' comment, boys are eternal. Shakespeare does indeed work to represent Leontes' vision as a fantasy, one of reproduction as reproducing homoeroticism, but that does not mean that we should be blind either to the ideological purpose of that work or to its cost. The events of the play show quite clearly that the fairy-tale ending of the play is entirely dependent on Mamillius's death. The birth of Perdita signals the replacement of a boy with a girl, with the result that Mamillius becomes unnecessary, and it is significant that it is the news of his death that makes Leontes repent (III.ii.142–5), whereas in *Pandosto* it is the queen's death (261). Shakespeare's change to Greene suggests to me that his focus is not on heterosexual romance but rather on reproduction. Considered from this point of view, Mamillius is merely the first to die. A narrative that concentrates on the marriage of the protagonists and that ends with that marriage in effect preserves the lovers as a young couple; a narrative that concentrates on reproduction makes clear not just how fleeting but also how unimportant wedded bliss really is.

As I have said, the birth of Perdita marks the beginning of the end of the narrative deadlock between Leontes and Polixenes. The way in which the birth is announced emphasizes its importance:

> [*Emilia*]   She is, something before her time, deliver'd.
> *Paulina.*   A boy?
> *Emilia.*   A daughter. (II.ii.23–4)

The choice in this exchange is between a boy, a male potentially connected to other boys in the same way that the young Leontes was connected to Polixenes, or a daughter, a female who is instantly situated in the context of reproduction and familial relationships. Perdita's birth is accompanied by the emergence of a female world to parallel the male world with which the play has been concerned until this point, both in its actual setting at the Sicilian court and in its pastoral recollections. Our first sight of the female world comes in the first scene of the second act, in which we see Hermione and her ladies surrounding Mamillius, a tableau that reverses the second scene of the first act, in which we see the kings and their men surrounding Hermione. In Act II, scene iii, Paulina, carrying the young princess, bursts in upon Leontes and his men, an event that calls forth a flood of misogynistic comments from Leontes, much of it centred on the male fear of domination by women. Paulina's incursion into the male world signals the completion of the shift from a society based on male homosociality to one based on reproduction. To say this is to present the movement of the play in the most general terms; what distinguishes *The Winter's Tale* from many of the other works that could be described in this way is that the shift can only be accomplished by rewriting the pastoral. Rather than abandoning the pastoral altogether and focusing on a world of courtly love and marriage (a movement that would recall the ending of *As You Like It*), Shakespeare, developing Greene's narrative, presents a pastoral of reproduction that replaces the traditional all-male pastoral just as Perdita has already by this point in the play replaced Mamillius and just as she and Florizel will eventually replace their fathers.[45]

The pastoral scenes begin in the third act, but when the character Time appears at the beginning of the fourth act, he signals that this pastoral is subject to time. His interruption of the pastoral narrative parallels Paulina's interruption of the male world: in both cases, what we see is a sign of the transfer of power from the traditional pastoral to the marriage plot. Time loses no time in asserting his control over the narrative. In quick succession, he moves the action sixteen years into the future, brings us up to date with Leontes, shifts the scene to 'fair Bohemia' (21), reminds us of Florizel's existence, and then turns to Perdita: 'what to her adheres, which follows after,/ Is th'argument of Time' (IV.i.28–9). One way to sum up the first part of *The Winter's Tale* is to say that it tells a story that begins with the pastoral boyhood of Leontes and Polixenes and that ends with the deaths of Hermione and Mamillius and the estrangement of the two men. In returning to the pastoral world evoked by Polixenes, Shakespeare is able to begin the story again and to tell it in such a way that it can end happily. This is repetition with a difference that will solve everything. The second scene of the fourth act, for instance, recalls the first scene of the play. Once again, Camillo and another man speak affectionately to each other. This time, however, the second man is not another lord, but the king Polixenes and what was originally a conversation between equals has become a conversation in which a man asks a more powerful man for a favour that is refused, although the refusal itself is affectionate: 'As thou lov'st me, Camillo, wipe not out the rest of thy services by leaving me now' (IV.ii.10–11).[46] The friendship of Camillo and Polixenes suggests that homosociality can now only exist when it is a part of the social hierarchy. Furthermore, while in the first scene Camillo and Archidamus spoke about Leontes' son, Mamillius, now Camillo and Polixenes speak about the latter's son, Florizel, who was conspicuously absent from the first scene. The most important change of all is that while Mamillius was discussed in isolation, Florizel is discussed in connection with the shepherd's 'daughter of most rare note' (IV.ii.42), whom he is pursuing and whom we know to be the daughter of Leontes and Hermione.

By rewriting not just the traditional pastoral but also the narrative he himself established in the first part of *The Winter's Tale*, Shakespeare emphasizes change, which will be the main theme of the last two acts of the play. What is in some ways the most significant change is announced by Florizel in his first speech in the play:

These your unusual weeds to each part of you
Does give life a life; no shepherdess, but Flora
Peering in April's front. This your sheep-shearing
Is as a meeting of the petty gods,
And you the queen on't. (IV.iv.1–5)

This change is the one represented by Perdita, who is presented as someone whose identity cannot be summed up. In the famous speech later on in the scene in which Florizel stresses the excellence of all the things she does –

    Each your doing
(So singular in each particular)
Crowns what you are doing in the present deeds,
That all your acts are queens (IV.iv.143–6) –

the impression given is one of an almost Protean changeability. Florizel states that Perdita is always changing, but it might be even more to the point to say that she embodies change. By change in this context I mean both the impending change to her own circumstances that will bring about the resolution of the play's plot and also (and more generally) the very idea of change that makes narrative possible and that will end the stasis of the homosocial pastoral. The trope of the infant who is brought up in humble circumstances until his or her true position can be realized goes back at least as far as the stories of Oedipus and Christ, but the closest contemporary parallel (although the story is not nearly so developed) is Spenser's Pastorella. As was the case with her, Perdita turns out to be a character who cannot be contained by the pastoral genre. In both Book VI of the *Faerie Queene* and *The Winter's Tale*, the recognition that the shepherdess is really a woman of high social status signals the end of the pastoral.

The beginning of the ending can be seen in the third line of Florizel's first speech. The sheep he mentions recall the lambs in Polixenes' recollection of his boyhood. Obviously, for the lambs to become sheep they must have been subjected to time, and the emphasis on time in Act IV, scene iv is extraordinarily heavy. It begins with the reference to April in line 3 and continues with references to months, to times of year, and to the suitability of certain kinds of flowers to certain times of life (IV.iv.78–9, 106–8, 112–16). This discussion establishes a parallel between people and flowers and the effect is to emphasize that both are subject to time, since both people and flowers grow and decay. One way to describe what is accomplished in this mapping of human and floral life onto time is to say that these kinds of life have become elements in a narrative; the parallel is thus one more sign of the entry of the pastoral into narrative time in the second half of *The Winter's Tale*. This is exactly what has happened with the lambs that are now sheep (and of course, sheep, along with flowers and men, are one of the basic elements of pastoral poetry). Furthermore, whereas Polixenes' description of himself and Leontes as lambs 'that did frisk i'th'sun' evoked a world of pure play, the fully grown sheep in this scene are being turned to human use and profit. In this scene, Shakespeare juxtaposes two human uses of nature – sheep-shearing and the grafting of flowers to which Perdita objects:

> I'll not put
> The dibble in earth to set one slip of them;
> No more than were I painted I would wish

This youth say 'twere well, and only therefore
Desire to breed by me. (IV.iv.99–103)

This comment, Perdita's final one in the discussion with Polixenes, suggests that she sees reproduction as yet another example of the use of nature.

The wool taken from the sheep can also be read as a tacit acknowledgment of the existence of winter and thus of narrative time,[47] but there are explicit mentions of winter in the scene as well. The first is made by Perdita when she gives Polixenes and Camillo 'rosemary and rue; these keep/ Seeming and savor all the winter long' (IV.iv.74–5). As Johnson suggests, the presence in this scene of these two men has a significance beyond the obvious significance to the plot: 'That Camillo and Polixenes should intrude upon this heterosexual pastoral suggests that this "natural" sheep-shearing feast is in some way anathema to the earlier male Eden in which twinned lambs never had to face the shearer.'[48] That is, their presence underlines the metaphoric equivalence of the sheep with the lambs of Polixenes' speech that I suggested earlier. As well, by associating the two men with winter Shakespeare signals the end of *The Winter's Tale* as a site of homoerotic space. When Polixenes responds to Perdita's speech by saying 'well you fit our ages/ With flow'rs of winter' (IV.iv.78–9), he acknowledges what we could describe as the end, not only of his story, but also of the possibility of the male couple. At this point, it is instructive to consider the visual tableau: we see two couples, one consisting of two old – or, at any rate, middle-aged – men and one consisting of a young man and a young woman, with various more-or-less anonymous rustics cavorting in the background among their sheep. The tableau as a whole could be called The Triumph of Heterosexuality, although this triumph was achieved (or, at least, inevitable) long before the sheep-shearing scene. Camillo and Polixenes are not a couple in the sense that Perdita and Florizel are or in the sense that Polixenes and Leontes were. Rather, they are a king and one of his attendant lords, a very faint reflection of the original couple formed by Polixenes and Leontes all those years ago.

Camillo's decision to help Perdita and Florizel escape is also a reflection – in this case, of his decision to help Polixenes escape sixteen years before. Whereas before the characters fled from Sicily to Bohemia and thus from Leontes, now they flee from Bohemia to Sicily and to Leontes; and whereas before Camillo fled with a man, now he is accompanied

by a heterosexual couple. At his first meeting with the lovers, Leontes
makes a speech that draws our attention to the idea of repetition:

> Were I but twenty-one,
> Your father's image is so hit in you
> (His very air) that I should call you brother,
> As I did him, and speak of something wildly
> By us perform'd before. (V.i.126–30)[49]

This is the beginning of the speech. Next, Leontes turns to Perdita and
then laments his losses, but he ends this speech as he began it: by
speaking of his desire to see Polixenes again (V.i.134–8). Still, it is clear
that what appears to be the return of Polixenes to Sicily and thus
potentially a new beginning for the love between the kings is actually
another repetition with a difference. Polixenes came to Sicily attended
by men; Florizel, the young version of his father, has come to Sicily with
a woman. From this point on, the ending of the play is not in doubt (if
indeed it ever was): the young couple will marry and this marriage is
the most important example in the play of repetition with a difference.
The love between Leontes and Polixenes is repeated by Perdita and
Florizel, but they are able to reproduce and thus to be of use both
dynastically and narratively.

In marrying, Perdita and Florizel do not only repeat their father,
however. In the speech I quoted above Leontes exclaims over Florizel's
resemblance to his father; in the next scene Paulina's steward, relating
the ways in which Perdita's true identity was recognized, speaks of 'the
majesty of the creature in resemblance of the mother' (V.ii.35–6). Visually, then, Shakespeare gives us a young version of Polixenes and
Hermione. Leontes' jealousy at the beginning of the play, which has
come to seem inexplicable even to him, can now perhaps be more fully
explained. It was simultaneously jealousy of Polixenes, because he had
sex with Hermione, and jealousy of Hermione, because she had sex
with Polixenes, as I said above; on the other hand, it was not jealousy at
all but rather a prophecy. The reproduction highlighted in *The Winter's
Tale*'s second half is, as it turns out, the reproduction of Polixenes and
Hermione. In effect, Leontes' tortured visions of the two having sex
were glimpses into the future, glimpses of the marriage that will only
take place after the play's conclusion. This marriage will, in a sense,
reproduce both Leontes and Polixenes, but Leontes will only have
posterity through the female line. With this in mind, I want to look

again at his first speech to Florizel:

> Your mother was most true to wedlock, Prince,
> For she did print your royal father off,
> Conceiving you. (V.i.124–6)

This is a depiction of reproduction that presents the father as passive and the mother as active. Furthermore, the fact that Leontes adduces Florizel's resemblance to Polixenes as evidence of his mother's fidelity suggests that his thinking has not changed very much since the first act. And when we consider that Perdita looks like Hermione, we can see that for Leontes the question of whether he is the father of his children is still to some extent unsettled even at the end of the play. At the very least, Perdita's lack of resemblance to Leontes emphasizes that he is shut out of the heterosexual union that is the only thing that can end the play.

Looked at from this point of view, Hermione's resurrection, which has occasioned so much discussion, could be considered as a strategy to disguise Leontes' exclusion. Even Polixenes, as an older version of Florizel, has at least a visual place with the happy couple. Nevertheless, rather than ending the play by being shut off from the rest of the characters, as Melantius is at the end of *The Maid's Tragedy*, Leontes is able to take part in the final tableau by the side of Hermione. What I really want to discuss at this point, however, is another event in the ending of *The Winter's Tale*, one that – like the return of Hermione – has no equivalent in *Pandosto*. This is the marriage of Camillo and Paulina – in its own way, as surprising a plot twist as Hermione's return. At the very end of the play, after she has brought all the characters together, Paulina does something unusual. Up until this point in the play, Paulina has always spoken on behalf of either Hermione or Perdita and she has not seemed particularly bothered by her widowhood. Now, when she has achieved everything she wanted, she speaks about herself:

> I, an old turtle,
> Will wing me to some wither'd bough, and there
> My mate (that's never to be found again)
> Lament till I am lost. (V.iii.132–5)

In response, Leontes says, 'Thou shouldst a husband take by my consent,/ As I by thine a wife' (V.iii.136–7) and proposes Camillo, who, he hints, has already thought of the match: 'For him, I partly know his mind' (V.iii.142). It should surprise us both that Leontes presents Paulina's marriage to Camillo as parallel to his reunion with Hermione and that he claims to know the mind of someone he has not seen for sixteen years.

What Leontes' speech conceals is the purpose this marriage serves in *The Winter Tale*'s negotiations with homoeroticism. For most of the play, Camillo and Paulina have been instrumental in moving the plot along and in keeping the memory of the events represented at the beginning of the play fresh. What is more, the ending of the play could not have happened without them, and the characters whose story the play could be said to narrate (those who would normally be described as the main characters, that is to say Leontes, Polixenes, Hermione, Perdita, and Florizel) are revealed at various points in the second half of the play to have been dependent on them. Camillo and Paulina have also – and for my purposes, crucially – continued, although in different forms, the homosociality that is so prominent in the play's first scenes, the former with Polixenes and the latter with Hermione. The union of Perdita and Florizel signals the end of the attention paid to homosociality, however, and now that Hermione has been restored to her family and Polixenes is primarily identified as the father of the groom, Camillo and Paulina are conspicuously isolated. By marrying them off, Shakespeare is able to provide one more example of how homosociality turns into hetero-sexuality. In lines 136 and 137, Leontes sets up a parallel between himself, on one hand, and Paulina, on the other, but I think a better parallel for Camillo and Paulina is with Florizel and Perdita. Along with Mamillius, these four are the only characters in *The Winter's Tale*, even including very minor ones like Mopsa and Dorcas, not to have Greek names. Thus, the four people who are going to get married at the end of the play all have Latinate names. The change from Greek to Latin can be seen chronologically as a change from old to new; in literary terms it can be seen as a change from a literature focusing on homo-sociality and homoeroticism to one that is increasingly concerned with heteroeroticism. And, of course, what Shakespeare leaves behind by using Latinate names is the pastoral, which traditionally uses only Greek names. The change, in other words, marks the new and heteroerotic dispensation under which not only the characters of the play but the pastoral genre as a whole will have to exist.

The reason for giving Mamillius a Latin name may not seem obvious, but I think it lies in the possibilities he embodies, or rather embodied.

At the beginning of Act V, when the news comes to Leontes that Florizel and his princess are in Sicily, Paulina says,

> Had our prince,
> Jewel of children, seen this hour, he had pair'd
> Well with this lord; there was not full a month
> Between their births. (V.i.115–18)

The reference to Mamillius emphasizes the all-important substitution of a girl for a boy that will finally take place when Perdita enters, and the reference to the closeness in birth of the two sons emphasizes their similarity, as opposed to the all-important difference between male and female in the union of Perdita and Florizel. Nevertheless, the passage still testifies to the possibility that things might have worked out differently. If we are to consider the boys as twins, then we have to recall that Polixenes and Leontes were originally like 'twinned lambs.' And while Paulina may use 'pair'd' simply to denote a similarity, the word cannot be stripped of its erotic charge. Connected in this case not by their births but by their Latinate names, Mamillius and Florizel are the couple whose story Shakespeare cannot tell, even in a narrative categorized as a winter's tale. Even the possibility of this story can only be mentioned once Mamillius is dead, when, that is, he has become a suitable subject for an elegy.

Postscript

Thoughout this book I have looked at old literature from my own contemporary perspective and drawn many conclusions. In the last few decades, it has become a truism to point out that this sort of inquiry is always biased, and as is the case with many truisms, this one bears repeating. In her article on women in Shakespeare's history plays, Phyllis Rackin issues a useful formulation of the problem: 'The questions with which we approach the past are the questions that trouble us here and now, the answers we find (even when couched in the words of old texts) the products of our own selection and arrangement.'[1] In this book, I have been concerned with precisely the issues raised by Rackin: What are the questions that have troubled people in their own here and now? What do people hope to find in old texts? What have they selected and arranged and how?[2] My own way of answering these questions has been close to Umberto Eco's formulation of what a reader does:

> Since the intention of the text is basically to produce a model reader able to make conjectures about it, the initiative of the model reader consists in figuring out a model author that is not the empirical one and that, in the end, coincides with the intention of the text. Thus, more than a parameter to use in order to validate the interpretation, the text is an object that the interpretation builds up in the course of the circular effect of validating itself on the basis of what is makes up as its result.[3]

In Eco's view, readers become writers in that they produce their own text, or at least their own version of an existing text. The new version will confirm their view (their reading) of the original. In these respects, the scholarly reader who analyses Virgil's *Eclogues* is doing the same sort of thing, *mutatis mutandis*, as Spenser or Barnfield or any of the many other pastoral poets since Virgil. Eco's emphasis on the power of the reader can be seen as a cause for celebration and this aspect of my book is very important to me. As I wrote in the introduction, one of the things I want to do is to consider how readers might interpret texts in order to construct homoerotic spaces, however covert or temporary those spaces might be. In part, I have been trying to recover a homoerotic tradition that is not secret – in fact, many of the works I have discussed and many others that could have been included in my book are central to our literary tradition. Still, this is not the whole story about homoeroticism in literature or about the sorts of imagery found in representations of homoeroticism. In the twentieth century, discussions of homosexual men have usually employed images of mourning. These images have often been traced to Freud, whose theories have been understood to say that homosexuality is a pernicious form of arrested development. Later writers transferred homosexuality from this relatively neutral category to the category of disease, and by the time of the popular fiction and movies produced after the Second World War, the disease had become fatal. More recently, of course, the rise of the AIDS pandemic in the 1980s has strengthened the connection between homosexuality and mourning.

This association is now so common that it has assumed the status of a natural fact. My point is not that there are never any reasons for the association – the fact of AIDS proves otherwise – but rather that it is to a great extent the result of the Renaissance adoption of tropes, images, and genres from classical literature as means to write about passionate connections between men. What may be perceived as self-evidently natural (e.g., homosexuality = death) is really cultural and historical, and as a part of culture this equation has been and still is the site of many interpretative battles. As examples of the combatants in these battles, I would mention both readers like myself, trying to find, restore, reclaim a homoerotic literary tradition and the generations of homophobic scholars who have produced countless disingenuous introductions (as in 'Speculation as to the nature of Whitman's sexuality has rocketed high above the facts,'[4] a statement that would certainly be true of speculation that he was heterosexual) and countless obfuscatory translations (as in most of the Loeb Classical Library). Attempts to clear some of Western literature's most favoured texts and authors from the suspicion of being 'that way' persist, but it is now possible to find scholars and translators who do not try to suppress the evidence of homoeroticism in the texts with which they are concerned and scholars and translators who actually celebrate this evidence.

A good deal of recent scholarship has focused on the role of the reader from feminist and queer perspectives and has taken as its starting point the idea that how we read is a function of who we are. In a recent article on pedagogy, for instance, Deborah P. Britzman points out that '[r]eading practices ... are socially performative' and adds that 'part of the performance might well be the production of normalcy ... if techniques of reading begin from a standpoint of refusing the unassimilability of difference and the otherness of the reader.'[5] The introductions and translations to which I have just referred would obviously fit into this class. Yet Britzman does suggest another way of reading, one that would lead the reader to think about his or her otherness and perhaps even to 'creat[e] a queer space where old certainties made no sense.'[6] This latter is more the model I have tried to follow in this book, although unlike Britzman and most analysts of reading practices I have concentrated on readers who are also writers. The 'queer spaces' created by the readers I have mentioned have become texts in their own right, subject to reading and to re-imagining by other readers. Still, there is a problem here: the spaces I have looked at have, as a rule, been temporary spaces, concerned with – and made possible by – death and other kinds of loss. For reasons that are simultaneously personal and political, I want to end this book with a look at a homoerotic space that is happy. My choice is Theocritus's twelfth idyll, a poem that is particularly interesting and useful to me because of its concern with placing the love affair that is the poem's subject in an existing tradition of homoeroticism and with extending that tradition into the future.[7]

Just before I turn to the idyll, I want to point out (or admit) that this book has tacitly presented a process with three chronologically organized stages: classical poets write poetry, Renaissance poets read those poems and write their own, and now, at the beginning of the twenty-first century, I write a scholarly analysis that takes its place in a long tradition of scholarly analyses of these poems. This form reflects my own interests and abilities, or limitations. In fact, the process of writing poems arising from a contemplation of classical poetry continues. I would like here to mention two particularly good examples of this sort of poem, both written quite recently by Canadian poets. Anne Carson's *Autobiography of Red* translates and transforms the fragments of Stesichoros's epic about Geryon, the monster whose cattle were stolen by Heracles as the tenth of his labours and who was subsequently killed by him. Here is her rendition of that death:

> Arrow means kill It parted Geryon's skull like a comb Made
> The boy neck lean At an odd slow angle sideways as when a
> Poppy shames itself in a whip of Nude breeze[8]

In their depiction of a young man's death and in their use of the image of the poppy familiar from Catullus and the *Aeneid* these lines could easily fit into the rest of my book, but Carson goes on to expand the fragments and to tell the story of Geryon and Heracles as lovers. *Autobiography of Red* ends (in South America) in a way that takes old narratives in new directions. Her fusion of old and new in content is reflected in her brilliant use of form; in the extract above, for instance, the words seem to hover between ancient Greek and modern English and the capital letters we have all been trained to read as indicating the first word of a line of poetry (and this was not the case with ancient Greek poetry) appear within lines. In other words, *Autobiography of Red* refuses to be either a brand-new poem or a translation. The new does not replace the old, but exists by its side.

The other poem is Lisa Robertson's *Debbie: An Epic*. In this revision and analysis of (and also tribute to) the great poet whom she addresses at one point as 'Virgil, sweetheart,'[9] Robertson, like Carson, sometimes rewrites the original words themselves. For instance, in a way that implicitly plays on the relationship between text and textile and that also highlights her own feminist interests, she turns Aeneas's famous line, 'forsan et haec olim meminisse iuuabit' (perhaps one day even this will be pleasant to remember; I.203) into 'maybe even this dress shall some day/ be a joy to repair' (339–40). Near the end of the book Robertson puts a particularly good example of her approach into the mouth of Debbie herself:

> I dreamt that Virgil mapped my lavish sleep
> I read the curbs of epic lust's *dérive*
> And there, saw myself.
> Precocious closure sculpts

Thin difference, thin frock.
I greet an ornament. Hello shepherdess! Lend me a bit of that stuff. That
fancy stuff. So Virgil, this is how it is. ('Appendix: Debbie's Folly')

Despite the obvious differences in form and in point of view between
my work on the one hand and Carson's and Robertson's on the other
(and the two poets are also very different from each other), I would like
to think that there are similarities as well. Reading and refashioning
poetry is something that is always being done and something that is
always still to do. This is another reason for my decision to end this
book with a discussion of Theocritus's twelfth idyll, as it stresses continuity and shows that matters of personal concern are not only of
personal concern and do not become irrelevant with the deaths of the
people involved.

The poem begins with the speaker directly addressing his lover: 'You've
come, o lovely youth. After two days and nights, you've come' (1–2). A
list of comparisons follows (3–7), after which the speaker says that his
delight in the return of his lover is equal to the amount by which spring,
for example, is preferred to winter (8). The comparisons begin with the
seasons (spring and winter), include fruit (apple and wild plum), women
(virgin and thrice-married woman), and animals (both ewe and lamb
and fawn and calf), and end with birds (nightingale and all other birds).
Although human beings are positioned centrally in this list, they are only
one of the comparisons. Theocritus presents humans and, in particular,
his own love as a natural fact, as something that takes place in a natural
environment. Like the music in the much more famous first idyll, the
speaker's love appears to arise naturally from the contemplation and
even the imitation of nature. The connection between these idylls is
suggested by the fact that the speaker says, 'I run to you like a traveller to
the shade of the oak in the heat of the sun' (8–9). Having already established the shade of a tree as the natural place for poetry to come into
being, Theocritus now links it to love.

After this declaration, the speaker makes a wish, the first of several
in the poem. His frequent use of the optative mood gives the idyll a
certain wistfulness, but he is not wistful about the love itself. His
concern is for the future, long after he and his lover will be dead:

If only equal loves might inspire both our minds, so that we could become
a song and a saying to all: 'There were two men in earlier times. One was
the lover, as the Amyclaeans might say; in contrast, the other, as a Thessalian

might say, was the lover. They loved each other under an equal yoke. They were golden men then: the one who was loved loved in return.' (10–16)

What strikes me most about these lines is the speaker's desire to become a song. As in the first idyll, Theocritus emphasizes the transition from life to art. What differentiates this from the first idyll, however, is the emphasis on posterity: it is not just that the love between the two men will result in a song, but that this song will be for the benefit of those who come after them (and these people are at least grammatically male). Taken as a whole, the first section of the twelfth idyll demonstrates that the speaker sees his love as being at once part of nature and part of a specifically homoerotic literary tradition. Although both these things would have seemed obvious to Theocritus, the idea of homoeroticism as natural and the idea that there is a homoerotic tradition in literature have been energetically suppressed in the millennia since the poem was written. I want to comment on some of my choices in translating the idyll. One of the distinctive features of the original is the use of the adverb *palin* (14 and 16), which I have rendered first as 'in contrast' and second as 'then' (in a temporal sense). Liddell and Scott give three main meanings for *palin*: 'back' or 'backwards,' as in palindrome; to signal a contradiction, as in palinode; and 'again' or 'in turn,' as in palimpsest. It could be argued that Theocritus's two uses here hover among those meanings, but the basic sense of going back, of repeating, draws attention to the reciprocity of the relationship between the lovers.

I have chosen to underscore this reciprocity in my translation of lines 13 and 14, in which the distinctive feature is Theocritus's use of synonyms. He uses two words for 'might say' and two for 'lover.' The two verbs (*phaie* and *eipoi*, respectively) are very similar in meaning and usage and his use of two words is probably not significant. The words for lover are uncommon, however, and I would like to consider them in greater detail. The two synonyms are closely connected both to each other and to the verb in line ten, which I have translated as 'inspire.' This verb is a form of *pneo* and means literally 'breathe' or 'breath forth' (as does 'inspire' itself, of course). The first word for lover (13) is *eispnelos*, which is a substantive form of *eispneo*, 'breathe upon' (literally, 'breathe into'). The second word for lover – it is also the usual title for the idyl – is *aites*, from *aio*, 'breathe.' The two words are almost indistinguishable in meaning. The interchangeability of the synonyms is heightened, since it is not clear how, or even if, the synonyms correspond to the distinction between lover and beloved familiar from the Attic terms *erastes* and *eromenos*. Theocritus separates these synonyms only by giving each its dialect origin. This aspect of the poem may well be the one that suprises us most now, trained as we have been in the past few years by scholars like David M. Halperin to regard the crucial sexual dichotomy in ancient Greece not as the one between heteroeroticism and homoeroticism but as that between penetrator and penetrated or between persons of high and low status. Although Halperin's work – and much of the other recent work on sexuality in the ancient world – is very valuable, perhaps Stan Persky has a point when he says, in his discussion of the *Symposium*, that he 'suspect[s] that the Athenians themselves had a more various idea of what to do in bed than some scholars credit them with.'[10] Scholars are readers too, and although our own reading of ancient poetry may be informed by them, as mine has been by Halperin, scholarly analysis is only one kind of reading practice. In its depiction of a love that appears not to be hierarchical at all, the twelfth idyll might be taken to gesture toward a different way of understanding Greek love.

I think what Theocritus is suggesting (and hoping) is that the love between these men will find expression even across the barriers of time and language. This is the wish he expresses just after this passage:

> If only, Father, son of Cronos, if only, ageless immortals, it might come to pass that after two hundred generations someone would tell me by the Acheron from which there is no return: 'The story of you and your beautiful lover is now on all lips, and especially on the youths'.' But all these things the gods above will decide as they wish. (17–23)

The repetition of 'if only' (*ei gar*), the reference to the gods as 'ageless immortals' (*ageroi athanatoi*, which contrasts with the statement at the beginning of the poem that lovers quickly grow old [*geraskousin*] when their beloveds are absent), the description of Acheron as a place from which no traveller returns, and the acknowledgment of divine power all stress the transience of human life and make the possible survival more impressive and moving and a greater tribute to the power of art. It is also significant that the song that the love has become is described as an object that literally passes through a man's mouth (*dia stomatos*). Here also Theocritus stresses mutuality, but this time his particular emphasis is on the physical side of their relationship. The equal love shared by the men begins as a verbal construct that we read and that describes an emotion and a physical relationship. Within the poetic frame, the speaker hopes (and even foresees) that his love will become a verbal construct once again and, also once again, something physical in the mouths of men. The poem and the story it tells become a kiss.

Kissing is, in fact, the subject of the poem's final section. The speaker informs us that the 'men of Megaran Nisaea' (27) are blessed because they honour the memory of 'Diocles, lover of boys' (28–9). Whereas before the speaker has looked to the future, here he draws on the past and places his poem in an existing homoerotic tradition. Diocles is honoured because he died in battle to save the youth he loved. The Megarans have erected a tomb to him that is the focal point of a ritual that keeps his memory alive in a way that he would have appreciated: 'Always around his grave at the beginning of spring, youths compete to win the prize in kissing. Whoever puts his lips most sweetly to other lips goes home to his mother weighed down with garlands' (30–3). The speaker sees the judge's task as difficult, although enviable, and says that he must pray to 'bright-eyed Ganymede for a mouth like the Lydian touchstone, by which moneychangers tell if gold is real or false' (35–7). The reference to money-changing may seem jarring to us, but the mention of gold and the idea that we establish what is valuable by comparisons and competitions recall the imagined description of the lovers as golden in line 17 and the comparisons in lines 4–6. The idea of choosing and cherishing what is valuable is central to the poem.

At thirty-seven lines, this is one of the shortest of the idylls,[11] yet its scope is very broad. Part of this scope is linguistic. For instance, the use of dialect terms of lovers in lines 13 and 14 (*eispnelos* and *aites*) can be seen as a way of making the poem accessible to readers who know different forms of Greek. The use of dialect in these lines is especially noticeable because this is the only one of Theocritus's poems to be written in Ionic rather than in Doric. Thus, to a reader of the idylls as a whole, the poem is already marked as dialectal. The scope of the poem is also geographical, something that is connected to, but not identical with, the dialectal scope. The geographical range is something we can see in Theocritus's own life, as he was from Syracuse and lived in both Cos and Alexandria. This range is reflected within the poem: the speaker mentions Amyclaea, Thessaly, Niseae, Attica, and Lydia, as well as heaven and the underworld, which are beyond geographical space altogether. Finally, there is the temporal range. The poem goes from the mythical (or at least distant) past to the historical past (Diocles) to the present and ultimately to both an unspecified future (the men who will tell their story) and a specified one (two hundred generations in the future), as well as mentioning the gods, who as 'ageless immortals' are beyond time. The reference to Ganymede is particularly interesting in this context. As a human who was granted immortality because of the power of his beauty over Zeus, Ganymede is the precedent for the sort of immortality the speaker desires for his love. He is an example of the triumphant power of homoeroticism.

Yet as everyone knows, the power of homoeroticism has not been a popular topic and narratives of homoeroticism have tended to be melancholy. As I noted in the introduction, even the story of Ganymede is only a triumphant one in celestial terms: the moral of the story could be that a man must give up his humanity in order to be happy with another man. Poems that depict a joyful homoeroticism in the here and now have always been rare and have not been well received or widely published (or taught). In the course of writing this book I have been mindful that I have concentrated almost exclusively on the literature of sorrow. My book could, I suppose, be taken to suggest that sorrow is a necessary component of the literature of homoeroticism. I do not believe this is true, however, and for both personal and political reasons I wanted to end the book with a brief discussion of the twelfth idyll, a poem that celebrates the love between two men and places that love in a tradition of celebratory homoeroticism. As I see it, Theocritus's point is that love between men is something that occurs in all places and at all times and that is passed on orally: by poetry and by kissing.

NOTES

Introduction

1 *The History of Sexuality*, trans. R. Hurley (New York: Vintage, 1980), 100–1.
2 The best account here is Anthony Grafton and Lisa Jardine's *From Humanism to the Humanities: Education and the Liberal Arts in Fifteenth and Sixteenth-Century Europe* (Cambridge, MA: Harvard University Press, 1986); for their account of the introduction of Greek, see 99–121.
3 *Homosexual Desire in Shakespeare's England: A Cultural Poetics* (Chicago: University of Chicago Press, 1991), 83.
4 See, for instance, Erasmus's famous analysis of the second eclogue in *De ratione studii*, *Collected Works*, vol. 24, ed. C.R. Thompson (Toronto: University of Toronto Press, 1978), 686–7. For a discussion of the Erasmus passage, see Jonathan Goldberg, 'Colin to Hobbinol: Spenser's Familiar Letters,' in R.R. Butters, J.M. Clum, and M. Moon, eds, *Displacing Homophobia: Gay Male Perspectives in Literature and Language* (Durham, NC: Duke University Press, 1989), 107–26.
5 'Marlowe and Constructions of Renaissance Homosexuality,' *Canadian Review of Comparative Literature* 21 (1994), 33.
6 All translations are my own. This is not because I feel that my translations are particularly poetic; rather, since all translation is to some extent interpretation, I wished to make my interpretation as clear as possible.
7 For two very interesting recent discussions of what is sometimes called transgressive reading, see Vivien Jones, 'The Seduction of Conduct: Pleasure and Conduct Literature,' in R. Porter and M.M. Roberts, eds, *Pleasure in the Eighteenth Century* (London: Macmilan, 1996), 108–32, and Mark D. Jordan, *The Invention of Sodomy in Christian Theology* (Chicago: University of Chicago Press, 1997), esp. 92–113.

8 *The Practice of Everyday Life*, trans. S. Rendall (Berkeley: University of California Press, 1984), 117.
9 Ibid., 34.
10 *The Light in Troy: Imitation and Discovery in Renaissance Poetry* (New Haven: Yale University Press, 1982), 53.
11 See ibid., esp. chaps 10, 12, and 13.
12 See *The History of Sexuality*, esp. 42–4.
13 *Homosexuality in Renaissance England* (London: Gay Men's Press, 1982), 59.
14 Ibid., 60.
15 'Marlowe and Constructions of Renaissance Homosexuality,' 43.
16 *Homosexuality in Renaissance England*, 60. For another objection to this point of view, see Alan Stewart, *Close Readers: Humanism and Sodomy in Early Modern England* (Princeton: Princeton University Press, 1997), esp. 123ff.
17 *Sodometries: Renaissance Texts, Modern Sexualities* (Stanford: Stanford University Press, 1992), 69.
18 For an example of this kind of reading, see Forrest Tyler Stevens's 'Erasmus's "Tigress": The Language of Friendship, Pleasure, and the Renaissance Letter,' in J. Goldberg, ed., *Queering the Renaissance* (Durham, NC: Duke University Press, 1994), 126.
19 *Homosexuality in Renaissance England*, 37.
20 '"To Serve the Queere": Nicholas Udall, Master of Revels,' in *Queering the Renaissance*, 169; see also 166–70.
21 'Homosexuality and the Signs of Male Friendship,' in *Queering the Renaissance*, 42–7.
22 *The Homosexual Literary Tradition: An Interpretation* (New York: Revisionist Press, 1974), 127.
23 *Between Men: English Literature and Male Homosocial Desire* (New York: Columbia University Press, 1985), 1.
24 John Boswell makes this point in his discussion of working with classical sources. See *Christianity, Social Tolerance, and Homosexuality* (Chicago: University of Chicago Press, 1980), 47. For a similar statement, see Mario DiGangi, *The Homoerotics of Early Modern Drama* (Cambridge: Cambridge University Press, 1997), esp. 43–4.
25 *De copia, Collected Works*, vol. 24, ed. C.R. Thompson (Toronto: University of Toronto Press, 1978), 492–3.
26 *Transuming Passion: Ganymede and the Erotics of Humanism* (Stanford: Stanford University Press, 1991), 40.
27 Ibid., 106. For a different look at the association between sodomy and art (and artists) in the Italian Renaissance, see Michael Rocke, *Forbidden*

Friendships: Homosexuality and Male Culture in Renaissance Florence (New York: Oxford University Press, 1996), 134–6. Rocke also tells the anecdote about Cellini and Bandinelli (136).

28 *Transuming Passion*, 106.
29 Ibid., 140n24.
30 *Epistemology of the Closet* (New York: Harvester Wheatsheaf, 1991), 144n14.
31 *Death, Desire and Loss in Western Culture* (New York: Routledge, 1998), xii.
32 It is curious that Dollimore – apart from a brief discussion of 'Adonais' – ignores the elegy altogether.
33 *On the Naïve and Sentimental in Literature*, trans. H. Watanabe-O'Kelly (Manchester: Carcanet, 1981), 48.
34 'Landscape in Greek Poetry,' *Yale Classical Studies* 15 (1957), 7.
35 *What Is Pastoral?* (Chicago: University of Chicago Press, 1996), 31.
36 'New English Sodom,' in *Queering the Renaissance*, 332.
37 This strategy is almost as old as ancient Greece. For two interesting discussions of the use of this strategy since the Renaissance, see Linda Dowling, *Hellenism and Homosexuality in Victorian Oxford* (Ithaca: Cornell University Press, 1994) and Byrne R.S. Fone, 'This Other Eden: Arcadia and the Homosexual Imagination,' *Journal of Homosexuality* 8:3/4 (1982–3), 13–34.
38 *Love between Men in English Literature* (New York: St Martin's, 1996), 88.
39 *Virgil's Eclogues: Landscapes of Experience* (Ithaca: Cornell University Press, 1974), 35.
40 *Before Pastoral: Theocritus and the Ancient Tradition of Bucolic Poetry* (New Haven: Yale University Press, 1983), 38.
41 *The Making of Jacobean Culture: James I and the Renegotiation of Elizabethan Literary Practice* (Cambridge: Cambridge University Press, 1997), 53.
42 Ibid., 54.
43 Ibid., 51. I chose to cite Perry as his is one of the most recent statements of the view that the pastoral is especially artificial. Examples could easily have been adduced from almost everyone who has ever written on the pastoral.
44 *Sodomy and Interpretation: Marlowe to Milton* (Ithaca: Cornell University Press, 1991), 199–200.
45 'The Book of Good Love? Design versus Desire in *Metamorphoses* 10,' *Ramus* 17 (1988), 121–2.
46 *Pastoral and the Poetics of Self-contradiction: Theocritus to Marvell* (Cambridge: Cambridge University Press, 1994), 8. Haber is developing Halperin's point in *Before Pastoral* that bucolic verse derives from epic

verse. Halperin takes as his starting point the fact that the *Idylls* are written in the dactylic hexameters of classical epic.

47 *Elegy and Paradox: Testing the Conventions* (Baltimore: Johns Hopkins University Press, 1994), 169.

48 'The Origin of Genres,' *New Literary History* 8 (1976–7), 160.

49 The best discussion of elegy as substitution is in Peter M. Sacks, *The English Elegy: Studies in the Genre from Spenser to Yeats* (Baltimore: Johns Hopkins University Press, 1985). See especially 1–37.

50 *Death, Desire and Loss in Western Culture*, 318.

51 Ibid., 319.

52 *Issues of Death: Mortality and Identity in English Renaissance Tragedy* (Oxford: Clarendon Press, 1997), 246.

53 'O queen, you order me to renew an unspeakable sorrow.' *Aeneid*, in *Opera*, ed. R.A.B. Mynors (Oxford: Clarendon, 1969), II.3. All references to the works of Virgil are to this edition.

Chapter 1: Classical Pastoral and Elegy

1 For an interesting discussion of definitions of pastoral as a genre and of the distinction between pastoral and bucolic, see Halperin's *Before Pastoral: Theocritus and the Ancient Tradition of Bucolic Verse*. For a problematization of questions of genre and origin in pastoral with reference to the *Eclogues*, see Charles Martindale's excellent 'Green Politics: The Eclogues,' in C. Martindale, ed., *The Cambridge Companion to Virgil* (Cambridge: Cambridge University Press, 1997), 107–9.

2 *Idylls*, in *Bucolici Graeci*, ed. A.S.F. Gow (Oxford: Oxford University Press, 1952), I.1–3, 7–8. All references are to this edition.

3 The word the Goatherd uses to describe Thyrsis's music is *melos*, which can mean either a song or the music to which the song is set. The former is more common; in any case, as the poem progresses there is a clear distinction between the Goatherd's piping and Thyrsis's singing.

4 *The English Elegy*, 14.

5 *Poetry and Myth in Ancient Pastoral: Essays on Theocritus and Virgil* (Princeton: Princeton University Press, 1981), 6.

6 *What Is Pastoral?* 81. Alpers cites the first idyll here.

7 *The Green Cabinet* (Berkeley: University of California Press, 1969), 118.

8 'Introduction,' in *Theocritus: Idylls and Epigrams* (New York: Atheneum, 1982), xix.

9 *Theocritus' Pastoral Analogies: The Formation of a Genre* (Madison: University of Wisconsin Press, 1991), 95.

10 *Placing Sorrow* (Chapel Hill: University of North Carolina Press, 1976), xxvii–xxix.
11 *Poetry and Myth in Ancient Pastoral*, 36.
12 *Elegy and Paradox*, 5.
13 'Theocritus, *Idyll* I: 81–91,' *Journal of Hellenic Studies* 89 (1969), 122.
14 Ibid.
15 *Theocritus at Court* (Leiden: E.J. Brill, 1979), 128.
16 *The Green Cabinet*, 64.
17 For a good analysis of the cup and a useful survey of criticism, see Gutzwiller, *Theocritus' Pastoral Analogies*, 88–94.
18 For an interesting discussion of the implications of this line, see G. Zuntz, 'Theocritus' I.95f.,'*Classical Quarterly* 10 (1960), 37–40.
19 There may be a further play on words here since the adjective *pikros* has the basic meaning of sharp and piercing and derives ultimately from *peuke*. Like *pitus* in line 1, *peuke* is a word for the pine tree that provides the shade necessary for pastoral singing.
20 For a detailed discussion of the shifts of diction in this poem, see Donald J. Mastronarde, 'Theocritus Idyll 13: Love and the Hero,' *Transactions of the American Philological Association* 99 (1968), esp. 279–81.
21 Ibid., 285.
22 *Poetry and Myth in Ancient Pastoral*, 59.
23 *Before Pastoral*, 234–5.
24 *Theocritus at Court*, 48n24. The reference is to the *Agamemnon* of Aeschylus.
25 The penultimate line is curiously ambiguous: when Virgil says that the 'summa ... uillarum culmina' are smoking, does he mean that the smoke is rising from hearths or that the farmhouses themselves are on fire? Perhaps we should take this as an example of Meliboeus's statement: 'en quo discordia ciuis / produxit miseros' (see how civil discord has brought forth miseries; 71–2).
26 *In Vergilii* Bucolica *et* Georgica *Commentarii*, ed. G. Thilo (Hildesheim: Georg Olms, 1961), 18, n. to Ecloga Secunda, line 1. All references to Servius are to this passage.
27 *Don Juan*, in *Poetical Works*, ed. F. Page (Oxford: Oxford University Press, 1970), I.XLII.7–8.
28 As Michael C.J. Putnam points out, the contrast is set up by the collocation of 'formosum' and 'pastor.' See *Virgil's Pastoral Art* (Princeton: Princeton University Press, 1970), 83.
29 *Virgil's* Eclogues: *Landscapes of Experience*, 144.
30 *Pastoral and the Poetics of Self-contradiction*, 38.

31 For a fuller discussion of this passage, see Putnam, *Virgil's Pastoral Art*, 109–10.

32 *Virgil's* Eclogues, 97n25.

33 *Virgil's Pastoral Art*, 112.

34 See ibid., 342–3 and 379–80.

35 Gallus's poems were thought to have been lost, but in 1978 a fragment (in which he complains about Lycoris) was found in Egypt. See R.D. Anderson, P.J. Parsons, and R.G.M. Nisbet, 'Elegiacs by Gallus from Qaṣr Ibrîm,' *Journal of Roman Studies* 69 (1979), 125–55.

36 *The Rhetoric of Imagination: Genre and Poetic Memory in Virgil and Other Latin Poets*, trans. C. Segal (Ithaca: Cornell University Press, 1986), 108.

37 *Virgil's* Eclogues, 160.

38 Conte points out that the verb 'concedere' is used in comedies to signal an exit. Gallus's use of it can thus be seen as another way for Virgil to suggest that the tenth eclogue is in part an examination of literary genres. See *The Rhetoric of Imagination*, 123n25.

39 *Virgil's Pastoral Art*, 346–8.

40 'The "Dying Gallus" and the Design of *Eclogue* 10,' *Classical Philology* 91 (1996), 131.

41 *Virgil's Pastoral Art*, 381.

42 *The Rhetoric of Imagination*, 126.

43 Ibid., 108.

44 *The Chaonian Dove: Studies in the* Eclogues, Georgics, *and* Aeneid *of Virgil* (Leiden: E.J. Brill, 1986), 32.

45 *Virgil's Pastoral Art*, 388.

46 Conte points out that the ending of the tenth eclogue can be read as Virgil's insistence that he has done what Apollo told him to do at the beginning of the sixth eclogue. See *The Rhetoric of Imagination*, 124n8.

Chapter 2: The *Aeneid* and the Persistence of Elegy

1 *Iliad*, ed. A.T. Murray (London: Heinemann, 1985), I.1. All references are to this edition.

2 When Achilles is finally ready to fight again, he tells Agamemnon that it is time to end the quarrel that began 'for the sake of a girl' (XIX.58).

3 *One Hundred Years of Homosexuality: and Other Essays on Greek Love* (New York: Routledge, 1990), 84.

4 'Lacan and Literature: Imaginary Objects and Social Order,' *Massachusetts Review* 22 (1981), 70.

5 The word Patroclus uses for a game of dice (*astragaloisi*) refers to what dice

were often made from: ankle bones. While his statement in lines 80–1 mentions the place where Achilles will die, his choice of words here foreshadows the part of the body where Achilles will be fatally wounded.

6 Achilles is *'prenea ... tanussas/ en konieis,'* while Hector is *'en koni ektanusas proprenea.'* The differences between the two phrases are great enough that Homer cannot be said to be using a stock phrase.

7 Of course, this would hardly be Priam's aim.

8 'Ganymede and Virgilian Ekphrasis,' *American Journal of Philology* 116 (1992), 436.

9 *Virgil* (Oxford: Oxford University Press, 1986), 94.

10 *The Rhetoric of Imagination*, 171–2. For an interesting recent discussion of this question, see Ellen Oliensis, 'Sons and Lovers: Gender and Sexuality in Virgil's Poetry,' in C. Martindale, ed., *The Cambridge Companion to Virgil* (Cambridge: Cambridge University Press, 1997), 309.

11 *Virgil's Iliad: An Essay on Epic Narrative* (Cambridge: Cambridge University Press, 1984), 112–14. Significantly, the first instance of vatic empathy in the poem is addressed to Dido (IV.408–11).

12 The adjective 'pius' is often misunderstood to mean that Nisus's love for Euryalus was not sexual. This error is apparently the result of assuming that 'pius' has the same Christian connotations as the modern English 'pious.' The Latin adjective has a range of meanings, including religious (although obviously not in the Christian sense), dutiful, kind, and gentle. The best discussion of the story of Nisus and Euryalus is John F. Makowski, 'Nisus and Euryalus: A Platonic Relationship,' *Classical Journal* 85 (1989–90), 1–15.

13 *The* Aeneid (London: Allen and Unwin, 1987), 18.

14 *The Child and the Hero: Coming of Age in Catullus and Vergil* (Ann Arbor: University of Michigan Press, 1997), 48.

15 *Catullus*, ed. C.J. Fordyce (Oxford: Oxford University Press, 1961), XI.22–4 and XLII.39–47. All references to Catullus are to this edition.

16 *Greek Lyric*, vol. 1, *Sappho and Alcaeus*, ed. D.A. Campbell (Cambridge, MA: Harvard University Press, 1982), Sappho 105(c).

17 See, for instance, Homer's use of it in his description of the death of one of Priam's sons (*Iliad* VIII.306–7).

18 *The Choice of Achilles: The Ideology of Figure in the Epic* (Stanford: Stanford University Press, 1992), 175.

19 *Virgil's Iliad*, 118.

20 *The Child and the Hero*, 51.

21 *Virgil's Iliad*, 90.

22 *The Rhetoric of Imagination*, 189–90.

232 Notes to pages 78–89

23 The plucking is a development of the intertexuality with Catullus, who says that the flower 'tenui carptus defloruit ungui' (fades when it is plucked by a tender fingernail; LXII.43).

24 *Redeeming the Text: Latin Poetry and the Hermeneutics of Reception* (Cambridge: Cambridge University Press, 1993), 42.

25 *Virgil's Iliad*, 45.

26 *Virgil's* Aeneid *and the Tradition of Hellenistic Poetry* (Berkeley: University of California Press, 1987), 100.

27 *The Epic Successors of Virgil: A Study in the Dynamics of a Tradition* (Cambridge: Cambridge University Press, 1993), 34.

28 *Virgil's* Aeneid, 100.

29 *Orpheus Dis(Re)Membered: Milton and the Myth of the Poet-Hero* (Sheffield: Sheffield Academic Press, 1996), 99.

Chapter 3: The Space of the Tomb

1 For a helpful discussion of Castiglione's Latin poems that includes translations of several of them (although not of 'Alcon'), see Joseph S. Salemi, 'Selected Latin Poems of Baldassare Castiglione,' *Allegorica* 6:2 (1981), 102–48.

2 *Milton and the Tangles of Neaera's Hair: The Making of the 1645* Poems (Columbia: University of Missouri Press, 1997), 2. Revard's discussion of the poem is on pages 226–36.

3 '"Will you rend our ancient love asunder?": Lesbian Elegy in Donne, Marvell, and Milton,' *ELH* 54 (1987), 847.

4 *Pastoral Process: Spenser, Marvell, Milton* (Stanford: Stanford University Press, 1998), 3.

5 'The name of the game / the game of the name: Sign and Self in Castiglione's *Book of the Courtier*,' *Journal of Medieval and Renaissance Studies* 18 (1988), 22–3, 24.

6 Castiglione studied Greek at Milan with Demetrios Chalcondylas, who edited the idylls, and he must have known Greek literature well. See José Guidi, 'Thyrsis ou la cour transfigurée,' in André Rochon, ed., *Ville et campagne dans la littérature italienne de la renaissance*, vol. 2 (Paris: Université de la Sorbonne Nouvelle, 1977), 153–4.

7 'Selected Latin Poems of Castiglione,' 102.

8 'When We Dead Awaken: Writing as Re-Vision,' In *On Lies, Secrets, and Silence: Selected Prose 1966–1978* (New York: W.W. Norton, 1979), 40–1.

9 'The Latin Pastorals of Milton and Castiglione,' *PMLA* 50 (1935), 481.

10 'Alcon,' in T.P. Harrison, Jr, ed., *The Pastoral Elegy* (Austin: University of Texas Press, 1939). All references are to this edition.

11 I have translated 'viduatus' as 'deprived of' (its basic sense), but the word also means 'widowed' and is the ancestor of modern Italian 'vedova' and cognate to English 'widow.' Castiglione's choice of this word – as opposed to 'orbatus,' which also means 'deprived of,' highlights the romantic implications of the passage.

12 Harrison capitalizes 'Superos' in line 63, so that it means 'the gods above'; without the capital it would mean 'the lands above.'

13 The wording of line 22 – 'serae ... decedere nocti' – is very close to the passage in the *Georgics* in which Virgil discusses signs of sickness in sheep, and the allusion may be significant. Virgil says that if a shepherd sees a sheep 'serae solam decedere nocti' (either 'retiring only late at night' or retiring by itself late at night'; III.467), he should kill it instantly before the contagion spreads.

14 If Harrison is correct in his assumption that Leucippus is Castiglione's brother, who died the year after Falcone, then the substitution of Leucippus for Iolas mirrors the earlier replacement of Leucippus for Alcon.

15 *Courtly Performances: Masking and Festivity in Castiglione's* Book of the Courtier (Detroit: Wayne State University Press, 1978), 215n28.

16 See Bent Juel-Jensen, 'The Poet Earl of Surrey's Library,' *The Book Collector* 5 (1956), 172n67.

17 For a thorough discussion of the relationship between Surrey and Richmond, see W.A. Sessions, *Henry Howard, the Poet Earl of Surrey* (Oxford: Oxford University Press, 1999), esp. chaps. 3 and 4.

18 The best account of Surrey as innovator and renovator is W.A. Sessions, 'Surrey's Wyatt: Autumn 1542 and the New Poet,' in P.C. Herman, ed., *Rethinking the Henrician Era: Essays on Early Tudor Texts and Contexts* (Urbana: University of Illinois Press, 1994), 168–92. The two best discussions of Surrey's achievement with blank verse are O.B. Hardison, 'Tudor Humanism and Surrey's Translation of the *Aeneid*,' *Studies in Philology* 83 (1986), 237–60, and Arturo Cattaneo, *L'ideale umanistico: Henry Howard, Earl of Surrey* (Bari: Adriatica Editrice, 1991), chap. 3.

19 For a discussion of this imprisonment, see Sessions, *Henry Howard, the Poet Earl of Surrey*, 129–30.

20 'Norfolk sprang thee,' in *Poems*, ed. E. Jones (Oxford: Oxford University Press, 1964), 10. All references to the poems of Surrey are to this edition.

21 'Truth and Mourning in a Sonnet by Surrey,' *ELH* 50 (1983), 516.

22 For a discussion of the homoeroticism of this sonnet, see Jonathan Crewe, *Trials of Authorship: Anterior Forms and Poetic Reconstruction from Wyatt to Shakespeare* (Berkeley: University of California Press, 1990), 64–7.

23 All references to Chaucer's poems are to *The Riverside Chaucer*, 3rd ed., ed. L.D. Benson (Boston: Houghton Mifflin, 1987).

24 *The Poems of Henry Howard, Earl of Surrey*, ed. F.M. Padelford (New York: Haskell, 1966), 9.
25 'Surrey's Five Elegies: Rhetoric, Structure, and the Poetry of Praise,' *PMLA* 91 (1976), 24.
26 *By Mourning Tongues: Studies in English Elegy* (Ipswich and Totowa, NJ: Boydell Press and Rowan and Littlefield, 1977), 2.
27 *Placing Sorrow*, 28.
28 Ibid., xiii.
29 *The English Elegy*, 8.
30 Ibid., 37.
31 Quoted in Edwin Casady, *Henry Howard, Earl of Surrey* (New York: MLA, 1938), 57.
32 'Contexts in Surrey's Poetry,' *ELR* 4 (1974), 41–2.
33 Ibid., 51.
34 Ibid., 52.
35 W.A. Sessions, *Henry Howard, Earl of Surrey* (Boston: Twayne, 1986), 130.
36 *Trials of Authorship*, 72.
37 'Contexts in Surrey's Poetry,' 45.
38 *The English Lyric from Wyatt to Donne* (Princeton: Princeton University Press, 1967), 71.
39 *Henry Howard, Earl of Surrey*, 128.
40 'Thomas Wyatt and Henry Surrey: Dissonance and Harmony in Lyric Form,' *New Literary History* 1 (1969–70), 396.
41 *Medieval to Renaissance in English Poetry* (Cambridge: Cambridge University Press, 1985), 318, 320.
42 'Contexts in Surrey's Poetry,' 52–3.
43 *Henry Howard, Earl of Surrey*, 129.
44 *Grief and English Renaissance Elegy* (Cambridge: Cambridge University Press, 1985), 70.
45 'Portraits of an Artist: Milton's Changing Self-Image,' *Milton Studies* 19 (1984), 179.
46 'High Pastoral Art in *Epitaphium Damonis*,' *Milton Studies* 19 (1984), 153.
47 'Milton and Diodati: An Essay in Psychodynamic Meaning,' *Milton Studies* 7 (1975), 152.
48 'Imitation in *Epitaphium Damonis*,' *Milton Studies* 19 (1984), 170.
49 'Milton and Diodati,' 131.
50 'Epitaphium Damonis,' in *Complete Poems and Major Prose*, ed. M.Y. Hughes (Indianapolis: Odyssey, 1957), 1–2. All references to the poems of Milton are to this edition.
51 Milton's other reference to Hylas occurs in *Paradise Regained* when Satan tempts Christ:

> in order stood
> Tall stripling youths rich clad, of fairer hue
> Than *Ganymede* or *Hylas*. (II.351–3)

Like a reference to Ganymede, a reference to Hylas is an allusion, clear to anyone with a classical education, to homoeroticism. For an analysis of the significance of the allusion, see Claude J. Summers, 'The (Homo)Sexual Temptation in *Paradise Regained*,' in R.-J. Frontain, ed., *Reclaiming the Sacred: The Bible in Lesbian and Gay Culture* (New York: Haworth Press, 1997), 45–69.

52 For a good discussion of the importance of the refrain, see Ralph W. Condee, 'The Structure of Milton's "Epitaphium Damonis,"' *Studies in Philology* 62 (1965), 577–94.

53 'Milton and Diodati,' 132.

54 *Opera*, ed. E.C. Wickham (Oxford: Oxford University Press, 1901), II.viii.21. The line is 'te suis matres metuunt iuvenci' (mothers fear you because of their young sons [literally, bullocks]). The poem is addressed to the courtesan Barine.

55 'Milton and the Sexy Seals: A Peephole into the Horton Years,' *Early Modern Literary Studies* 1:3 (1995), 5.3–4, 6–7.

56 See, for instance, Catullus 2, in which the poet envies Lesbia's sparrow its access to its mistress's body. Catullus quickly kills off the bird; see Catullus 3.

57 *Placing Sorrow*, 185.

58 *Forbidden Friendships*, 3. This book provides numerous examples of this association.

59 For the view that Italy does not pose any problems to Milton, see Revard, *Milton and the Tangles of Neaera's Hair*, 227–9.

60 'Sion's Bacchanalia: An Inquiry into Milton's Latin in the *Epitaphium Damonis*,' *Milton Studies* 16 (1982), 125.

61 'Portraits of an Artist,' 183.

62 'High Pastoral Art,' 150.

63 Ibid., 159.

64 '"Written Encomiums": Milton's Latin Poetry in Its Italian Context,' in M.A. DiCesare, ed., *Milton in Italy: Context, Images, Contradictions* (Binghamton, NY: Medieval and Renaissance Texts and Studies, vol. 90, 1991), 525.

65 'The *Consolatio* in Milton's Funeral Elegies,' *Huntington Library Quarterly* 34 (1970–1), 247.

66 This image of Diodati evokes a well-known passage from the *Georgics*:
> felix qui potuit rerum cognoscere causas
> atque metus omnis et inexorabile fatum

subiecit pedibus strepitumque Acherontis auari

(Happy is he who can know the causes of things and put every fear and inexorable fate and the roaring of greedy Acheron under his feet; II.490–2.)

As the contrast in the Virgilian passage is between this rather intellectual happiness and the simpler happiness of rural life, Milton may intend to suggest that Diodati is transcending the pastoral world altogether.

67 'The *Consolatio* in Milton's Funeral Elegies,' 247–8.

68 'Sion's Bacchanalia,' 128.

69 '"Lycidas," "Epitaphium Damonis," the Empty Dream, and the Failed Song,' in *Acta Conventus Neo-Latini Lovaniensis* (Leuven and Munich: Leuven University Press and Wilhelm Fink Verlag, 1973), 450.

70 *Unediting the Renaissance: Shakespeare, Marlowe, Milton* (London: Routledge, 1996), 218.

Chapter 4: Pastoral and the Shrinking of Homoerotic Space

1 And long after the Renaissance. The homoerotic elegy is one of the central genres of English poetry: Gray's elegy, Tennyson's *In Memoriam*, and the poems of Wilfred Owen are some of the most famous examples of this long and rich tradition.

2 Perhaps the most memorable example of the heterosexualization of the pastoral comes from Thomas Nashe's 'The Choice of Valentines.' The last line of the poem is an alteration of the last line of Virgil's third eclogue ('claudite iam riuos, pueri; sat prata biberunt'; close the watercourses, boys, the fields have drunk enough). Nashe renders this as 'Claudite iam rivos Priape, sat prata biberunt.' In this version, the 'rivos' are the liquids that gush from the dildo (addressed as Priapus) and the 'prata' are the female genitalia.

3 The best discussion of this is Richard Helgerson, *Self-Crowned Laureates: Spenser, Jonson, Milton, and the Literary System* (Berkeley: University of Cali-fornia Press, 1983). For a more politically inflected look at the topic see Robert Lane, *Shepheards Devises: Edmund Spenser's* Shepheardes Calender *and the Institutions of Elizabethan Society* (Athens: University of Georgia Press, 1993). For a sensible account of some of the problems with this criticism, see Ted Brown, 'Pride and Pastoral in *The Shepheardes Calender*,' in D.G. Allen and R.A. White, eds, *Subjects on the World's Stage: Essays on British Literature of the Middle Ages and Renaissance* (Newark: University of Delaware Press, 1995), 100–15, esp. 100–2.

4 Critical discussions of the homoeroticism of *The Shepheardes Calender* have tended to deal primarily (and sometimes exclusively) with the character of Hobbinol. The most famous of these is Jonathan Goldberg, 'Colin to Hobbinol: Spenser's Familiar Letters,' in R.R. Butters, J.M. Clum, and M. Moon, eds, *Displacing Homophobia: Gay Male Perspectives in Literature and Culture* (Durham, NC: Duke University Press, 1989), 107–26. For a somewhat different approach, see Richard Rambuss, 'The Secretary's Study: The Secret Designs of *The Shepheardes Calender*,' *ELH* 59 (1992), 313–35. The best recent discussions of Spenser's use of Virgil and Chaucer are John Watkins, *The Specter of Dido: Spenser and Virgilian Epic* (New Haven: Yale University Press, 1995) and Anthony M. Esolen, 'The Disingenuous Poet Laureate: Spenser's Adoption of Chaucer,' *Studies in Philology* 87 (1990), 285–311, although Esolen's emphasis is on the *Faerie Queene*.

5 'Januarye,' in *Poetical Works*, ed. J.C. Smith and E. de Selincourt (Oxford: Oxford University Press, 1983), 49–50. All references to Spenser's poems are to this edition.

6 Here as elsewhere it is hard to know what to make of E.K. Most of the criticism of E.K. is condemnatory in tone, but this may be changing. For recent discussions of E.K., see Frances M. Malpezzi, 'E.K., A Spenserian Lesson in Reading,' *Connotations* 4 (1994–5), 181–91, and Peter C. Herman, 'Poets, Pastors, and Antipoetics: A Response to Frances M. Malpezzi, "E.K., A Spenserian Lesson in Reading,"' *Connotations* 6 (1996–7), 316–25.

7 'The Secretary's Study,' 329.

8 'Colin to Hobbinol,' 108.

9 This passage seems to lead inexorably to the composition of the *Faerie Queene*, but the *Amoretti* (especially the seventy-fourth sonnet with its union of the three Elizabeths) could be said to provide another way to bring together the poet's own love for a woman with his desire to celebrate the queen.

10 For a good discussion of this passage see David R. Shore, *Spenser and the Poetics of Pastoral: A Study of the World of Colin Clout* (Kingston and Montreal: McGill-Queen's University Press, 1985), 75.

11 'Spenser's Farewell to Dido: The Public Turn,' in A.F. Kinney, ed., *Classical, Renaissance, and Postmodernist Acts of the Imagination: Essays Commemorating O.B. Hardison* (London: Associated University Presses, 1996), 113.

12 Spenser was not the first poet to write a formal elegy with a female subject. See Celeste Marguerite Schenk, *Mourning and Panegyric: The Poetics of Pastoral Ceremony* (University Park: Pennsylvania State University Press, 1988).

13 *Spenser and the Politics of Pastoral*, 101.

14 'Ploughing Virgilian Furrows: The Genre of *Faerie Queene* VI,' *John Donne Journal* 1 (1982), 158.

15 The name Thestylis itself is significant. In the second eclogue, this is the name given to the woman who makes salads for the reapers in the shade while Corydon wanders under the noon sun speaking of his love for Alexis. Spenser may wish us to see his Thestylis as a symbol of domesticity and heterosexuality; when he uses the names Corydon and Alexis later in the poem he may wish us to understand that these names have been purged of homoerotic connotations. This seems particularly clear in the case of the Corydon in Book VI of the *Faerie Queene*, whose distinguishing characteristic is his love for Pastorella.

16 For a discussion of the similarities of Book VI to the *Odyssey* as a heterosexual epic, see Donald Cheney, 'Colin Clout's Homecoming: The Imaginative Travels of Edmund Spenser,' *Connotations* 7 (1997–8), 146–58, esp. 156–7.

17 Very little is known of Barnfield's life. What we do know we owe to Andrew Worrall's painstaking research. See his 'Biographical Introduction: Barnfield's Feast of "all Varietie,"' in George Klawitter and Kenneth Borris, eds, *The Affectionate Shepherd: Celebrating Richard Barnfield* (Selinsgrove, PA: Susquehanna University Press, 2001), 25–40.

18 *Greenes Funeralls* was ascribed to 'R.B. Gent' on its title page. For a defence of Barnfield as the author, see George Klawitter, 'Introduction,' in *Richard Barnfield: The Complete Poems* (London and Toronto: Associated University Presses, 1990), 26. All references to the poems of Barnfield are to this edition. For the argument that Barnfield was the author of 'Orpheus His Journey to Hell,' see Wes Folkerth, 'The Metamorphosis of Daphnis: The Case for Richard Barnfield's *Orpheus*,' in *The Affectionate Shepherd: Celebrating Richard Barnfield*, 305–31. See also A. Leigh DeNeef, 'The Poetics of Orpheus: The Text and a Study of *Orpheus His Journey to Hell* (1595),' *Studies in Philology* 89 (1992), 20–70. Even if these poems and the others listed as Dubia were added to the canon of his work, it would not be a large canon.

19 In his groundbreaking article on Barnfield, Scott Giantvalley has a good, if brief, discussion of the sexual quality of the poems and the importance of this quality. See 'Barnfield, Drayton, and Marlowe: Homoeroticism and Homosexuality in Elizabethan Literature,' *Pacific Coast Philology* 16:2 (1981), 18–19. Klawitter's loving explication of the sexual implications of Barnfield's imagery fills the notes to his edition.

20 '"Ile hang a bag and bottle at thy back": Barnfield's Homoerotic Advocacy and the Construction of Homosexuality,' in *The Affectionate Shepherd: Celebrating Richard Barnfield*, 202–3.

21 Giantvalley has a good discussion of how Barnfield makes his pastoral
   poetry English. See 'Barnfield, Drayton, and Marlowe,' 16–17. See also
   Charles Crawford, 'Richard Barnfield, Marlowe, and Shakespeare,' *Notes
   and Queries* 8 (1901), 217–19 and 277–9, as well as Klawitter's notes. The
   best treatment of Barnfield's use of classical poetry is still Montague
   Summers's introduction to his edition, *The Poems of Richard Barnfield*
   (London: Fortune Press, [1936]).

22 *Complete Works of Christopher Marlowe*, 2 vols., ed. Fredson Bowers (Cambridge: Cambridge University Press, 1973). All references to Marlowe are
   to this edition.

23 The statement is so famous that it hardly counts as a quotation, but
   Barnfield may have been interested in Caesar's bisexuality as well. See
   Suetonius, *Divus Iulius*, ed. H.E. Butler and M. Cary (Oxford: Clarendon
   Press, 1927), chaps. 2 and 49–52, particularly Suetonius's comment that
   'Curio pater ... omnium mulierum virum et omnium virorum mulierem
   appellat' (the elder Curius calls him the husband of all women and the
   wife of all men; 52.3).

24 *Richard Barnfield, Colin's Child* (Tallahassee: Florida State University
   Studies, 1963), 19n4.

25 *Astrophil and Stella, The Poems of Sir Philip Sidney*, ed. W.A. Ringler, Jr
   (Oxford: Clarendon Press, 1982), XIV.14.

26 Klawitter sees this as a *poème à clef*. See his introduction 30–1, his notes *ad
   loc.*, and his 'Barnfield's Penelope Devereux, Exalted and Reviled,' in *The
   Affectionate Shepherd: Celebrating Richard Barnfield*, 62–82. I do not find his
   interpretation particularly convincing.

27 'Tradition and the Individual Sodomite: Barnfield, Shakespeare, and
   Subjective Desire,' in C.J. Summers, ed., *Homosexuality in Renaissance and
   Enlightenment England: Literary Representations in Historical Context* (New
   York: Haworth Press, 1992), 46. See also 'Ile hang a bag and bottle at thy
   back,' 205–6.

28 Sonnet 20, *The Riverside Shakespeare*, ed. G.B. Evans (Boston: Houghton
   Mifflin, 1974), 13–14. All references are to this edition. The theory that this
   sonnet shows that the speaker's love is not sexual has been questioned.
   See Joseph Pequigney, *Such Is My Love: A Study of Shakespeare's Sonnets*
   (Chicago: University of Chicago Press, 1985), 30–41. For the conventional
   view, see Helen Vendler, *The Art of Shakespeare's Sonnets* (Cambridge, MA:
   Belknap Press, 1997), 13–14 and 128–9.

29 Raymond-Jean Frontain connects the praise of blackness with the Song of
   Solomon as part of his argument that 'Barnfield seeks to authorize
   homoeroticism by vesting it in religiously approved language.' See '"An
   Affectionate Shepheard sicke for Love": Barnfield's Homoerotic Appro-

priation of the Song of Solomon,' in *The Affectionate Shepherd: Celebrating Richard Barnfield*, 112.

30 Critics tend to assume that homoerotic poetry is pederastic even when there is no textual evidence for any age difference. In 'Teares,' as in the second eclogue and, for that matter, most pastoral poems, there is nothing to indicate that the men in question are of different ages. See 'Barnfield, Drayton, and Marlowe,' 14–15.

31 In marked contrast to his usual assiduity, Klawitter does not appear to see any sexual imagery in these lines.

32 For an interesting discussion of this epistle, see 'Tradition and the Individual Sodomite,' 46–50.

33 *Richard Barnfield, Colin's Child*, 52.

34 'Barnfield's Certain Sonnets 8,' *Explicator* 57 (1998), 14.

35 *Delia with the Complaint of Rosamond* (Menston: Scolar Press, 1969). All references are to this edition.

36 Frederic W. Moorman says that Browne may have been the translator of a French prose romance that appeared in 1647 (Browne died around 1645). The attribution is not certain, however. See *William Browne: His* Britannia's Pastorals *and the Pastoral Poetry of the Elizabethan Age* (Strassburg: Karl J. Trübner, 1897), 18. This is still the only full-length study of Browne. The most thorough discussion of Browne since Moorman is in Joan Grundy, *The Spenserian Poets: A Study in Elizabethan and Jacobean Poetry* (London: Edward Arnold, 1969).

37 'On the Countess Dowager of Pembroke,' in *The Poems of William Browne of Tavistock*, ed. Gordon Goodwin (London: Lawrence and Bullen, 1894). All references are to this edition.

38 Readers who are confused by the narrative of *Britannia's Pastorals* are advised to consult the helpful summary in Moorman, *William Browne*, chap. 2.

39 For a good discussion of this point, see Sukanta Chaudhuri, *Renaissance Pastoral and Its English Developments* (Oxford: Oxford University Press, 1989), 323–38.

40 Browne wrote *Britannia's Pastorals* when he was at the Inns of Court. As is the case with many Stuart pastorals, it has been assumed that its characters are portraits of the authors and his friends. In his book on Francis Beaumont, Charles Mills Gayley says that Doridon and Remond represent Beaumont and Fletcher. See *Francis Beaumont: Dramatist* (London: Duckworth, 1914), 140–3. Gayley's book is a mine of information on the social and artistic aspects of the Inns of Court in Beaumont's time. For a more recent treatment of this subject, see James Doelman's introduction to *Early Stuart Pastoral* (Toronto: Centre for Reformation and Renaissance Studies, 1999).

41 Browne prepared for the allusion by referring to Hero and Leander in lines 430–2.
42 *Francis Beaumont: Dramatist*, 141.
43 The essentially homophobic belief that the myth of Narcissus equates homoeroticism with self-love is so prevalent as to pass almost unnoticed. For a helpful and interesting corrective, see Steven Bruhm, *Reflecting Narcissus: A Queer Aesthetic* (Minneapolis: University of Minnesota Press, 2001).
44 Moorman, *William Browne*, 101.
45 *Francis Beaumont: Dramatist*, 138. Moorman also identifies Alexis with Ferrar (*William Browne*, 128–9). I have been unable to trace the identification any further.
46 *Aubrey's Brief Lives*, ed. O.L. Dick (London: Secker and Warburg, 1950), 21.
47 Spenser's influence is important throughout *Britannia's Pastorals*, but Doridon has already explicitly modelled himself on Colin Clout (with reference to Colin's songs to Rosalind) in the third song of the first book (I.3.179–94).
48 See Gordon Goodwin (vol. 2, 333, note *ad loc.*). He calls the epigram 'pseudo-Virgilian,' but Browne would presumably have thought it genuine.

Chapter 5: Idylls and Kings

1 *The Homoerotics of Early Modern Drama*, 137. For an interesting discussion of one of Fletcher's plays from this angle, see Goran Stanivukovic, '"The blushing shame of souldiers": The Eroticism of Heroic Masculinity in John Fletcher's *Bonduca*,' in A.P. Williams, ed., *The Image of Manhood in Early Modern Literature: Viewing the Male* (Westport, CT: Greenwood Press, 1999), 41–54.
2 *Sexuality and Form: Caravaggio, Marlowe, and Bacon* (Chicago: University of Chicago Press, 2000), 26.
3 *The Maid's Tragedy*, ed. R.K. Turner, Jr, *The Dramatic Works in the Beaumont and Fletcher Canon*, vol. 2 (Cambridge: Cambridge University Press, 1970), I.i.12–14. All references are to this edition.
4 *Poets on Fortune's Hill: Studies in Sidney, Shakespeare, Beaumont and Fletcher* (London: Faber and Faber, 1952), 106.
5 For a good discussion of this pessimism, see William Shullenberger, '"This for the most wrong'd of women": A Reappraisal of *The Maid's Tragedy*,' *Renaissance Drama* n.s. 13 (1982), 131–56.
6 *Jacobean Revenge Tragedy and the Politics of Virtue* (Newark: University of Delaware Pres, 1999), 44.

7 *Tragedies of Tyrants: Political Thought and Theater in the English Renaissance* (Ithaca: Cornell University Press, 1990), 167.

8 '"This for the most wrong'd of women,"' 143.

9 For an excellent discussion of the erotic aspects of this speech, see Lisa Hopkins, '"A place privileged to do men wrong": The Anxious Masculinity of *The Maid's Tragedy*,' in *The Image of Manhood in Early Modern Literature*, 58.

10 *Court and Country Politics in the Plays of Beaumont and Fletcher* (Princeton: Princeton University Press, 1990), 183–4; see also 194ff. for a more detailed discussion of the similarities between Amintor and Aspatia. For a characterization of Evadne's behaviour as masculine, see *Jacobean Revenge Tragedy and the Politics of Virtue*, 131.

11 '"A place privileged to do men wrong,"' 55.

12 Melantius has already made the connection between fighting and eroticism in his description of the masque as 'soft and silken warres' (I.i.41). A similar connection is made by Dula when she says to Evadne, 'Madame shall we undresse you for this fight?/ The wars are nak't that you must make to night' (II.i.1–2). Beaumont and Fletcher force the audience to pay attention to what was almost a dead metaphor in the literature of their time.

13 'Staging the Feminine Performance of Desire: Masochism in *The Maid's Tragedy*,' *Papers on Language and Literature* 31 (1995), 317.

14 The best discussion of the masque is Michael Neill, '"The Simetry, Which Gives a Poem Grace": Masque, Imagery, and the Fancy of *The Maid's Tragedy*,' *Renaissance Drama* n.s. 3 (1970), 111–34. See also *Court and Country Politics in the Plays of Beaumont and Fletcher*, 186.

15 '"A place privileged to do men wrong,"' 56. This substitution also foreshadows the substitution at the end of the play when Lysippus takes his brother's place as king of Rhodes.

16 '"A maidenhead, *Amintor*, at my yeares": Chastity and Tragicomedy in the Fletcher Plays,' in G. McMullan and J. Hope, eds, *The Politics of Tragicomedy: Shakespeare and After* (London: Routledge, 1992), 93.

17 'Staging the Feminine Performance of Desire,' 318.

18 *Jacobean Revenge Tragedy and the Politics of Desire*, 130.

19 '"A place privileged to do men wrong,"' 64.

20 'On the Sources of *The Maid's Tragedy*,' *Modern Language Notes* 31 (1916), 503.

21 For a good analysis of the story of Harmodius and Aristogeiton and its use in Greek culture, see Michael W. Taylor, *The Tyrant Slayers: The Heroic Image in Fifth Century B.C. Athenian Art and Politics* (New York: Arno, 1981).

22 *Plutarch's Moralia*, trans. P. Holland (London: J.M. Dent, 1911). One of the stories that mentions Harmodius and Aristogeiton ('Of Intemperate Speech or Garrulity') tells how the harlot Leaena refused, even under torture, to implicate the other conspirators. This may have provided hints for the story of Evadne.

23 '"This for the most wrong'd of women,"' 132.

24 *The Body Embarrassed: Drama and the Disciplines of Shame in Early Modern England* (Ithaca: Cornell University Press, 1993), chap. 1, esp. 44–50.

25 In II.i (the scene of the wedding night), Evadne and Aspatia are together on stage as the women wait for Amintor to arrive. The meeting of the three seems inevitable, but Evadne leaves after line 108, Amintor enters after 109, Aspatia leaves after 124, and Evadne returns at line 137. Thus, in a manner that would on stage recall a bedroom farce, Beaumont and Fletcher contrive to avoid the meeting of the three characters.

26 '"This for the most wrong'd of women,"' 151.

27 '"A place privileged to do men wrong,"' 71.

28 See, for example, Stephen Orgel, 'The Poetics of Incomprehensibility,' *Shakespeare Quarterly* 42 (1991), 431–7 and the following series of connected articles: David Laird, 'Competing Discourses in *The Winter's Tale*,' *Connotations* 4 (1994–5), 25–43; Maurice Hunt, 'Modern and Postmodern Discourses in Shakespeare's *The Winter's Tale*: A Response to David Laird,' *Connotations* 5 (1995–6), 83–4; and Laird, 'An Answer to Maurice Hunt's "Modern and Postmodern Discourses in Shakespeare's *The Winter's Tale*,"' *Connotations* 6 (1996–7), 246–50. An excellent article that approaches this topic through, among other things, the allusion to Giulio Romano, is Elisabetta Cori's '"Deceiv'd in that which seems so": L'iconografia dell'illusione in *The Winter's Tale*,' *Strumenti Critici* n.s. 14 (1999), 1–34.

29 For a discussion of the play that considers Renaissance theories of genres and makes reference to pastoral, see Robert Henke, '*The Winter's Tale* and Guarinian Dramaturgy,' *Comparative Drama* 27 (1993–4), 197–217.

30 'Time, Sexual Love, and the Uses of Pastoral in *The Winter's Tale*,' *Modern Language Quarterly* 33 (1972), 6.

31 'Ganymedes and Kings: Staging Male Homosexual Desire in *The Winter's Tale*,' *Shakespeare Studies* 26 (1998), 189 and 198–9.

32 *Pandosto*, in *The Life and Complete Works in Prose and Verse of Robert Greene, M.A.*, vol. 4, ed. A.B. Grosart (New York: Russell and Russell, 1964), 234. All references are to this edition.

33 For an interesting discussion of Shakespeare's use of settings, see Michele Marrapodi, '"Of that fatal country": Sicily and the Rhetoric of Topography in *The Winter's Tale*,' in M. Marrapodi et al., eds, *Shakespeare's Italy: Func-*

tions of Italian Locations in Renaissance Drama (Manchester: Manchester University Press, 1993), 213–28. The best study of Shakespeare's adaptation of Greene is Claudia Corti, 'Quando dire è fare: Da *Pandosto* a *The Winter's Tale*,' *Rivista di Letterature Moderne e Comparate* n.s. 44 (1991), 19–44.

34 '"Verily Bearing Blood": Pornography, Sexual Love, and the Reclaimed Feminine in *The Winter's Tale*,' *Essays in Theatre* 9 (1990–1), 63.

35 *Dream Works: Lovers and Families in Shakespeare's Plays* (Toronto: University of Toronto Press, 1987), 195.

36 Michael W. Price has published an intriguing note on the significance of this passage, which he relates to the play's concern with linguistic indeterminacy. See 'Shakespeare's *The Winter's Tale* I.2.1–9,' *The Explicator* 52 (1993–4), 140–2.

37 The ambiguities in Polixenes' speeches, the queen's obvious affection for him, and the fact that he has been in Sicily long enough to be the father of the child she is carrying (to say nothing of the fact that nine months really is a long time for a king to be away from his kingdom) all indicate that Leontes' jealousy is not strictly speaking baseless, as it is often said to be. Still, Shakespeare has made the situation noticeably less ambiguous than it was in *Pandosto*, in which various things occur that might reasonably appear to a husband as evidence of adultery; see *Pandosto*, 237–8.

38 A similar desire to deny homoeroticism occurs in discussions of Helena's reproachful speech to Hermia in *A Midsummer's Night's Dream* (III.ii.195–219). Shakespeare does nothing to prevent readings of that relationship or of the one between Leontes and Polixenes as sexual. One of the few critics even to consider the possibility that the boyhood friendship between Leontes and Polixenes was sexual is Murray M. Schwartz. See 'Leontes' Jealousy in *The Winter's Tale*,' *American Imago* 30 (1973), 251–2.

39 'Metacriticism and Materiality: The Case of Shakespeare's *The Winter's Tale*,' *ELH* 58 (1991), 290.

40 'The Providential Tempest and the Shakespearean Family,' in M.M. Schwartz and C. Kahn., eds, *Representing Shakespeare: New Psychoanalytic Essays* (Baltimore: Johns Hopkins University Press, 1980), 233. There are many similar judgments; see Stockholder, *Dream Works*, 185, and Lawrence Danson, '"The Catastrophe is a Nuptial": The Space of Masculine Desire in *Othello*, *Cymbeline*, and *The Winter's Tale*,' *Shakespeare Survey* 46 (1994), 78. I have chosen to single out these writers because their work is in other respects so good.

41 *Love between Men in English Literature* (New York: St Martin's, 1996), 58. His treatment of *The Winter's Tale* is to be found on 56–8.

42 *Character and Motive in Shakespeare: Some Recent Appraisals Examined* (London: Longman, Greene, and Co., 1949), 35. Stewart's approach is heavily Freudian; for a similar analysis without the Freud (and without references to Stewart), see John Ellis, 'Rooted Affection: The Genesis of Jealousy in *The Winter's Tale*,' *College English* 25 (1963–4), 545–7. Since then, analyses of this subject have tended to proceed along psychoanalytic lines. The most famous are Murray M. Schwartz, 'Leontes' Jealousy in *The Winter's Tale*' (see n. 38 above) and its continuation, '*The Winter's Tale*: Loss and Transformation,' *American Imago* 32 (1975), 145–99. See also René Girard, 'The Crime and Conversion of Leontes in *The Winter's Tale*,' *Religion and Literature* 22:2/3 (1990), 193–219.

43 'Ganymedes and Kings,' 199.

44 For an intriguing discussion of Leontes' anxieties about paternity, see Stanley Cavell, *Disowning Knowledge in Six Plays of Shakespeare* (Cambridge: Cambridge University Press, 1987), esp. 195 and 212–14.

45 What I am describing here is both a narrative and a generic reversal. For a study of the play that discusses a different kind of reversal and that concentrates on the character of Paulina, see Andrew Gash, 'Shakespeare, Carnival and the Sacred: *The Winter's Tale* and *Measure for Measure*,' in R. Knowles, ed., *Shakespeare and Carnival: After Bakhtin* (London: Macmillan, 1998), esp. 189–97.

46 Johnson argues that the character of Camillo is intended to have a certain homoerotic resonance and points out that as cupbearer to Leontes he has the same function as Ganymede in relation to Zeus; see 'Ganymedes and Kings,' 204–5. It may be significant that the character in Greene who is equivalent to Camillo is called Franion (see *Pandosto*, 240), a word that means a wanton young man but that is used of a woman by Spenser in the *Faerie Queene* (V.iii.22) and may thus have seemed androgynous to Shakespeare.

47 In writing this scene Shakespeare may have recalled Marlowe's 'The Passionate Shepherd to his Love,' another pastoral with an awareness of winter (at least in the six-stanza version first published in 1600 in *Englands Helicon*):
    A gowne made of the finest wooll,
    Which from our pretty Lambes we pull,
    Fayre lined slippers for the cold. (13–15)

48 'Ganymedes and Kings,' 204.

49 This is the speech cited by Schwartz when he argues for a sexual component in the boyhood relationship of Leontes and Polixenes. See n. 38 above.

2464664646 Notes to pages 216–23

Postscript

'Foreign Country: The Place of Women and Sexuality in Shakespeare's Historical World,' in R. Burt and J.M. Archer, eds, *Enclosure Acts: Sexuality, Property, and Culture in Early Modern England* (Ithaca: Cornell University Press, 1994), 68. For an article that focuses on this issue with particular reference to Spenser, see Jim Ellis, 'Desire in Translation: Friendship in the Life and Work of Spenser,' *English Studies in Canada* 20 (1994), 171–85, esp. 180–2.
2 One way to assess the centrality of these questions (and especially of the last) to my own work is to remember that both selection and arrangement are English equivalents for the Greek '*eklego*,' which was taken into Latin and eventually became the English 'eclogue.'
3 'Overinterpreting Texts,' in S. Cellini, ed., *Interpretation and Overinterpretation* (Cambridge: Cambridge University Press, 1992), 54.
4 James E. Miller, 'Introduction,' in *Complete Poetry and Selected Poetry of Walt Whitman* (Boston: Houghton Mifflin, 1959), xxxii. This example was chosen at random. I would like to make two points about it: first, although Miller's introduction is over forty years old and thus does not represent the cutting edge of Whitman criticism, it would be naive to think that scholars have, as a group, moved beyond this sort of thing; second, although there are now many studies of Whitman that are not afraid to discuss his sexuality, Miller's edition is still likely to be the undergraduate's copy of Whitman.
5 'Queer Pedagogy and Its Strange Techniques,' in J.L. Ristock and C.G. Taylor, eds, *Inside the Academy and Out: Lesbian / Gay / Queer Studies and Social Action* (Toronto: University of Toronto Press, 1998), 55.
6 Ibid.
7 My interest in this poem does not appear to be shared: the twelfth idyll has attracted almost no critical attention and as a rule it has only been translated in complete editions of Theocritus. There is a double translation (into French and into heterosexual terms) by the French Renaissance poet Jean Vauquelin de la Fresnaie. See his *Idillies et Pastoralles. I.76, Les Diverses Poésies*, vol. 2 (Geneva: Slatkin, 1968).
8 *Autobiography of Red* (New York: Vintage, 1999), 13.
9 *Debbie: An Epic* (Vancouver: New Star Books, 1997), 166. All references are to this edition. This is Robertson's third book; her second also dealt with Virgil and the pastoral. See *Xeclogue* (Vancouver: Tsunami Editions, 1993).
10 *Autobiography of a Tattoo* (Vancouver: New Star Books, 1997), 170.
11 Only four of the thirty idylls attributed to Theocritus are shorter: IX (36 lines), XIX (8 ll.), XXVIII (25 ll.), and XXX (32 ll.). Many are much longer.

WORKS CITED

Allman, Eileen. *Jacobean Revenge Tragedy and the Politics of Virtue*. Newark: University of Delaware Press, 1999.

Alpers, Paul. *What Is Pastoral?* Chicago: University of Chicago Press, 1996.

Anderson, R.D., P.J. Parsons, and R.G.M. Nisbet. 'Elegiacs by Gallus from Qaṣr Ibîm.' *Journal of Roman Studies* 69 (1979), 125–55.

Aubrey, John. *Aubrey's Brief Lives*. Ed. Oliver Lawson Dick. London: Secker and Warburg, 1950.

Barkan, Leonard. *Transuming Passion: Ganymede and the Erotics of Humanism*. Stanford: Stanford University Press, 1991.

Barnfield, Richard. *The Poems of Richard Barnfield*. Ed. Montague Summers. London: Fortune Press, [1936].

– *The Complete Poems*. Ed. George Klawitter. London and Toronto: Associated University Presses, 1990.

Beaumont, Francis, and John Fletcher. *The Maid's Tragedy*. Ed. Robert K. Turner, Jr. *The Dramatic Works in the Beaumont and Fletcher Canon*. Volume 2. Cambridge: Cambridge University Press, 1970.

Borris, Kenneth. '"Ile hang a bag and bottle at thy back": Barnfield's Homoerotic Advocacy and the Construction of Homosexuality.' In George Klawitter and Kenneth Borris, eds, *The Affectionate Shepherd: Celebrating Richard Barnfield*, 193–248. Selinsgrove, PA: Susquehanna University Press, 2001.

Boswell, John. *Christianity, Social Tolerance, and Homosexuality*. Chicago: University of Chicago Press, 1980.

Boyle, A.J. *The Chaonian Dove: Studies in the* Eclogues, Georgics, *and* Aeneid *of Virgil*. Leiden: E.J. Brill, 1986.

Bray, Alan. *Homosexuality in Renaissance England*. London: Gay Men's Press, 1982.

- 'Homosexuality and the Signs of Male Friendship.' *History Workshop Journal* 29 (1990), 1–19. Reprinted in Jonathan Goldberg, ed., *Queering the Renaissance*, 40–61. Durham: Duke University Press, 1994.
Bredbeck, Gregory M. *Sodomy and Interpretation: Marlowe to Milton*. Ithaca: Cornell University Press, 1991.
- 'Tradition and the Individual Sodomite: Barnfield, Shakespeare, and Subjective Desire.' In Claude J. Summers, ed., *Homosexuality in Renaissance and Enlightenment England: Literary Representations in Historical Context*, 41–68. New York: Haworth Press, 1992.
Briggs, William Dinsmore. 'On the Sources of *The Maid's Tragedy*.' *Modern Language Notes* 31 (1916), 502–3.
Britzman, Deborah P. 'Queer Pedagogy and Its Strange Techniques.' In Janice L. Ristock and Catherine G. Taylor, eds, *Inside the Academy and Out: Lesbian / Gay / Queer Studies and Social Action*, 49–71. Toronto: University of Toronto Press, 1988.
Brown, Ted. 'Pride and Pastoral in *The Shepheardes Calender*.' In David G. Allen and Robert A. White, eds, *Subjects on the World's Stage: Essays on British Literature of the Middle Ages and the Renaissance*, 100–15. Newark: University of Delaware Press, 1995.
Browne, William. *The Poems of William Browne of Tavistock*. Ed. Gordon Goodwin. 2 vols. London: Lawrence and Bullen, 1894.
Bruhm, Stephen. *Reflecting Narcissus: A Queer Aesthetic*. Minneapolis: University of Minnesota Press, 2001.
Bruss, Neal H. 'Lacan and Literature: Imaginary Objects and Social Order.' *Massachusetts Review* 22 (1981), 62–92.
Bushnell, Rebecca. *Tragedies of Tyrants: Political Thought and Theater in the English Renaissance*. Ithaca: Cornell University Press, 1990.
Byron, George Gordon, Lord. *Poetical Works*. Ed. Frederick Page. Oxford: Oxford University Press, 1970.
Campbell, Gordon. 'Imitation in *Epitaphium Damonis*.' *Milton Studies* 19 (1984), 165–77.
Carson, Anne. *Autobiography of Red*. New York: Vintage, 1999.
Casady, Edwin. *Henry Howard, Earl of Surrey*. New York: MLA, 1938.
Castiglione, Baldassare. 'Alcon.' In Thomas Perrin Harrison, Jr, ed., *The Pastoral Elegy*. Austin: Texas University Press, 1939.
Cattaneo, Arturo. *L'ideale umanistico: Henry Howard, Earl of Surrey*. Bari: Adriatica Editrice, 1991.
Catullus. *Catullus*. Ed. C.J. Fordyce. Oxford: Oxford University Press, 1961.
Cavell, Stanley. *Disowning Knowledge in Six Plays of Shakespeare*. Cambridge: Cambridge University Press, 1987.

Chaucer, Geoffrey. *The Riverside Chaucer*. 3rd ed. Ed. Larry D. Benson. Boston: Houghton Mifflin, 1987.

Chaudhuri, Sukanta. *Renaissance Pastoral and Its English Developments*. Oxford: Oxford University Press, 1989.

Cheney, Donald. 'Colin Clout's Homecoming: The Imaginative Travels of Edmund Spenser.' *Connotations* 7 (1997–8), 146–58.

Clausen, Wendell. *Virgil's Aeneid and the Tradition of Hellenistic Poetry*. Berkeley: University of California Press, 1987.

Condee, Ralph W. 'The Structure of Milton's "Epitaphium Damonis."' *Studies in Philology* 62 (1965), 577–94.

Conte, Gian Biagio. *The Rhetoric of Imagination: Genre and Poetic Memory in Virgil and Other Latin Poets*. Trans. Charles Segal. Ithaca: Cornell University Press, 1986.

Cori, Elisabetta. '"Deceiv'd in that which seems so": L'iconografia dell'illusione in "The Winter's Tale."' *Strumenti Critici* n.s. 14 (1999), 1–34.

Corti, Claudia. 'Quando dire è fare: Da *Pandosto* a *The Winter's Tale*.' *Rivista di Letterature Moderne e Comparate* n.s. 44 (1991), 19–44.

Crawford, Charles. 'Richard Barnfield, Marlowe, and Shakespeare.' *Notes and Queries* 8 (1901), 217–19 and 277–9.

Crewe, Jonathan. *Trials of Authorship: Anterior Forms and Poetic Reconstruction from Wyatt to Shakespeare*. Berkeley: University of California Press, 1990.

Danby, John F. *Poets on Fortune's Hill: Studies in Sidney, Shakespeare, Beaumont and Fletcher*. London: Faber and Faber, 1952.

Daniel, Samuel. *Delia with the Complaint of Rosamond*. Menston: Scolar Press, 1969.

Danson, Lawrence. '"The Catastrophe is a Nuptial": The Space of Masculine Desire in *Othello*, *Cymbeline*, and *The Winter's Tale*.' *Shakespeare Survey* 46 (1994), 69–79.

Davis, Walter R. 'Contexts in Surrey's Poetry.' *English Literary Renaissance* 4 (1974), 40–55.

De Certeau, Michel. *The Practice of Everyday Life*. Trans. Steven Rendall. Berkeley: University of California Press, 1984.

DeNeef, A. Leigh. 'Ploughing Virgilian Furrows: The Genres of *Faerie Queene* VI.' *John Donne Journal* 1 (1982), 151–66.

– 'The Poetics of Orpheus: The Text and a Study of *Orpheus His Journey to Hell* (1595).' *Studies in Philology* 89 (1992), 20–70.

DiGangi, Mario. *The Homoerotics of Early Modern Drama*. Cambridge: Cambridge University Press, 1997.

Doelman, James. 'Introduction.' In *Early Stuart Pastoral*, 7–14. Toronto: Centre for Reformation and Renaissance Studies, 1999.

Dollimore, Jonathan. *Death, Desire and Loss in Western Culture*. New York: Routledge, 1998.

Dowling, Linda. *Hellenism and Homosexuality in Victorian Oxford*. Ithaca: Cornell University Press, 1994.

Eco, Umberto. 'Overinterpreting Texts.' In Stefan Cellini, ed., *Interpretation and Overinterpretation*, 45–66. Cambridge: Cambridge University Press, 1992.

Ellis, Jim. 'Desire in Translation: Friendship in the Life and Work of Spenser.' *English Studies in Canada* 20 (1994), 171–85.

Ellis, John. 'Rooted Affection: The Genesis of Jealousy in *The Winter's Tale*.' *College English* 25 (1963–4), 545–7.

Erasmus, Desiderius. *Collected Works*. Volume 24. Ed. Craig R. Thompson. Toronto: University of Toronto Press, 1978.

Esolen, Anthony M. 'The Disingenuous Poet Laureate: Spenser's Adoption of Chaucer.' *Studies in Philology* 87 (1990), 235–311.

Falconer, Rachel. *Orpheus Dis(Re)Membered: Milton and the Myth of the Poet-Hero*. Sheffield: Sheffield Academic Press, 1996.

Finkelpearl, Philip J. *Court and Country Politics in the Plays of Beaumont and Fletcher*. Princeton: Princeton University Press, 1990.

Folkerth, Wes. 'The Metamorphosis of Daphnis: The Case for Richard Barnfield's Orpheus.' In George Klawitter and Kenneth Borris, eds, *The Affectionate Shepherd: Celebrating Richard Barnfield*, 305–31. Selinsgrove, PA: Susquehanna University Press, 2001.

Fone, Byrne R.S. 'This Other Eden: Arcadia and the Homosexual Imagination.' *Journal of Homosexuality* 8:3/4 (1982–3), 13–34.

Foucault, Michel. *The History of Sexuality*. Volume 1. Trans. Robert Hurley. New York: Vintage, 1980.

Frontain, Raymond-Jean. '"An Affectionate Shepheard sicke for Love": Barnfield's Homoerotic Appropriation of the Song of Solomon.' In George Klawitter and Kenneth Borris, eds, *The Affectionate Shepherd: Celebrating Richard Barnfield*, 99–114. Selinsgrove, PA: Susquehanna University Press, 2001.

Gash, Andrew. 'Shakespeare, Carnival and the Sacred: *The Winter's Tale* and *Measure for Measure*.' In Ronald Knowles, ed., *Shakespeare and Carnival: After Bakhtin*, 177–210. London: Macmillan, 1998.

Gayley, Charles Mills. *Francis Beaumont: Dramatist*. London: Duckworth, 1914.

Giantvalley, Scott. 'Barnfield, Drayton, and Marlowe: Homoeroticism and Homosexuality in Elizabethan Literature.' *Pacific Coast Philology* 16:2 (1981), 9–24.

Girard, René. 'The Crime and Conversion of Leontes in *The Winter's Tale.*' *Religion and Literature* 22:2/3 (1990), 193–219.

Goldberg, Jonathan. 'Colin to Hobbinol: Spenser's Familiar Letters.' In Ronald R. Butters, John M. Clum, and Michael Moon, eds, *Displacing Homophobia: Gay Male Perspectives in Literature and Language*, 107–26. Durham, NC: Duke University Press, 1989.

– *Sodometries: Renaissance Texts, Modern Sexualities.* Stanford: Stanford University Press, 1992.

Grafton, Anthony, and Lisa Jardine. *From Humanism to the Humanities: Education and the Liberal Arts in Fifteenth and Sixteenth-Century Europe.* Cambridge, MA: Harvard University Press, 1986.

Gransden, K.W. *Virgil's Iliad: An Essay on Epic Narrative.* Cambridge: Cambridge University Press, 1984.

Greene, Robert. *Pandosto.* In Alexander B. Grosart, ed., *The Life and Complete Works in Prose and Verse of Robert Greene, M.A.* Vol. 4. New York: Russell and Russell, 1964.

Greene, Thomas. *The Light in Troy: Imitation and Discovery in Renaissance Poetry.* New Haven: Yale University Press, 1982.

Griffin, Jasper. *Virgil.* Oxford: Oxford University Press, 1986.

Griffiths, Frederick T. *Theocritus at Court.* Leiden: E.J. Brill, 1979.

Grundy, Joan. *The Spenserian Poets: A Study in Elizabethan and Jacobean Poetry.* London: Edward Arnold, 1969.

Guidi, José. 'Thyrsis ou la cour transfigurée.' In André Rochon, ed., *Ville et campagne dans la littérature italienne de la renaissance*, vol. 2, 141–86. Paris: Université de la Sorbonne Nouvelle, 1977.

Gutzwiller, Kathryn J. *Theocritus' Pastoral Analogies: The Formation of a Genre.* Madison: University of Wisconsin Press, 1991.

Haan, Estelle. '"Written Encomiums": Milton's Latin Poetry in Its Italian Context.' In Mario A. DiCesare, ed., *Milton in Italy: Contexts, Images, Contradictions*, 521–47. Binghamton: Medieval and Renaissance Texts and Studies, vol. 90, 1991.

Haber, Judith. *Pastoral and the Poetics of Self-contradiction: Theocritus to Marvell.* Cambridge: Cambridge University Press, 1994.

Hale, John K. 'Sion's Bacchanalia: An Inquiry into Milton's Latin in the *Epitaphium Damonis.*' *Milton Studies* 16 (1982), 113–50.

– 'Milton and the Sexy Seals: A Peephole into the Horton Years.' *Early Modern Literary Studies* 1:3 (1995), 5.1–12.

Halperin, David M. *Before Pastoral: Theocritus and the Ancient Tradition of Bucolic Poetry.* New Haven: Yale University Press, 1983.

– *One Hundred Years of Homosexuality: And Other Essays on Greek Love*. New York: Routledge, 1990.

Hammill, Graham L. *Sexuality and Form: Caravaggio, Marlowe, and Bacon*. Chicago: University of Chicago Press, 2000.

Hammond, Paul. *Love between Men in English Literature*. New York: St Martin's Press, 1996.

Hardie, Philip. *The Epic Successors of Virgil: A Study in the Dynamics of a Tradition*. Cambridge: Cambridge University Press, 1993.

Hardison, O.B. 'Tudor Humanism and Surrey's Translation of the *Aeneid*.' *Studies in Philology* 83 (1986), 237–60.

Harrison, Thomas Perrin, Jr. 'The Latin Pastorals of Milton and Castiglione.' *PMLA* 50 (1935), 480–93.

Helgerson, Richard. *Self-Crowned Laureates: Spenser, Jonson, Milton, and the Literary System*. Berkeley: University of California Press, 1983.

Henke, Robert. '*The Winter's Tale* and Guarinian Dramaturgy.' *Comparative Drama* 27 (1993–4), 197–217.

Herman, Peter C. 'Poets, Pastors, and Antipoetics: A Response to Frances M. Malpezzi, "E.K., A Spenserian Lesson in Reading."' *Connotations* 6 (1996–7), 316–25.

Hine, Daryl. 'Introduction.' In *Theocritus: Idylls and Epigrams*. New York: Atheneum, 1982.

Holstun, James. '"Will you rend our ancient love asunder": Lesbian Elegy in Donne, Marvell, and Milton.' *English Literary History* 54 (1987), 835–67.

Homer. *Iliad*. Ed. A.T. Murray. London: Heinemann, 1985.

Hopkins, Lisa. '"A place privileged to do men wrong": The Anxious Masculinity of *The Maid's Tragedy*.' In Andrew P. Williams, ed., *The Image of Manhood in Early Modern Literature: Viewing the Male*, 55–72. Westport, CT: Greenwood Press, 1999.

Horace. *Opera*. Ed. Edward C. Wickham. Oxford: Oxford University Press, 1901.

Horton, Ronald. 'Spenser's Farewell to Dido: The Public Turn.' In Arthur F. Kinney, ed., *Classical, Renaissance, and Postmodern Acts of the Imagination: Essays Commemorating O.B. Hardison, Jr*, 105–15. London: Associated University Presses, 1996.

Hunt, Maurice. 'Modern and Postmodern Discourses in Shakespeare's *The Winter's Tale*: A Response to David Laird.' *Connotations* 5 (1995–6), 83–94.

Janan, Micaela. 'The Book of Good Love? Design versus Desire in *Metamorphoses* 10.' *Ramus* 17 (1988), 110–37.

Jentoft, C.W. 'Surrey's Five Elegies: Rhetoric, Structure, and the Poetry of Praise.' *PMLA* 91 (1976), 23–32.

Johnson, Nora. 'Ganymedes and Kings: Staging Male Homosexual Desire in
    The Winter's Tale.' Shakespeare Studies 26 (1998), 187–217.
Jones, Vivien. 'The Seduction of Conduct: Pleasure and Conduct Literature.'
    In Roy Porter and Marie Mulvey Roberts, eds, *Pleasure in the Eighteenth
    Century*, 108–32. London: Macmillan, 1996.
Jordan, Mark D. *The Invention of Sodomy in Christian Theology.* Chicago:
    University of Chicago Press, 1997.
Juel-Jensen, Bent. 'The Poet Earl of Surrey's Library.' *The Book Collector* 5
    (1956), 172.
Kahn, Coppélia. 'The Providential Tempest and the Shakespearean Family.' In
    Murray M. Schwartz and Coppélia Kahn, eds, *Representing Shakespeare: New
    Pyschoanalytic Essays*, 217–43. Baltimore: Johns Hopkins University Press,
    1980.
Klawitter, George. 'Barnfield's Penelope Devereux, Exalted and Reviled.' In
    George Klawitter and Kenneth Borris, eds, *The Affectionate Shepherd: Cele-
    brating Richard Barnfield*, 62–82. Selinsgrove, PA: Susquehanna University
    Press, 2001.
Knedlik, Janet Leslie. 'High Pastoral Art in *Epitaphium Damonis.' Milton
    Studies* 19 (1984), 149–63.
Labriola, Albert C. 'Portraits of an Artist: Milton's Changing Self-Image.'
    Milton Studies 19 (1984), 179–94.
Laird, David. 'Competing Discourses in *The Winter's Tale.' Connotations* 4
    (1994–5), 25–43.
– 'An Answer to Maurice Hunt's "Modern and Postmodern Discourses in
    Shakespeare's *The Winter's Tale."' Connotations* 6 (1996–7), 246–50.
Lambert, Ellen Zetzel. *Placing Sorrow.* Chapel Hill: University of North
    Carolina Press, 1976.
Lane, Robert. *Shepheards Devises: Edmund Spenser's* Shepheardes Calender *and
    the Institutions of Elizabethan Society.* Athens: University of Georgia Press,
    1993.
Leach, Eleanor Winsor. *Virgil's* Eclogues: *Landscapes of Experience.* Ithaca:
    Cornell University Press, 1974.
Leòn Alfar, Cristina. 'Staging the Feminine Performance of Desire: Masochism
    in *The Maid's Tragedy.' Papers on Language and Literature* 31 (1995), 313–33.
Lindenbaum, Peter. 'Time, Sexual Love, and the Uses of Pastoral in *The
    Winter's Tale.' Modern Language Quarterly* 33 (1972), 3–22.
Makowski, John F. 'Nisus and Euryalus: A Platonic Relationship.' *Classical
    Journal* 85 (1989–90), 1–15.
Malpezzi, Frances M. 'E.K., A Spenserian Lesson in Reading.' *Connotations* 4
    (1994–5), 181–91.

Marcus, Leah. *Unediting the Renaissance: Shakespeare, Marlowe, Milton*. London: Routledge, 1996.

Marlowe, Christopher. *The Complete Works of Christopher Marlowe*. 2 volumes. Ed. Fredson Bowers. Cambridge: Cambridge University Press, 1973.

Marrapodi, Michele. '"Of that fatal country': Sicily and the Rhetoric of Topography in *The Winter's Tale*.' In Michele Marrapodi et al., eds, *Shakespeare's Italy: Functions of Italian Locations in Renaissance Drama*, 213–28. Manchester: Manchester University Press, 1993.

Martindale, Charles. *Redeeming the Text: Latin Poetry and the Hermeneutics of Reception*. Cambridge: Cambridge University Press, 1993.

– 'Green Politics: The *Eclogues*.' In Charles Martindale, ed., *The Cambridge Companion to Virgil*, 107–24. Cambridge: Cambridge University Press, 1997.

Mastronarde, Donald J. 'Theocritus Idyll 13: Love and the Hero.' *Transactions of the American Philological Association* 99 (1968), 273–90.

McCandless, David. '"Verily Bearing Blood": Pornography, Sexual Love, and the Reclaimed Feminine in *The Winter's Tale*.' *Essays in Theatre* 9 (1990–1), 61–81.

McLuskie, Kathleen. '"A maidenhead, *Amintor*, at my yeares": Chastity and Tragicomedy in the Fletcher Plays.' In Gordon McMullan and Jonathan Hope, eds, *The Politics of Tragicomedy: Shakespeare and After*, 92–121. London: Routledge, 1992.

Miller, James E., Jr. 'Introduction.' In *Complete Poetry and Selected Prose of Walt Whitman*. Boston: Houghton Mifflin, 1959.

Milton, John. *Complete Poems and Major Prose*. Ed. Merritt Y. Hughes. Indianapolis: Odyssey, 1957.

Moorman, Frederic W. *William Browne: His* Britannia's Pastorals *and the Pastoral Poetry of the Elizabethan Age*. Strassburg: Karl Trübner, 1897.

Morris, Harry. *Richard Barnfield, Colin's Child*. Tallahassee: Florida State University Studies, 1963.

Morse, William R. 'Metacriticism and Materiality: The Case of Shakespeare's *The Winter's Tale*.' *English Literary History* 58 (1991), 283–304.

Nashe, Thomas. *The Unfortunate Traveller and Other Works*. Ed. J.B. Steane. Harmondsworth: Penguin, 1985.

Neill, Michael. '"The Simetry, Which Gives a Poem Grace": Masque, Imagery, and the Fancy of *The Maid's Tragedy*.' *Renaissance Drama* n.s. 3 (1970), 111–34.

– *Issues of Death: Mortality and Identity in English Renaissance Tragedy*. Oxford: Clarendon Press, 1997.

Nichols, Fred J. '"Lycidas," "Epitaphium Damonis," the Empty Dream, and the Failed Song.' In *Acta Conventus Neo-Latini Lovaniensis*, 445–52. Leuven and Munich: Leuven University Press and Wilhelm Fink Verlag, 1973.

Norton, Rictor. *The Homosexual Literary Tradition: An Interpretation*. New York: Revisionist Press, 1974.

Oliensis, Ellen. 'Sons and Lovers: Gender and Sexuality in Virgil's Poetry.' In Charles Martindale, ed., *The Cambridge Companion to Virgil*, 294–311. Cambridge: Cambridge University Press, 1997.

Orgel, Stephen. 'The Poetics of Incomprehensibility.' *Shakespeare Quarterly* 42 (1991), 431–7.

Ostriker, Alicia. 'Thomas Wyatt and Henry Surrey: Dissonance and Harmony in Lyric Form.' *New Literary History* 1 (1969–70), 387–405.

Parry, Adam. 'Landscape in Greek Poetry.' *Yale Classical Studies* 15 (1957), 3–29.

Paster, Gail Kern. *The Body Embarrassed: Drama and the Disciplines of Shame in Early Modern England*. Ithaca: Cornell University Press, 1993.

Pequigney, Joseph. *Such Is My Love: A Study of Shakespeare's Sonnets*. Chicago: University of Chicago Press, 1985.

Perkell, Christine G. 'The "Dying Gallus" and the Design of *Eclogue* 10.' *Classical Philology* 91 (1996), 128–40.

Perry, Curtis. *The Making of Jacobean Culture: James I and the Renegotiation of Elizabethan Literary Practice*. Cambridge: Cambridge University Press, 1997.

Persky, Stan. *Autobiography of a Tattoo*. Vancouver: New Star, 1997.

Peterson, Douglas L. *The English Lyric from Wyatt to Donne*. Princeton: Princeton University Press, 1967.

Petrini, Mark. *The Child and the Hero: Coming of Age in Catullus and Vergil*. Ann Arbor: University of Michigan Press, 1997.

Pigg, Daniel F. 'Barnfield's Certain Sonnets 8.' *The Explicator* 57 (1998), 14–17.

Pigman, G.W., III. *Grief and English Renaissance Elegy*. Cambridge: Cambridge University Press, 1985.

Pittinger, Elizabeth. '"To Serve the Queere": Nicholas Udall, Master of Revels.' In Jonathan Goldberg, ed., *Queering the Renaissance*, Durham, NC: Duke University Press, 1994. 162–89.

Plutarch. *Plutarch's Moralia*. Trans. Philemon Holland. London: J.M. Dent, 1911.

Price, Michael W. 'Shakespeare's *The Winter's Tale* I.2.1–9.' *The Explicator* 52 (1993–4), 140–2.

Putnam Michael C.J. *Virgil's Pastoral Art*. Princeton: Princeton University Press, 1970.

– 'Ganymede and Virgilian Ekphrasis.' *American Journal of Philology* 116 (1992), 419–40.

Rackin, Phyllis. 'Foreign Country: The Place of Women and Sexuality in Shakespeare's Historical World.' In Richard Burt and John Michael Archer, eds, *Enclosure Acts: Sexuality, Property, and Culture in Early Modern England*, 68–95. Ithaca: Cornell University Press, 1994.

Rambuss, Richard. 'The Secretary's Study: The Secret Designs of *The Shepheardes Calender*.' *English Literacy History* 59 (1992), 313–35.

Rebhorn, Wayne A. *Courtly Performances: Masking and Festivity in Castiglione's Book of the Courtier*. Detroit: Wayne State University Press, 1978.

Regosin, Richard L. 'The name of the game / the game of the name: Sign and Self in Castiglione's *Book of the Courtier*.' *Journal of Medieval and Renaissance Studies* 18 (1988), 21–47.

Revard, Stella P. *Milton and the Tangles of Neaera's Hair: The Making of the 1645 Poems*. Columbia: University of Missouri Press, 1997.

Rich, Adrienne. 'When We Dead Awaken: Writing as Re-Vision.' In *On Lies, Secrets, and Silence: Selected Prose 1966–1978*, 33–49. New York: W.W. Norton, 1979.

Robertson, Lisa. *Xeclogue*. Vancouver: Tsunami Editions, 1993.

– *Debbie: An Epic*. Vancouver: New Star Books, 1997.

Rocke, Michael. *Forbidden Friendships: Homosexuality and Male Culture in Renaissance Florence*. New York: Oxford University Press, 1996.

Rosenmeyer, Thomas G. *The Green Cabinet*. Berkeley: University of California Press, 1969.

Sacks, Peter M. *The English Elegy: Studies in the Genre from Spenser to Yeats*. Baltimore: Johns Hopkins University Press, 1985.

Salemi, Joseph S. 'Selected Latin Poems of Baldassare Castiglione.' *Allegorica* 6:2 (1981), 102–48.

Sappho. *Greek Lyric, I: Sappho and Alcaeus*. Ed. David A. Campbell. Cambridge, MA: Harvard University Press, 1982.

Saslow, James M. *Ganymede in the Renaissance: Homosexuality in Art and Society*. New Haven: Yale University Press, 1986.

Schenk, Celeste Marguerite. *Mourning and Panegyric: The Poetics of Pastoral Ceremony*. University Park: Pennsylvania State University Press, 1988.

Schiller, Friedrich. *On the Naive and Sentimental in Literature*. Trans. Helen Watanabe-O'Kelly. Manchester: Carcanet, 1981.

Schwartz, Murray M. 'Leontes' Jealousy in *The Winter's Tale*.' *American Imago* 30 (1973), 250–73.

– '*The Winter's Tale*: Loss and Transformation.' *American Imago* 32 (1975), 145–99.

Sedgwick, Eve Kosofsky. *Between Men: English Literature and Male Homosocial Desire*. New York: Columbia University Press, 1985.
– *Epistemology of the Closet*. New York: Harvester Wheatsheaf, 1991.
Segal, Charles. *Poetry and Myth in Ancient Pastoral: Essays on Theocritus and Virgil*. Princeton: Princeton University Press, 1981.
Servius. *In Vergilii* Bucolici *et* Georgica *Commentarii*. Ed. Georg Thilo. Hildesheim: Georg Olms, 1961.
Sessions, W.A. *Henry Howard, Earl of Surrey*. Twayne's English Authors Series. Boston: Twayne, 1986.
– 'Surrey's Wyatt: Autumn 1542 and the New Poet.' In Peter C. Herman, ed., *Rethinking the Henrician Era: Essays on Early Tudor Texts and Contexts*, 168–92. Urbana: University of Illinois Press, 1994.
– *Henry Howard, the Poet Earl of Surrey: A Life*. Oxford: Oxford University Press, 1999.
Shakespeare, William. *The Riverside Shakespeare*. Ed. G. Blakemore Evans. Boston: Houghton Mifflin, 1974.
Shaw, W. David. *Elegy and Paradox: Testing the Conventions*. Baltimore: Johns Hopkins University Press, 1994.
Shawcross, John T. 'Milton and Diodati: An Essay in Psychodynamic Meaning.' *Milton Studies* 7 (1975), 127–63.
Shore, David R. *Spenser and the Poetics of Pastoral: A Study of the World of Colin Clout*. Kingston and Montreal: McGill-Queen's University Press, 1985.
Shullenberger, William. '"This for the most Wrong'd of women": A Reappraisal of *The Maid's Tragedy*.' *Renaissance Drama* n.s. 13 (1982), 131–56.
Sidney, Sir Philip. *The Poems of Sir Philip Sidney*. Ed. William A. Ringler, Jr. Oxford: Oxford University Press, 1982.
Smith, Bruce R. *Homosexual Desire in Shakespeare's England: A Cultural Poetics*. Chicago: University of Chicago Press, 1991.
Smith, Eric. *By Mourning Tongues: Studies in English Elegy*. Ipswich and Totowa, NJ: Boydell Press and Rowman and Littlefield, 1977.
Snyder, Susan. *Pastoral Process: Spenser, Marvell, Milton*. Stanford: University of Stanford Press, 1998.
Spearing, A.C. *Medieval to Renaissance in English Poetry*. Cambridge: Cambridge University Press, 1985.
Spenser, Edmund. *Poetical Works*. Ed. J.C. Smith and E. de Selincourt. Oxford: Oxford University Press, 1983.
Stanivukovic, Goran. '"The blushing shame of souldiers": The Eroticism of Heroic Masculinity in John Fletcher's *Bonduca*.' In Andrew P. Williams, ed., *The Image of Manhood in Early Modern Literature: Viewing the Male*, 41–54. Westport, CT: Greenwood Press, 1999.

Stevens, Forrest Tyler. 'Erasmus's "Tigress": The Language of Friendship, Pleasure, and the Renaissance Letter.' In Jonathan Goldberg, ed., *Queering the Renaissance*, 124–40. Durham, NC: Duke University Press, 1994.

Stewart, Alan. *Close Readers: Humanism and Sodomy in Early Modern England.* Princeton: Princeton University Press, 1997.

Stewart, J.I.M. *Character and Motive in Shakespeare: Some Recent Appraisals Examined.* London: Longmans, Green and Co., 1949.

Stockholder, Kay. *Dream Works: Lovers and Families in Shakespeare's Plays.* Toronto: University of Toronto Press, 1987.

Suetonius. *Divus Iulius.* Ed. H.E. Butler and M. Cary. Oxford: Clarendon Press, 1927.

Summers, Claude J. 'Marlowe and Constructions of Renaissance Homosexuality.' *Canadian Review of Comparative Literature* 21 (1994), 27–44.

– 'The (Homo)sexual Temptation in *Paradise Regained.*' In Raymond-Jean Frontain, ed., *Reclaiming the Sacred: The Bible in Lesbian and Gay Culture*, 45–69. New York: Haworth, 1997.

Surrey, Henry Howard, Earl of. *Poems.* Ed. Emrys Jones. Oxford: Oxford University Press, 1964.

– *The Poems of Henry Howard, Earl of Surrey.* Ed. Frederick Morgan Padelford. Rev. ed. New York: Haskell, 1966.

Taylor, Michael W. *The Tyrant Slayers: The Heroic Image in Fifth Century B.C. Athenian Art and Politics.* New York: Arno, 1981.

Theocritus. *Idylls.* In *Bucolici Graeci.* Ed. A.S.F. Gow. Oxford: Oxford University Press, 1952.

Todorov, Tzvetan. 'The Origin of Genres.' *New Literary History* 8 (1976–7), 159–70.

Vauquelin, Jean, Sieur de la Fresnaie. *Idillies et Pastoralles. Les Diverses Poésies.* Vol. 2. Geneva: Slatkine, 1968.

Vendler, Helen. *The Art of Shakespeare's Sonnets.* Cambridge, MA: Belknap Press, 1997.

Virgil. *Opera.* Ed. R.A.B. Mynors. Oxford: Clarendon, 1969.

Warner, Michael. 'New English Sodom.' In Jonathan Goldberg, ed., *Queering the Renaissance*, 330–58. Durham, NC: Duke University Press, 1994.

Watkins, John. *The Specter of Dido: Spenser and Virgilian Epic.* New Haven: Yale University Press, 1995.

West, Michael. 'The *Consolatio* in Milton's Funeral Elegies.' *Huntington Library Quarterly* 34 (1970–1), 233–49.

Williams, F.J. 'Theocritus, *Idyll* I: 81–91.' *Journal of Hellenic Studies* 89 (1969), 121–3.

Williams, R.D. *The Aeneid.* London: Allen and Unwin, 1987.

Wofford, Susanne Lindgren. *The Choice of Achilles: The Ideology of Figure in the Epic*. Stanford: Stanford University Press, 1992.

Worrall, Andrew. 'Biographical Introduction: Barnfield's Feast of "all Varietie."' In George Klawitter and Kenneth Borris, eds, *The Affectionate Shepherd: Celebrating Richard Barnfield*, 25–40. Selinsgrove, PA: Susquehanna University Press, 2001.

Zitner, S.P. 'Truth and Mourning in a Sonnet by Surrey.' *English Literary History* 50 (1983), 509–29.

Zuntz, G. 'Theocritus I.95 f.' *Classical Quarterly* 10 (1960), 37–40.

INDEX